Laurel & Hardy

in

"BIG QUIZNESS"

by Robert McFerren & Tracie McFerren
Illustrated by Robert McFerren

Editor/JoAnn Jones

Plumtree
Publishing

LAUREL & HARDY IN BIG QUIZNESS

FIRST EDITION 1997

Published by
Plumtree Publishing,
9420 Stratton Rd.,
Salem, OH 44460-7618
U.S.A.

Picture Credits: The Larry Bell Collection

Printed in the United States of America
Cover design by Robert McFerren

Library of Congress Cataloging in Publication Data
McFerren, Robert
McFerren, Tracie
Laurel & Hardy
Reference: Trivia and Fact
Library of Congress Catalog Card Number: 97-97019
ISBN 0-9660323-0-6

In the undertaking of such an overwhelming project as this book, one finds out how good of friends he or she really has. In the truest essence of Stan and Ollie – loyal friends through thick and thin – are the following people. To all of you, we are eternally grateful.

THIS BOOK IS DEDICATED TO . . .

OUR FAMILY

• James and Margie McFerren, our parents, who introduced us to the Boys at a very early age.
• Cris McFerren (Robert's wife), whose help on this book is immeasurable. Thanks for all your help and support.
• Jordan, Zachary and Tucker (Robert's children) – for being patient and understanding ("Is the book done YET?")
• Our sister and her family, Kelly and Joe Igro, Jennifer and Brad Rockwell

OUR FRIENDS

• Jo Ann Jones, our former high school teacher, for working so hard to edit this book. Even after all these years, you are still teaching us. We are proud to call you a dear and loyal friend. Our sincerest thanks for all your help.
• If there is ever a man to possess the true spirit of Laurel and Hardy, it is Larry Bell. He generously loaned us the use of his private collection of Laurel and Hardy memorabilia, which was a true inspiration to this book, since most of it once belonged to Stan Laurel. Thanks for all your help and support on this project.

Special thanks to:
• Jami Ketler, Janice Solmen, Bill Thompson, Victoria Turnage, Eric Grazier, Kenneth Croyle, for your help, guidance and encouragement.

ACKNOWLEDGEMENTS

Many thanks to:
Chris Seguin, Bram Reijnhoudt, Ned Comstock, Randy Skretvedt, Rob Stone, Rob Lewis, Dave Powers, and to Charles Lord, who answered the question that I've always wondered:
Whatever happened to Ollie's mom, Miss Emmie?

BIBLIOGRAPHY

Information in this book is compiled from numerous sources and personal observations based on the films. A special thanks goes out to the works of John McCabe, Randy Skretvedt and Glenn Mitchell.

Mr. Laurel and Mr. Hardy, John McCabe, Doubleday, 1961
The Comedy World of Stan Laurel, John McCabe, Doubleday, 1974
Babe: The Life of Oliver Hardy, John McCabe, Citadel Press, 1989
Laurel & Hardy, John McCabe (with Al Kilgore and Richard Bann), E.P. Dutton, 1975
Laurel and Hardy: The Magic Behind the Movies, Randy Skretvedt, Moonstone Press, 1987
The Laurel and Hardy Encyclopedia, Glenn Mitchell, B.T. Batsford Ltd., 1995
The Laurel and Hardy Book, Leonard Maltin, Curtis Books, 1973
The Intra-Tent Journal, Sons of the Desert, published quarterly by International Laurel & Hardy Society, U.S.A.
The Laurel & Hardy Magazine, produced by the Helpmates U.K. Tent
The Film Encyclopedia, Ephraim Katz, Harper & Row, 1979
The Encyclopedia of Film, James Monaco, Perigee Book, 1991
W.C. Fields: His Follies & Fortunes, Robert Lewis Taylor, Doubleday, 1949

CONTENTS

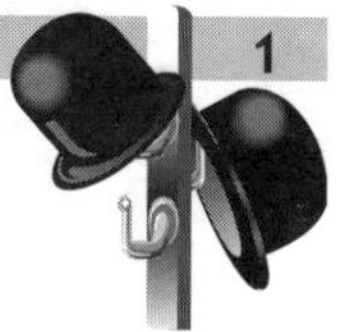

TO LAUREL & HARDY

Throughout our whole United States
You've recognized us all-time greats
And far from home, on foreign shores
You've been goodwill ambassadors.
You've done more in derby hats
Than high hats worn by diplomats
If we had more high men of mirth
We might once have peace on Earth

Written for 'This Is Your Life'

December 1, 1954

THE BOYS

Characterizations

Stan Laurel

Oliver Hardy

THE BOYS

Night Clothes

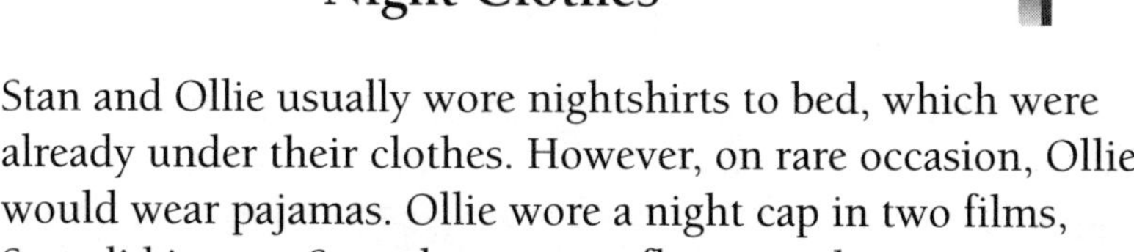

Stan and Ollie usually wore nightshirts to bed, which were already under their clothes. However, on rare occasion, Ollie would wear pajamas. Ollie wore a night cap in two films, Stan did in one. Stan always wore floppy socks.

The Boys wore their night clothes in 21 films:

- Leave 'Em Laughing
- Early to Bed
- Berth Marks
- They Go Boom
- Angora Love
- Brats
- The Laurel~Hardy Murder Case
- Laughing Gravy
- The Chimp
- County Hospital (Ollie)
- Scram!
- Sons of the Desert
- Oliver the Eighth
- Babes in Toyland
- The Live Ghost
- Bonnie Scotland
- Our Relations
- A Chump at Oxford
- Saps at Sea
- The Big Noise
- Atoll K

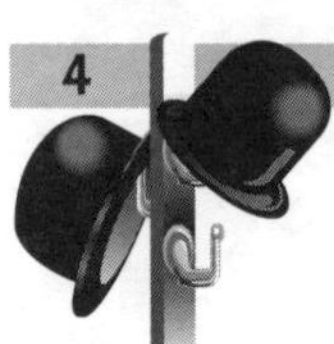

STAN & OLLIE
A Character Study

The Boys were true and loyal friends throughout all their films. Although they fought in many films like a married couple, they would defend and protect each other time and time again against attacks from the outside world. Some of the characteristics that made the Boys:

OLLIE'S MANNERISMS

Known for his genteel ways and Southern charm, he considered himself the leader of the two, always sticking by his half-witted friend. He had the grace and movements of a nimble ballerina.

♦ **The tie-twiddles:** A nervous and sometimes coy fluttering of his necktie at girls or angry opponents he has inadvertently wronged
♦ **Camera-glances:** Varying looks that take us into his confidence, as if to say, "Can you believe this"
♦ **His fingers:** If a stressful situation arises, Ollie nervously makes light of it, while rubbing his finger on a table or his jacket, or he will start to pick his nails
♦ **His hair:** Oil-slicked, with spit-curls

STAN'S MANNERISMS

His character was as simple as a child yet at times could have brief but brilliant ideas.

♦ **The eye-blink:** Caused by confusion, opens wide as if a sudden bolt of lightning has made it suddenly clear, but the idea fades as fast as it struck
♦ **Arms:** Attempts to fold arms in defiance, but never quite masters the technique
♦ **Head scratch:** The itching of his unwieldy hair could be a sign of joy or fear
♦ **Crying:** Whenever things go wrong, Stan will weep
♦ **White magic:** Stan has a knack for making the impossible suddenly possible. He could light his thumb afire, yet never get burned. Quite adept at hand tricks

OLLIE SAYS, STAN SAYS

Frequent or Favorite Phrases

OLLIE

- ♦ "Why don't you do something to help me?"
- ♦ "Here's another nice mess you've gotten me into."
- ♦ "Don't you think you're over stepping your bounds?"
- ♦ "Hmmm!"
- ♦ "... And nobody will be any the wiser."
- ♦ "I'll break your neck!"

STAN

- ♦ "You bet your life it's a good idea."
- ♦ ". . ." (blank stare)
- ♦ "Wait 'til I spit on me hands"
- ♦ "Oh, me apple!"
- ♦ "... Yes, Ma'am."

IN THE NEWS
1955 to 1965

TV Deals for Laurel and Hardy

BY LARRY WOLTERS

LAUREL-HARDY: While old Laurel and Hardy films have been on TV for years, their only live appearance was on Ralph Edwards' This Is Your Life.

Laurel

Hardy

That show revived interest in this great comedy team, in retirement nearly a decade.

As a result, NBC and Hal Roach Jr. are about ready to close a deal under which Stan and Oliver would turn out three 90 minute color films for which the network would underwrite most of the cost. The films would be premiered on NBC Spectaculars and then relased afterwards to theaters.

Stan and Ollie remained popular even in their later years. There was talk of a Laurel and Hardy television show featuring the Boys in 1955, but their ill health kept the show from ever being made.

An editorial cartoon that ran in the Los Angeles Times the week of Stan's death in 1965. Quite a fitting tribute to the comedy genius of the Boys.

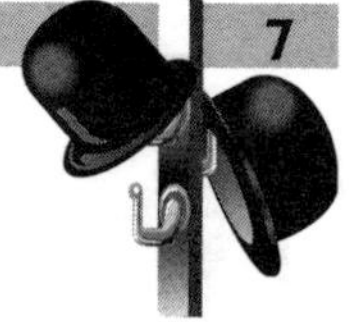

STILL SEEN TODAY

Recent Sightings

Although the Boys made their last film together in 1951, Stan and Ollie still can be seen today. Occasionally they appear in editorial cartoons in newspapers, in books, magazines, and even in newsletters devoted to the Boys in many languages around the world. Their films still air on television, and have been seen or mentioned on several TV shows in the United States and Britain in recent years.

©Chicago Tribune

Even today, Laurel and Hardy appear frequently in editorial cartoons, an easy interpretation for the reader usually showing incompetence of some government branch or official.

ON TELEVISION SHOWS IN THE U.S.

- **Seinfeld:** Jerry and George imitate Stan and Ollie on one episode.
- **Friends:** 'Leave 'Em Laughing' poster hangs on wall.
- **X-Files:** Agent Scully seen watching 'The Bullfighters'
- **Wings:** Wax dummy of Stan on one episode.
- **Mystery Science Theater 3000:** Mentions Boys often.
- **Perfect Strangers:** Did a tribute episode.

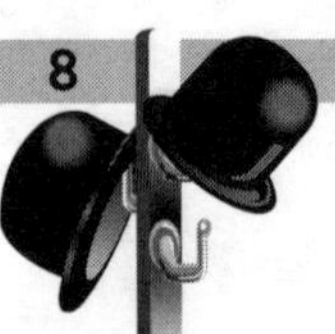

SPECIAL DAILY PASS

Hal Roach Studios, Inc.

HAL E. ROACH, PRESIDENT

A 2883

PASS ____________________

____

____

HAL ROACH STUDIOS, INC.

DATE ____________

(READ CONDITIONS ON REVERSE SIDE)

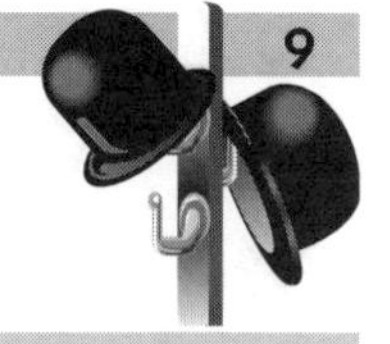

FILM TRIVIA

How Well Do You Know The Films?

Rate your performance in the ultimate trivia questions about the Boys. You think you know everything there is to know about Stan & Ollie? Think again! Keep track of your score as you go along so you can rate yourself on the trivia meter.

LUCKY DOG

♦ *Stan finds a stray dog.*

1. What are the two names Stan picks out for 'Lucky Dog'?

2. Name the dog show that Stan tries to get his dog into.

3. When Ollie refers to 'Bolsheviki candy,' what is he talking about?

4. What is Ollie's line of work?

5. What is Ollie's alias and where is he from?

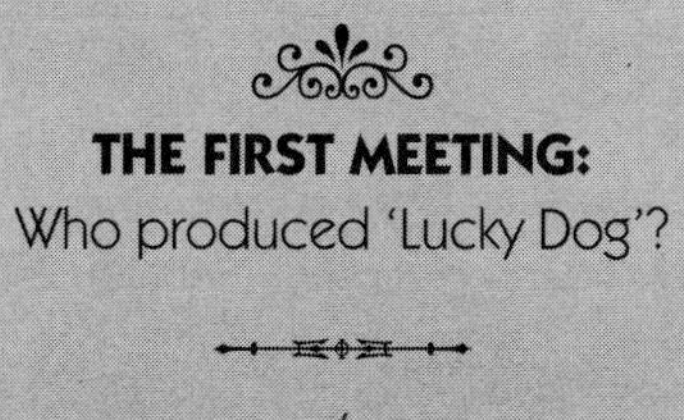

THE FIRST MEETING:
Who produced 'Lucky Dog'?

Bronco Billy Anderson

◆ 'Forty-Five Minutes from Hollywood' was originally considered to be part of the Glenn Tryon series for Hal Roach.

◆ 'Duck Soup' was originally titled 'Home From the Honeymoon,' written for the stage by Stan's father, A.J. Jefferson, in 1908.

FORTY-FIVE MINUTES FROM HOLLYWOOD

◆ *A family goes to Hollywood*

1. Stan had not yet captured his trademark "look." What is different about Stan's appearance in this film?

2. What does the bootlegger's card say?

3. What is Stan's occupation?

4. What is Ollie's occupation?

5. What is Glenn Tryon's character's name?

DUCK SOUP

◆ ***The Boys hide out in a mansion and are mistaken for the owners.***

1. 'Duck Soup' would later be remade into what two-reel film?

2. What is the reason the Boys hide out in the mansion?

3. What is the Boys' occupation?

4. What mode of transportation do Stan & Ollie use to avoid becoming 'volunteers'?

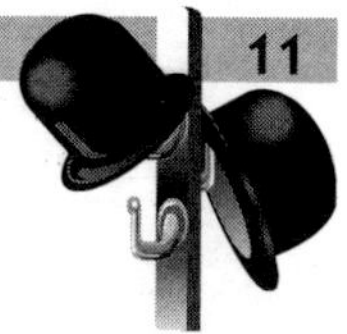

SLIPPING WIVES

♦ *Stan pretends to be having an affair with a woman to make her husband jealous.*

1. What is Stan's character's name?

2. What is Ollie's character's name?

3. Who does Stan pretend to be?

4. What is Stan's occupation?

5. What is Ollie's occupation?

6. This is later remade by the Boys as what film?

LOVE 'EM & WEEP

♦ *A married businessman is visited by an old flame who threatens blackmail.*

1. What is Stan's character's name?

2. This is later remade by the Boys as what film?

3. What is Ollie's character's name?

4. What is Fin's wife's name?

5. What time is Fin's dinner party with the Judge & meeting with ex-flame Mae Busch?

GEORGE STEVENS

He first worked as cameraman with the Boys on 'Slipping Wives' and continued to work with them for the next three years. He later went on to become an Oscar-winning director of such classic films as 'A Place in the Sun,' with Montgomery Clift and Elizabeth Taylor, and 'Giant,' with Rock Hudson , James Dean & Elizabeth Taylor.

HELLO, SAILOR:
How many of the Laurel & Hardy films are somehow boat-related (sailors, fishermen, etc.) ?

ANSWER:
Fourteen films.

- ♦ Why Girls Love Sailors
- ♦ Sailors, Beware!
- ♦ Putting Pants on Philip
- ♦ Two Tars
- ♦ Men O'War
- ♦ Any Old Port
- ♦ Towed in a Hole
- ♦ Sons of the Desert
- ♦ The Live Ghost
- ♦ Our Relations
- ♦ Saps at Sea
- ♦ Jitterbugs
- ♦ Nothing But Trouble
- ♦ Atoll K

WHY GIRLS LOVE SAILORS

♦ *Ollie, a sea captain, kidnaps Stan's girlfriend.*

1. What does Willie (Stan) have tattooed on his chest?

2. How does Willie scare the sailor who's kidnapping his fiancee?

3. What is Willie's fiancee's name?

WITH LOVE & HISSES

♦ ***The Boys are in the Army.***

1. What is Hardy's character's name and what is his rank?

2. What is Fin's name and rank?

3. What is Laurel's character's name?

4. The troops lose their clothes while swimmimg. How do they try to hide their nakedness?

5. What does the ending title card say about the troop being attacked by bees?

SUGAR DADDIES

♦ ***Fin wakes up and finds himself married.***

1. What are the three bad habits of Fin's new brother-in-law?
2. How much money did Fin's new in-laws want from him?
3. Where did Fin get married, and who was his best man?
4. What is Stan's occupation?
5. What is Ollie's occupation?

SAILORS, BEWARE!

♦ ***Stan helps nab jewel thieves.***

1. What is Stan's character's name and occupation?
2. What is Ollie's character's name and occupation?
3. What is unusual about Anita Garvin's baby?
4. What is Anita Garvin's character's name?
5. Lupe Velez appears with the Boys for the first time; what's her character's name?

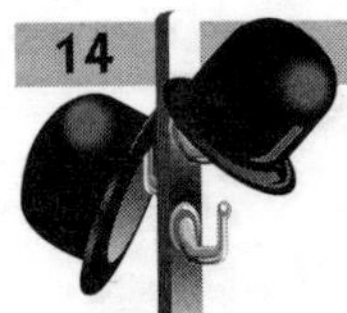

THE SECOND HUNDRED YEARS

♦ *The Boys escape from jail.*

1. What are Stan and Ollie's nicknames?

2. Stan asks another inmate to mail a letter for him. For how long is that inmate in jail?

3. Who plays the prison guard?

4. Who do Stan and Ollie pretend to be at the reception?

5. How many times do the Boys attempt to break out of jail?

CALL OF THE CUCKOOS

♦ ***Neighbors move away from next door oddballs.***

1. Name the family that lives next door to Laurel, Hardy, Charley Chase, and Jimmy Finlayson.

2. What are Laurel, Hardy, Charley Chase, and Fin training to be?

3. Why are Stan and Ollie's heads shaved for this film?

4. What does Stan try to shoot off of Ollie's head?

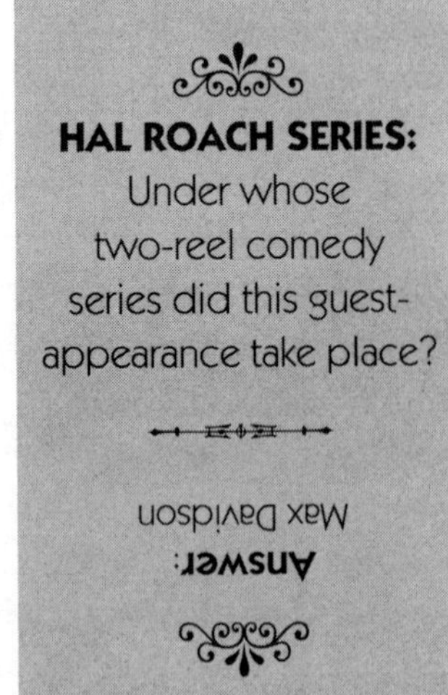

HAL ROACH SERIES:
Under whose two-reel comedy series did this guest-appearance take place?
Answer:
Max Davidson

DO DETECTIVES THINK?

♦ *The Boys are hired to protect Jimmy Finlayson from a killer.*

1. What is the name of the convict Judge Foozle (Fin) sentences?
2. What is the convict's sentence?
3. What is Stan's character's name?
4. What is Ollie's character's name?
5. This would be remade seven years later. Name the remake.

PUTTING PANTS ON PHILIP

♦ *Ollie is embarrassed by his Scottish relative.*

1. What is Ollie's character's name?
2. What is the name of the ship that Philip arrives on in the U.S.?
3. What size pants does Philip wear?
4. What is Philip's obsessive interest?
5. How is Philip related to Piedmont?
6. What is Piedmont's sister's name?

THE BATTLE OF THE CENTURY

♦ *A boxer turns into a pie fighter.*

1. Who is Stan's opponent in the boxing match?
2. How much does it cost Ollie to insure Stan?
3. How much does Ollie say he'll get for the bump on Stan's head?
4. What is Stan's alias as a boxer?
5. In the boxing circle, what is Stan known as?
6. How much money will the Boys get if Stan wins the fight?
7. How much will they make if Stan loses the fight?

LEAVE 'EM LAUGHING

♦ *Stan is ailing.*

1. What does the sign hanging above the bed say?
2. Who plays the Boys' landlord?
3. Who plays the traffic cop?
4. What is Stan's affliction?
5. What time of night does the opening title card say it is?

FLYING ELEPHANTS

♦ ***Prehistoric males must marry within the next 24 hours.***

1. How long ago is the setting for 'Flying Elephants'?

2. What is Stan's character's name?

3. What is Ollie's character's name?

4. What is Stan's occupation?

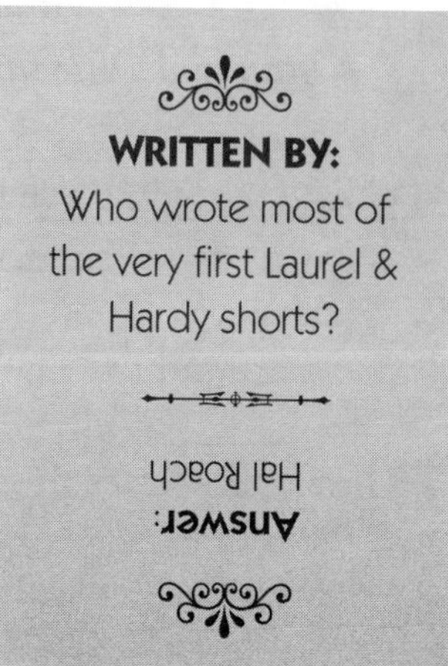

WRITTEN BY:
Who wrote most of the very first Laurel & Hardy shorts?
Answer:
Hal Roach

THE FINISHING TOUCH

♦ ***The Boys are building a house.***

1. How much does the house owner Sam Lufkin say he will pay the Boys if they can finish the house by noon next Monday?

2. What does Ollie accidentally swallow three times?

3. What does Ollie claim that the house is built as strong as?

4. Why do the Boys need to be quiet while building the house?

5. Who plays the nurse that keeps "sssshhhing" the Boys?

FROM SOUP TO NUTS

♦ *Stan and Ollie are servants at a posh dinner party.*

1. How does Stan serve the salad?

2. What piece of food does Mrs. Culpepper (Anita Garvin) chase around her plate?

3. How many times does Anita Garvin's tiara fall down?

4. This two-reeler was reworked into what film 12 years later?

5. What does Laurel and Hardy's business card say?

YOU'RE DARN TOOTIN'

♦ *Stan and Ollie lose their jobs as musicians.*

1. What instrument does Stan play?

2. What instrument does Ollie play?

3. What is the name of Stan and Ollie's landlord?

4. What is the boy's name at the dinner table who tells the landlady that Laurel and Hardy lost their jobs?

5. How many weeks has it been since Stan and Ollie paid their landlady rent?

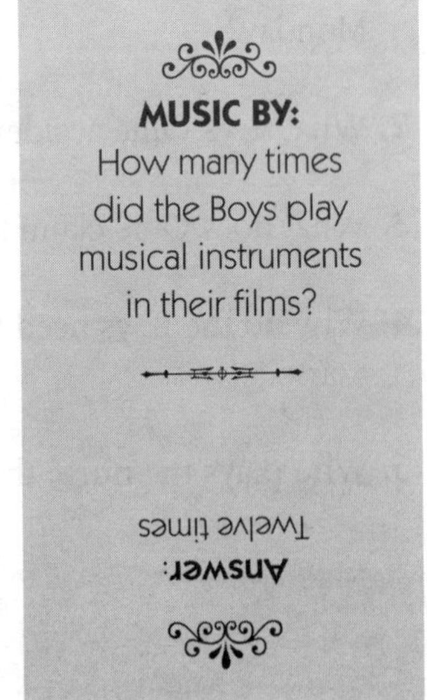

MUSIC BY:
How many times did the Boys play musical instruments in their films?
Answer:
Twelve times

THEIR PURPLE MOMENT

♦ ***The Boys go out to dinner without their wives and end up with two more problems.***

1. Where is Stan stashing his skimmings from his paycheck?

2. What is Mr. and Mrs. Pincher's (Stan and his wife's) house number?

3. How much does the bill at the restaurant total?

4. How many times does Stan (Mr. Pincher) cause the waiter to fall?

5. What do they order to eat at the restaurant?

6. How much is the fare for the taxi?

SHOULD MARRIED MEN GO HOME?

♦ ***Stan stops over at the Hardys' to get Ollie to play golf.***

1. Parts of this two-reeler would later be used again in what Laurel and Hardy film?

2. Instead of his toupee, what does Kennedy put on his head?

3. What does Stan's note say that he slips under Mr. and Mrs. Hardy's door?

4. What song does Stan ask Ollie if he can play on the phonograph?

EARLY TO BED

♦ ***Stan is trying to get Ollie to go to bed.***

1. A painting is hanging on the wall at Hardy Manor. This painting will be seen again four months later in the two-reel comedy 'Wrong Again.' What is the name of the painting?

2. Why does Ollie think Stan is "mad"?

3. How has Ollie become rich?

4. What is Stan's occupation?

5. Under what circumstances does Ollie say he'll go to bed?

TWO TARS

♦ ***The ship is docked, and the Boys look for a good time.***

1. What is Stan's rank?

2. What causes the traffic jam?

3. What is the name of the battleship to which the Boys are assigned?

4. Who plays the shopkeeper?

IN THE BEGINNING:
This film is notable for having two actors appear for the first time, but both would be in 56 films combined. Can you name the two actors?

Harry Bernard (26 films)
Baldwin Cooke (30 films)

HABEAS CORPUS

♦ *A mad scientist needs a body from the graveyard; enter Laurel and Hardy.*

1. Name the mad professor.

2. What is the professor's butler's name?

3. What time is it when Stan and Ollie go to the cemetery to snatch a body?

4. What street corner are the Boys on when Ollie climbs up the sign post?

5. What flies into Stan's face?

WE FAW DOWN

♦ *The Boys lie to their wives for a night out.*

1. Who does Ollie pretend is calling him?

2. Where does Ollie say his boss asks him and Stan to go?

3. What is the show at the theater?

4. What do the Boys want to do without their wives finding out?

5. This film idea would later be reused in which film?

LIBERTY

♦ ***Stan and Ollie escape from jail, but now they have on each other's pants.***

1. What is in Stan's pants that is causing him to jump?

2. On the high girders of a building being constructed, what does Ollie tell Stan to stop doing?

3. Who is the owner of the music shop?

4. Who is the actress seen entering the cab in this short?

THE ARTIST:
What English artist painted the painting 'Blue Boy'?

ANSWER

Thomas Gainsborough
(1727-1788)

BELIEVE IT OR NOT:
'Wrong Again' premiered on Feb. 23, 1929 — and Stan Laurel died exactly 36 years later to the day

WRONG AGAIN

♦ ***Two stablehands think they have found the stolen horse.***

1. How much is the reward for 'Blue Boy'?

2. What day of the week does the short take place?

3. What is the name of the stables?

4. What is the address of the owner of 'Blue Boy'?

5. Where are Laurel and Hardy told to put 'Blue Boy'?

THAT'S MY WIFE

♦ ***If Ollie is happily married, his rich uncle will leave him a fortune. Unfortunately, his wife just walked out.***

1. How long did Stan intend to drop in at the Hardys' and how long did he actually stay?

2. Where does Ollie's uncle take Ollie and "Magnolia" (Stan) out to dinner?

3. What is the name of the act that is performing at the restaurant?

4. Name Ollie's rich uncle.

5. Why does Stan pretend to be Ollie's wife?

BIG BUSINESS

♦ ***The Boys are door-to-door salesmen.***

1. What is the house number of the first house where the Boys stop?

2. What is Fin's house number?

3. What do Stan and Ollie sell?

4. Who plays the police officer?

5. Name the first item of Fin's that is destroyed.

♦ The only Laurel and Hardy film to be selected to The National Film Registry of the Library of Congress is 'Big Business'. This honor has been bestowed to only 175 films, ranging from D.W. Griffith's 'Birth of a Nation' to 'Star Wars.' Other comedians' works included in the Film Registry are W.C. Fields, Charlie Chaplin, Harold Lloyd, Fatty Arbuckle and the Marx Brothers.

UNACCUSTOMED AS WE ARE

♦ *Ollie brings Stan home for dinner as a surprise.*

THE NEW ERA:
An approriately entitled short, referring to the fact that this was Laurel & Hardy's very first talking picture.

1. What is Ollie's wife's name?

2. What is the name of the Hardy's neighbors?

3. Mrs. Hardy has a nickname for Ollie; what is it?

4. Name the actress who plays Mrs. Kennedy.

5. How many years does Ollie say he has known Stan?

6. This was later remade into what film?

DOUBLE WHOOPEE

♦ *A prince is coming to the hotel where the Boys work.*

1. How much of a tip does Stan get for opening the hotel door?

2. Name the taxi company that Charlie Hall drives for.

3. How many times does the prince fall into the elevator shaft?

4. On what street is the hotel located?

5. What are Stan's and Ollie's occupations?

BERTH MARKS

♦ ***The Boys have to catch a train for their next show.***

1. What is Stan and Ollie's occupation?

2. What town are the Boys going to for their vaudeville act?

3. At what train station do the Boys meet and at what time?

MEN O'WAR

♦ ***Sailors on shore leave enjoy an afternoon in the park.***

1. How much money do the Boys have to pay for the sodas?

2. How much does the bill come to?

3. What flavor soda does Ollie order for him and Stan to share?

4. What do the flirtatious ladies call Stan?

5. What article of clothing does the brunette (Anne Cornwall) lose?

6. What do Stan and Ollie think she lost?

PERFECT DAY

♦ ***A good day for a picnic – if they could just get there.***

1. Approximately how many times does Stan say "good-bye" in the film?

2. Approximately how many times does Ollie say "good-bye" in the film?

3. What day of the week does this film take place?

4. Who plays the aggressive neighbor that the Boys battle with?

THEY GO BOOM

♦ ***Ollie has the sniffles so Stan helps out.***

1. What time is it when 'They Go Boom' starts?

2. What does the sign above the bed say?

3. What is the brand name of the Boys' air mattress?

4. What does Ollie tell Stan he's liable to die of?

5. Who plays the Boys' landlord?

BACON GRABBERS

♦ *Stan & Ollie chase Edgar Kennedy for a change.*

1. What is the Boys' occupation?

2. What are Stan and Ollie repossessing from Kennedy?

3. What does Stan pull out of his pocket?

4. What are Edgar Kennedy's first name and middle initial in this film?

THE HOOSE-GOW

♦ *The Boys go to prison.*

1. What does Stanley get stuck in his mouth?

2. Stan and Ollie protest their innocence to Tiny Sanford. What do they claim they were doing when arrested?

3. Ollie throws Stan's pick, which ends up in the radiator of the governor's car. How do the Boys fix the leaking radiator?

4. Who plays the governor?

ANGORA LOVE

♦ *A goat follows the Boys home.*

1. What is the goat's name?

2. Name the pet store owner.

3. How much do the Boys spend for the doughnuts?

4. How many years does Ollie say they'll go to prison for 'kid'napping?

5. What is Stan and Ollie's apartment number?

6. This film was later reworked into what similar two-reeler?

NIGHT OWLS

♦ *Laurel & Hardy break into the house of the chief of police.*

1. The Boys make such a ruckus outside the chief's house that they wake him up. What do they pretend to be?

2. What is the tune that the player piano starts playing?

3. Why do the Boys agree to break into the chief's house?

4. Who gets blamed for the robberies on Kennedy's beat?

SAD SONG:
Frank Holliday plays the nightclub singer whose sad song, 'The Curse of the Aching Heart,' makes Stan burst into tears. He also plays the policeman in 'Below Zero,' a prison guard in 'Pardon Us' and a guest at Ollie's party in 'Chickens Come Home.'

BLOTTO

♦ ***A night out on the town could prove deadly when Stan's wife catches up with them.***

1. What is the name of the club the Boys go to drink their "liquor"?

2. What is Stan's phone number?

3. How much money does Ollie spend calling Stan?

4. What does Stan put on his head?

BRATS

♦ ***The Boys are the boys.***

1. What song does Ollie sing to make the "brats" go to bed?

2. Stan and Ollie play checkers while watching their children. What else do they play?

3. Who cheats while playing checkers, and who wins?

4. What former co-star's picture can be seen on the mantel?

BELOW ZERO

♦ *Stan and Ollie are street musicians who feel fit as a fiddle when they find a wallet.*

1. What song are the Boys playing in the middle of winter?

2. Name the instruments that each plays.

3. What does Stan call the waiter?

4. In front of what building are the Boys playing?

HOG WILD

♦ ***Mrs. Hardy puts Ollie to work.***

1. What is the name of the Hardy's maid?

2. Before Ollie can leave with Stan, what does Mrs. Hardy demand he do?

3. What article of clothing does Ollie lose?

RADIO DAYS

What do Mrs. Hardy & Stan want to listen to on the radio?

Answer: Japan

THE LAUREL~HARDY MURDER CASE

♦ ***The heir to the Laurel estate must spend the night in the creepy house.***

1. Stan is questioned on his whereabouts on November 15th. What four 'months' does Stan name?

2. Ollie asks the detective if he notices the family resemblance between Stan and the portrait on the wall. Whose portrait is it?

3. On what road does the Laurel Mansion reside?

4. How much is the Ebenezer Laurel estate worth?

NAMESAKE

Names used in film titles:

Abbott & Costello:
10 times in 37 films

Laurel & Hardy:
1 time in 106 films

ANOTHER FINE MESS

♦ ***Boys must pretend to be the owners of a mansion.***

1. What is Colonel Wilburforce Buckshot's address?

2. What sports does Ollie tell Sir Plumtree he plays?

3. What four other names do the Boys call Plumtree?

4. How many business cards does Plumtree give to the Boys?

5. What part of Kentucky does Ollie tell Plumtree he's from?

BE BIG

♦ *The Boys trick their wives.*

1. Where are Laurel and Hardy planning to go on vacation with their wives?

2. How do the Boys get out of going on vacation with their wives?

3. Why are Stan and Ollie trying to get out of going on vacation with the wives?

4. Who plays the bell boy?

5. What item is Stan carrying with him to take on vacation?

CHICKENS COME HOME

♦ *Ollie's past comes back to haunt him as an old girlfriend threatens blackmail.*

1. The Boys have a different kind of occupation in this short. What do they do for a living?

2. What is Ollie's home phone number?

3. What time is the dinner party at the Hardy residence?

4. How many people are invited to the dinner party?

5. For what political office is Ollie running?

LAUGHING GRAVY

♦ *The landlord has only one stipulation when renting rooms — no dogs allowed!*

1. What are Stan and Ollie's house and apartment numbers?

2. How much does Stan's uncle leave him?

3. Name the two other Laurel & Hardy films in which the dog 'Laughing Gravy' appears.

4. Who plays the Boys' landlord?

OUR WIFE

♦ *Ollie is eloping and Stan is "helping".*

1. What is the brand name of the bug spray Stan sprays on Ollie's wedding cake?

2. What is Ollie's fiancee's name?

3. Ben Turpin plays the justice of the peace; what is his character's name?

4. In celebration of their marriage, what two items does Stan toss at Ollie and his fiancee?

5. What nickname does Ollie's fiancee give to him?

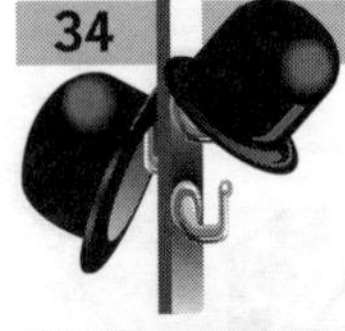

DID YOU KNOW?

♦ The prisoner marching in front of Ollie after they are recaptured is Hal Roach.

♦ Watch closely the scene of Stan & Ollie picking cotton – it will repeat itself right after the musical interlude.

♦ **Stan's prisoner number:** 44634

♦ **Ollie's prisoner number:** 44633

♦ The character's name Tiny Sandford plays in this film — Shields – after his close friend, Leroy Shields

PARDON US

♦ ***The Boys behind bars.***

1. How much is the reward for the recapture of Stan & Ollie who escaped from state prison?

2. When Professor Finlayson asks Stan how many times three goes into nine, what is Stan's response? What is Ollie's answer to the same question?

3. What was the date they escaped from prison?

4. How many times does Stan give the raspberry because of his loose tooth?

5. What was the Boys' occupation before they were arrested?

DAY BY DAY

♦ On what day of the month is this short set?

ANSWER:

The calendar seen hanging on the wall says the ninth

COME CLEAN

♦ ***Stan & Ollie stop a woman from committing suicide, but now she won't leave the Boys alone.***

1. What does the note say that Stan leaves for the Hardys?

2. Stan and Ollie go to get ice cream; what flavors does Charlie Hall say he has?

3. What flavors of ice cream is he out of?

4. What day of the week does Stan normally take a bath?

5. How much is the reward for turning in Mae Busch?

6. What's Stan going to do with his reward money?

ONE GOOD TURN

♦ ***The Boys try to help keep an old lady from being evicted.***

1. What were Stan and Ollie's total assets?

2. Stan claims his father is in the lumber business in a small way. What does his father do for a living?

3. How much does Billy Gilbert bid at the car auction?

4. What time does Stan tell the old man it is at the auction?

5. How much do the Boys think the lady owes Fin for rent?

IN THE NEWS

◆ What does the advertisement that Stanley is cutting out of the newspaper say?

ANSWER:

Big Spring Sale! Now is the time to buy fertilizer. Seeds, Hoses, Rakes. The Sunset Seed Co.

BEAU HUNKS

◆ ***Laurel & Hardy join the Foreign Legion to forget.***

1. What is the name of the band of villains who try to take over Fort Arid?

2. What is Stan's telephone number?

3. Why does Stan say he feels like Jeanie Weanie?

4. How many are going to attack the Fort?

5. What actress' photo is used for the character Jeanie Weanie?

HELPMATES

◆ ***When the wife's away, Ollie throws a party.***

1. What is Stan's phone number?

2. What is Ollie's house number?

3. What time is Ollie supposed to pick up his wife?

4. Where is Ollie's wife?

5. Why does Ollie need Stan to come over?

ANY OLD PORT

♦ *Stan has to box against an angry Mugsy Long.*

1. How much would the Boys make if Stan lasted four rounds in a boxing match against Mugsy Long?

2. How much did Ollie bet on Stan to lose the fight?

3. What does Hardy order to eat that Stan can't have since he has to fight later?

4. What are the Boys' occupations?

5. What is the name of Mugsy Long's Inn?

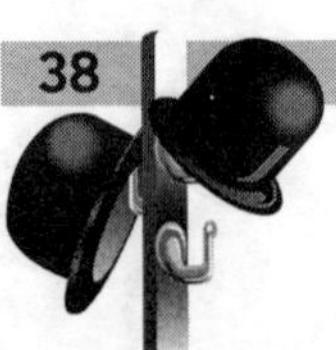

THE MUSIC BOX

♦ *Stan and Ollie deliver a piano.*

1. How much money did Stan and Ollie have to start their business?

2. What is the name of their business?

3. What is the address of the home where the piano is to be delivered?

4. What are all of Professor Theodore Von Schwarzenhoffen's titles?

5. What year was Stan and Ollie's company founded, and what is their motto?

6. What songs start to play on the player piano?

7. What is their horse's name?

HEAVE-HO

♦ The Music Box steps first appeared in the 1925 Hal Roach/Pathe comedy, 'Isn't Life Terrible' with Charley Chase & Oliver Hardy.

♦ The stairs are located between 923 & 935 Vendome St. in the Silver Lake area, Los Angeles, California.

♦ The Music Box steps have 131 steps.

CARRY ON

Stan & Ollie say "Heave — Ho" **31 times** in this three-reeler

THE CHIMP

♦ ***The circus is breaking up, and Stan and Ollie get Ethel, the chimp.***

1. What is the name of the circus?

2. Name three special things Ethel the chimp can do.

3. What do Stan and Ollie draw in the lottery as items they get to take from the circus?

4. What does Stan call the lion that chases them?

5. What is Tiny Sanford's character's name?

COUNTY HOSPITAL

♦ ***Stan pays Ollie a visit in the hospital.***

1. What hospital room is Ollie in?

2. What time of day does Stan visit Ollie?

3. Stan accidentally sits on a hypodermic needle which makes him drowsy. What was the room number of the patient who was supposed to receive the shot?

4. What does Stan bring Ollie in the hospital?

5. Which of Ollie's legs is broken?

SCRAM

◆ *The Boys in trouble with the law.*

1. What does the judge sentence the Boys to after they are caught sleeping in the park?

2. When asked by the judge how they plead, what does Ollie reply?

3. What is the name of the judge and his wife?.

4. How do the Boys end up in 'Arthur Housman's home?

5. How long a jail sentence would the Boys have received if the jails weren't already full?

PACK UP YOUR TROUBLES

◆ *Eddie's baby and the Boys.*

1. Why can't Ollie go fight in the war?

2. How do the Boys try to get out of going to war?

3. What branch of the military do they join?

4. How long do the Boys search through the phone book looking for Eddie's parents?

5. To make money the Boys run a lunch wagon. On what corner are they set up?

NEWSPAPERS

In their films:

◆ The Los Angeles Chronicle / 'Pack Up Your Troubles'

◆ Los Angeles Examiner / 'Going Bye-Bye'

◆ The Evening Blade / Saps at Sea

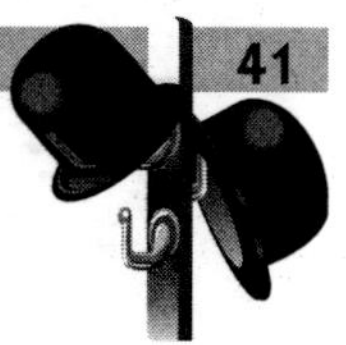

THEIR FIRST MISTAKE

♦ ***Stan acts as Ollie's marriage counselor.***

1. Stan has tickets to go to a bazaar. Whose bazaar is it and what are they giving away?

2. What show did Stan and Ollie go to the night before?

3. What is Stan being sued for by Ollie's wife?

4. Name Ollie's wife.

5. What is Hardy's boss' name?

6. What is Stan's solution to the Hardys' marital problems?

TOWED IN A HOLE

♦ ***Stan's idea to cut out the middleman almost works.***

1. What is the name of the junk yard where Stan and Ollie buy their fishing boat?

2. According to the sign on their truck, what is their specialty?

3. Name the game Stan plays on the wall below deck.

4. What is the Boys' occupation?

NAME GAME

♦ What is the name painted on the boat?

ANSWER:

Ruth – for Virginia Ruth Rogers – Stan's future wife.

TWICE TWO

♦ ***The Hardys are going over to the Laurels' for dinner.***

1. What flavor ice cream is Stan supposed to bring back from the store?

2. What is the second choice of ice cream Stan is supposed to get?

3. Where do Ollie and his wife plan to go to dinner after leaving the Laurel's house?

4. How many times does Stan call home about the ice cream?

5. After learning he is at the wrong store, why doesn't Stan go next door and buy the ice cream?

ME & MY PAL

♦ ***Ollie is about to be married, but Stan's gift is a distraction.***

1. At what time is Ollie to be married?

2. What four items does Stan have with him when he arrives at Ollie's house?

3. Where does Ollie want to go on his honeymoon, and where are the train tickets actually for?

4. What is the working time for the puzzle Stan bought for Ollie?

5. What is Fin's character's name?

THE DEVIL'S BROTHER

♦ ***Stanlio and Ollio decide to become bandits.***

1. How are the Boys going to be executed?

2. What is the name of the local tavern?

3. How much is the reward for the Ladyship's jewels?

4. How much is the reward for the bandit – Fra Diavolo?

5. Name the brand and year of wine the Boys go to the wine cellar to get.

6. Where and when does the story take place?

THE MIDNIGHT PATROL

♦ ***With the Boys on the police force, it's law & disorder.***

1. What is the address of the home being burglarized?

2. What other Laurel and Hardy comedy featured an address on Walnut Avenue?

3. What is the number of the squad car the Boys are driving?

4. Stan tells the burglar he is being arrested. What does he say the charge is?

5. The Boys actually make an arrest, but whom do they apprehend?

BUSY BODIES

♦ ***A day at the sawmill.***

1. What is the Boys' occupation?
2. When Ollie gets stuck in the window frame, Stan reads blueprints for what structure?
3. How does Stan get the brush full of glue off Ollie's face?
4. Who plays Stan and Ollie's foreman?
5. How do the Boys play music in their car?

DIRTY WORK

♦ ***Chimney sweeps are hired to clean the chimney of a mad scientist.***

1. How many years has Professor Noodle been working on his rejuvenation formula?
2. On what animal does Noodle first test the rejuvenation formula?
3. Name Professor Noodle's servant.
4. When Professor Noodle asks Ollie where Jessup is, what is Ollie's response?
5. What becomes of Ollie?

SONS OF THE DESERT

♦ ***The Boys' lodge is holding its annual convention – but their wives won't let them go.***

1. What song do the Sons of the Desert sing?

2. Where is the annual convention being held?

3. What is Stan & Ollie's tent name & number?

4. How many conventions have there been?

5. Where is Stan's wife?

6. What is Stan's wife's name?

7. What is Ollie's wife's name?

8. At Ollie's house, what magazine does Stan pretend to be reading?

9. How many "apples" has Stan eaten?

10. Where does Lottie want to go on vacation?

11. What kind of doctor does Stan get for Ollie, and what is his name?

12. What illness does the doctor say Ollie has?

13. Where is Charley Chase from and what is his tent number?

♦ William Seiter, the director of 'Sons of the Desert', worked with Laurel and Hardy just once and made one of the Boys' best films. However, he was fired as director from the Christmas classic 'The Bishop's Wife' with Cary Grant and David Niven. During his career, he directed Wheeler & Woolsey, W.C. Fields, the Marx Bros. and Abbott & Costello.

OLIVER THE EIGHTH

◆ ***Ollie is going to marry a crazy woman who plans to cut his throat.***

1. The Boys answer a widow's personal ad in which she's hunting for a husband. What is her P.O. box number?

2. What is Ollie's address?

3. What is the butler's name?

4. What are the Boys' occupations?

5. Why does Mae Busch kill men named Oliver?

GOING BYE-BYE!

◆ ***The Boys testify against Butch Long and he vows revenge.***

1. What is Stan and Ollie's phone number?

2. What does Butch threaten to do to the Boys when he breaks out of jail?

3. When the judge sentences Butch Long to life in prison, what is Stan's reply in the courtroom?

4. Where are Stan and Ollie planning a trip?

5. Stan puts an ad in the newspaper for someone to go along on their trip. What does the P.S. in the ad say?

THEM THAR HILLS

♦ ***Ollie needs to get away because of his health.***

LUNCHTIME

♦ What does Ollie prepare for lunch?

ANSWER:

Baked beans and coffee

1. What is Ollie's illness?

2. What does Billy Gilbert prescribe for Ollie?

3. Stan says the water tickles his throat. What is Ollie's reasoning for the tickle?

4. What is the name of the song Ollie hums?

5. Which of Ollie's feet has gout?

BABES IN TOYLAND

♦ ***Stannie Dum and Ollie Dee are toymakers.***

1. What are the three little pigs' names?

2. How much does Stan owe Ollie?

3. What month does this film take place?

4. What are Stan and Ollie found guilty of and what is their punishment?

5. What was Tom-Tom charged with?

6. Which of the three pigs was taken?

7. Name the evil villain.

THE LIVE GHOST

♦ ***The Boys shanghai a crew for a haunted ship.***

1. What time is it when Arthur Housman rings the bell on the ship?

2. What is the Boys' occupation before hijacking a crew for Walter Long?

3. What does Stan bet the sailors in the bar that they can't do?

4. Who is the first victim of Stan's bet?

TIT FOR TAT

♦ ***They open their own store and deal with their neighbor.***

1. Name Laurel and Hardy's store.

2. What is Charlie Hall's store name?

3. How much are pocket watches in the Boys' store?

4. What is unique about this Laurel & Hardy two-reeler?

5. What does Charlie Hall put in the marshmallows?

THE FIXER UPPERS

♦ *The Boys sell Christmas cards door-to-door and end up helping a woman in despair.*

1. How much does the woman (Mae Busch) offer Ollie to make her husband jealous?

2. What is her husband's name?

3. What are Mae Busch's address and phone number?

4. Name the cafe the Boys go to after her husband challenges Ollie to a duel to the death.

5. What do they order at the cafe?

6. At what time do the Boys start drinking, and when do they go "home"?

THICKER THAN WATER

♦ *Mrs. Hardy demands that Ollie do the dishes before he goes to the ballgame.*

1. How much money do the Hardys have saved up?

2. At the auction, how much do the Boys pay for the grandfather clock?

3. What magazine does Stan browse through to avoid Mrs. Hardy?

4. What is Ollie's doctor's name?

5. Approximately what time is it when Stan goes to visit Ollie in the hospital?

BONNIE SCOTLAND

♦ *Stan shows up for the reading of his grandfather's will.*

1. What is the attorney's name who reads the will?

2. What does Stan inherit?

3. What did Stan's grandfather die of? (And it's not a Tuesday)

4. Why don't the Boys have passports?

5. How do Stan and Ollie prove to the attorney who they are?

6. What are the Boys' prisoner numbers?

7. How much time did Stan and Ollie have left on their jail sentence when they escaped?

HAPPY BIRTHDAY

♦ A calendar can be seen hanging on the office wall with the date June 16 showing — Stan Laurel's birthday

8. Who made Ollie's pants?

9. What is the Boys' rank in the Army?

THE BOHEMIAN GIRL

♦ *A king's daughter is abducted by gypsies.*

COME AGAIN?

♦ The song 'Then You'll Remember Me' is not sung by the actor Antonio Moreno, who played Mae Busch's lover, but Felix Knight, who played Tom-Tom in 'Babes in Toyland.'

♦ Do you know who dubbed Stan's high-pitched singing voice? It was none other than Laurel & Hardy alumna Rosina Lawrence, who played Mary Roberts in 'Way Out West.'

1. What time is it when the Boys go into the village?

2. Name the game the Boys play to decide who gets to hold the money.

3. What is Darla Hood's character's name?

4. Who is Mrs. Hardy (Mae Busch) fooling around with behind Ollie's back?

5. How long does it take Stanley to make a malted milk?

6. What is the Count's name?

7. How many years pass in this film?

8. For what musical instrument is Ollie taking lessons?

OUR RELATIONS

♦ ***Stan and Ollie's long lost twin brothers show up.***

1. With who are the wives going to play bridge?

2. What is the name of the ship that Bert and Alf are on?

3. How much money do Bert and Alf give the chief engineer (James Finlayson) to start their savings?

4. How much does Fin give Stan and Ollie to have a "fling" on?

5. Where does the captain ask the Boys to bring the package?

6. What's the waiter's name at Denker's?

7. Name the two women that Bert and Alf meet at Denker's.

8. Where is Fin staying while the ship is docked?

9. What's the name of the pawn shop that Bert and Alf go to?

10. Where does Fin hide Bert and Alf's money?

11. What is the judge's name?

12. What is the name of the dinner club where Bert, Alf, Stan and Ollie all keep missing one another?

WAY OUT WEST

♦ ***The Boys deliver a deed, but to the wrong person.***

1. Where is Lola Marcel from?

2. What is the name of the saloon?

3. When Fin pushes $1 on the cash register, what rings up?

4. How does Stan stop the stage coach?

5. In what month is this film set?

6. What does Stan put in his shoe?

7. Ollie loses a heirloom necklace inside of his clothes. As he removes his clothes to look for it, what does Stan suggest he do?

8. What does Stan rest his head on in the saloon?

9. What is Mary Roberts' father's name?

10. Giving the deed to Lola is the second mistake the Boys make. What was the first?

11. How many times does Stan light his thumb?

12. Where do Ollie, Stan, and Mary plan to go from here?

13. What does Ollie want to eat when he gets there?

14. What does Stan want to eat when he gets there?

SWISS MISS

♦ *Stan and Ollie go to Switzerland to sell mousetraps.*

1. What mode of transportation do the Boys use?

2. What is the name of their business?

3. What is keeping Stan's bell from ringing?

4. How long have the Boys been in Switzerland?

5. What does Ollie order after dinner at the Alpen Hotel?

6. How does Stan finally get the St. Bernard to give him the brandy?

7. To prove that she is capable of playing the lead of a peasant girl in her husband's new opera, famous opera singer Anna Hoepfel (Della Lind) takes a job as what at the hotel?

8. What will the chef do if he catches the Boys with Anna?

BLOCK-HEADS

♦ *Ollie brings home an old Army buddy for supper.*

1. What is Ollie's apartment number?

2. How long had the war been over before Stan was found still guarding the trench?

3. What is the name of Mr. & Mrs. Hardy's neighbors?

4. Afraid that his wife won't believe his story on why the neighbor lady is in his pajamas, Ollie disguises her as what?

5. What names does Finlayson call Ollie that starts a fight?

THE FLYING DEUCES

♦ *The Boys join the Foreign Legion.*

1. What did Ollie say he wanted to come back as in another life?

2. After the plane crash, what did Ollie come back as?

3. Why do the Boys join the Foreign Legion?

4. What is the name of the tune which Ollie sings?

5. How many times does Stan hit his head on the sloped ceiling in their room?

R.I.P.

♦ In an unusual move in this film, Ollie is killed in a plane crash. Name another film in which both Stan & Ollie die.

The Midnight Patrol

A CHUMP AT OXFORD

♦ ***Stan gets hit on the head and is suddenly intelligent.***

1. As the Boys are hitchhiking, who stops to pick them up?

2. How much money do they have left when they go to the employment agency?

3. What is Anita Garvin's character's name?

4. What is she looking for?

5. What is the name of the bank that is robbed?

HEDGE MAZE HINTS

♦ When entering, go to the right, then the left, then to the right again. Then after you've been to the right, you keep going right until you come to a left turn again. Then you go right again, until you find yourself left on the right side.

If you keep to the right, you can't go wrong.

SAPS AT SEA

♦ ***The Boys rent a boat, but they end up being ship-jacked.***

1. Name the horn manufacturing company where Stan and Ollie work?

2. How many nervous breakdowns have there been that week?

3. Which horn always causes the breakdown?

4. What does the sign in the testing room say?

5. What is Ollie's ailment?

6. What does Fin recommend as a cure?

7. What instrument does Stan play?

8. Name the boat Stan and Ollie rent.

9. What is the goat's name?

10. What is the spy's name?

11. Who rents the boat to the Boys?

12. How much is the reward for Nick?

13. What is Nick Grainger's cell number?

14. How many guards did Nick kill?

RECIPE

Nick's Synthetic supper:

- **Sauce:** Red paint
- **Spaghetti:** String
- **Grated cheese:** Soap
- **Meatballs:** Sponge
- **Bacon:** Kerosene lamp wick
- **Biscuits:** Talcum powder
- **Coffee:** Tobacco

GREAT GUNS

♦ ***Stan and Ollie enlist to take care of their friend.***

1. How does Stan clip the lawn?

2. What is the name of Stan's pet raven?

3. How many things is Daniel Forrester allergic to?

4. What is Stan going to give Daniel for his birthday?

5. How old is Daniel?

6. What state is Daniel from?

7. Name Daniel's two aunts.

8. Where does Stan hide his raven during the inspection?

9. During war games, which side are the Boys on, blue or white?

ALL IN THE FAMILY

♦ Diana Rochelle, aka Margret Roach, who worked with the Boys in 'Swiss Miss' & 'A-Haunting We Will Go', was the daughter of Hal Roach.

A-HAUNTING WE WILL GO

♦ ***The Boys get caught up in an illegal scheme with gangsters.***

1. What is the Boys' occupation?

2. What is the name of the machine that makes money?

3. How much is Dante paying Stan & Ollie per week?

4. Where did the Boys want to go, and where did they end up?

AIR RAID WARDENS

♦ ***Since they can't enlist, the Boys become air raid wardens.***

1. How much do a shave, a haircut, and a shoe-shine cost?

2. What is the barber's name?

3. Which one of the following businesses didn't Stan & Ollie run in this film?

A. Laurel & Hardy Fertilizer
B. Laurel & Hardy Pet Shop
C. Laurel & Hardy Radio Shop
D. Laurel & Hardy Bicycles Inc. Ltd.

4. Kennedy is working on a jigsaw puzzle. What is it a picture of?

JITTERBUGS

♦ *The Boys are messed up in a gas scam, but they don't know it.*

1. What does it say on Stan and Ollie's trailer?

2. When Ollie swallows a harmonica, what song does Stan play by pushing on Ollie's stomach?

3. What are the Boys' occupations?

THE DANCING MASTERS

♦ *Stan and Ollie operate their own school.*

1. What do the Boys do for a living?

2. Who did actress Trudy Marshall play in this film?

3. What does Grant invent?

4. How does Ollie plan to help Grant get the money he needs for his invention?

MALCOLM ST. CLAIR

♦ He worked with Buster Keaton and Mack Sennett in the 1920s and ended up directing Laurel & Hardy's last four films with 20th Century-Fox.

THE BIG NOISE

♦ *Stan and Ollie are detectives hired to guard a new explosive.*

1. What items does Stan pull out of the suitcase?

2. Where do Stan and Ollie hide the bomb?

3. Who cheats when playing poker?

4. For what detective agency do the Boys work for?

5. This film uses two earlier films' ideas; can you name the two films?

NOTHING BUT TROUBLE

♦ *The Boys try to help out a boy king.*

1. Name the boy who is king.

2. What is Stan's occupation?

3. What is Ollie's occupation?

4. What country does the boy serve as king?

5. Who is trying to kill the king?

6. What sport does the king want to play more than anything?

THE BULLFIGHTERS

♦ ***The Boys are private detectives in Mexico.***

1. Where are Stan and Ollie from in 'The Bullfighters'?
2. Who are the Boys looking for in Mexico City?
3. What is Stan and Ollie's room number at the hotel?
4. What is the name of the famous Spanish bullfighter who is Stan's double?

ATOLL K

♦ ***Stanley inherits an island where the Boys decide to start their own republic.***

1. What is the name of the Boys' boat?
2. What book did Ollie read?
3. What is the name of their island?
4. What is the emblem on their country's flag?
5. Name the notaries that handled Stan's inheritance.

TRIVIA ANSWERS
See How Well You Did

So how did you do? Rate yourself below:

CORRECT ANSWERS	
0 - 100	**Terrible as Turpin**
101 - 200	**Simply Stanley**
201 - 300	**Excellent as Ollie**
301 - 400	**Fabulous as Fin**
400 - and up	**Great!!! You're an M.D., A.D., D.D.S., F.L.D., F.F.F. und F. !!!!!**

LUCKY DOG

1. Henry or Henrietta
2. Metropolitan Dog Fanciers Association Annual Exhibit
3. Dynamite
4. Bandit
5. Count De Chease from Switzerland

FORTY-FIVE MINUTES FROM HOLLYWOOD

1. A bushy mustache
2. Al K. Hall / Bootlegger / Name your poison
3. A starving actor
4. House detective
5. Orville

DUCK SOUP

1. 'Another Fine Mess'

2. They're hiding from the sheriff who is recruiting bums to fight forest fires

3. Bums

4. A stolen bicycle

SLIPPING WIVES

1. Ferdinand Flamingo

2. Jarvis

3. Mr. Lionel Ironsides, writer of fairy stories

4. A paint delivery man

5. The butler

6. 'The Fixer Uppers'

LOVE 'EM & WEEP

1. Romaine Rickets

2. 'Chickens Come Home'

3. Judge Chigger

4. Aggie

5. 7:00 p.m.

WHY GIRLS LOVE SAILORS

1. A ship (clipper)
2. Pulls his turtleneck up over his head and pretends to be a ghost
3. Nelly

WITH LOVE & HISSES

1. Top sergeant Banner
2. Captain Bustle
3. Cuthbert Hope
4. They hide behind a billboard
5. 'All's well that ends swell'

SUGAR DADDIES

1. He steals things, kills people, and eats with his knife
2. $50,000
3. He got married at the lion's cage at the circus, and the bartender was best man
4. Stan is a lawyer
5. Ollie is James Finlayson's butler

SAILORS BEWARE!

1. Chester Chaste / cab driver

2. Purser Cryder / ship's purser

3. He's not her baby; he's her midget husband pretending to be a baby so he can steal money and jewels

4. Madame Ritz

5. Baroness Behr

THE SECOND HUNDRED YEARS

1. Little Goofy and Big Goofy

2. 40 years

3. Tiny Sanford

4. Two French V.I.P.'s

5. Four times

CALL OF THE CUCKOOS

1. The Gimplewarts

2. Radio announcers

3. They had just filmed 'The Second Hundred Years' days before

4. An apple

DO DETECTIVES THINK?

1. Tipton Slasher

2. To death for killing two Chinamen (And I hope you choke!)

3. Ferdinand Finkleberry

4. Sherlock Pinkham

5. 'Going Bye-Bye!'

PUTTING PANTS ON PHILIP

1. Piedmont Mumblethunder

2. S.S. Miramar

3. 33

4. Girl chasing

5. Philip is Piedmont's nephew

6. Louise

THE BATTLE OF THE CENTURY

1. Thunder-Clap Callahan
2. $5
3. $1,000
4. Canvasback Clump
5. The Human Mop
6. $100
7. $5

LEAVE 'EM LAUGHING

1. 'Keep Smiling'
2. Charlie Hall
3. Edgar Kennedy
4. A toothache
5. 3 a.m.

FLYING ELEPHANTS

1. 6,000 years ago

2. Little Twinkle Star

3. Mighty Giant

4. A shootsman

THE FINISHING TOUCH

1. $500

2. Nails

3. Gibraltar

4. There is a hospital across the street

5. Dorothy Coburn

FROM SOUP TO NUTS

1. "Undressed"

2. A cherry

3. Six times

4. 'A Chump At Oxford'

5. "Laurel and Hardy - waiters. All we ask is a chance."

YOU'RE DARN TOOTIN'

1. The clarinet

2. The French horn

3. Sister MacPherson

4. Sturgeon

5. 14 weeks

THEIR PURPLE MOMENT

1. In a secret compartment in the pocket of the man in painting

2. 1750

3. $28.10

4. Fives times

5. Four big steaks

6. $22 and turns over to $22.10

SHOULD MARRIED MEN GO HOME?

1. 'Men O' War' (soda fountain)
2. A divot
3. "If you're not in when I come back, I'll know you are out, Stan."
4. 'The Maiden's Prayer'

EARLY TO BED

1. 'Blue Boy'
2. Stan falls face first into Ollie's birthday cake (and appears to be frothing at the mouth)
3. Ollie's rich uncle left him money
4. Ollie's butler
5. If Stan can catch him

TWO TARS

1. Ensign
2. Farming equipment ran out of gas in the middle of the road
3. Oregon
4. Charlie Hall

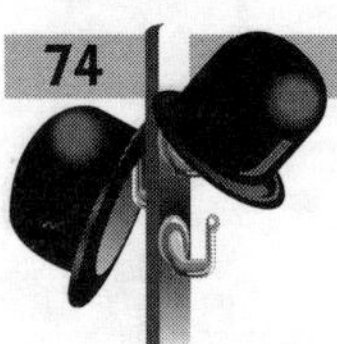

HABEAS CORPUS

1. Professor Padilla
2. Ledoux
3. Midnight
4. Hunter and Third
5. A bat

WE FAW DOWN

1. His boss
2. To the Orpheum Theater
3. The Great Navarro (a trick bicycle rider) and Hawaiian dancers
4. Play poker
5. 'Sons of the Desert'

LIBERTY

1. A crab
2. "Stop nipping"
3. James Finlayson
4. Jean Harlow

WRONG AGAIN

1. $5,000

2. Monday

3. The Piping Rock Riding Academy

4. 6 Collingwood Place

5. On the piano

THAT'S MY WIFE

1. Intended to stay for five minutes, but stayed for two years

2. The Pink Pup

3. Garrick and Lucille in 'The Pageant of Love'

4. Uncle Bernal

5. Uncle Bernal won't leave Ollie a dime if he's not happily married and Ollie's wife just left him, so Stan fills in.

BIG BUSINESS

1. 501

2. 281

3. Christmas trees

4. Tiny Sanford

5. Using a penknife, Stan cuts a chunk off Fin's door frame

UNACCUSTOMED AS WE ARE

1. Barbara
2. The Kennedys
3. Puzzoms
4. Thelma Todd
5. Five years
6. 'Block-Heads'

DOUBLE WHOOPEE

1. 25¢
2. The Independent Taxi Company
3. Three times
4. Broadway Street
5. Footman and doorman

BERTH MARKS

1. Vaudeville musicians
2. Pottsville
3. Santa Fe Station at 9:45 a.m.

MEN O'WAR

1. 15¢
2. 30¢
3. Frassasass, I mean Sassafras
4. General
5. Her gloves
6. Her underwear

PERFECT DAY

1. 36 times
2. 34 times
3. Sunday
4. Baldwin Cooke

THEY GO BOOM

1. 3 a.m.
2. 'Smile All The While'
3. Restwell Air Mattress
4. Ammonia
5. Charlie Hall

BACON GRABBERS

1. Repossession officers
2. Radio
3. A sandwich
4. Collis P.

THE HOOSE-GOW

1. An apple
2. "Only watching the raid"
3. They pour rice into the radiator
4. James Finlayson

ANGORA LOVE

1. Penelope
2. Mr. Caribeau
3. Their last dime
4. 10 years
5. 13
6. Laughing Gravy

NIGHT OWLS

1. Cats ("Meeeooowww")

2. 'Under the Anheuser Busch'

3. Kennedy blackmails them into doing it

4. Kennedy

BLOTTO

1. 'Rainbow Club'

2. Oxford 0614

3. 15¢ (calls him 3 times)

4. An ice bucket

BRATS

1. 'Go To Sleep My Baby'

2. Billiards

3. Ollie cheats, but Stan wins

4. Jean Harlow's

BELOW ZERO

1. 'In the Good Old Summertime'
2. Ollie - double bass; and Stan - organ
3. Gaston, instead of garcon
4. The Deaf and Dumb Institute

HOG WILD

1. Tillie
2. Install the radio aerial
3. Hat

THE LAUREL~HARDY MURDER CASE

1. November, Septober, Octember, Nowonder
2. General Grant
3. Dover Road
4. $3 million

ANOTHER FINE MESS

1. 1558 Poinsettia Avenue, Beverly Hills
2. Croquet, Parcheesi, and billiards
3. Appletree (twice), Figtree, Flagpole, and Crabtree
4. Six business cards
5. "Omaha, dear old Omaha"

BE BIG

1. Atlantic City
2. Ollie fakes an illness
3. The Boys' lodge is throwing a stag party in their honor
4. Charlie Hall
5. A toy sail boat

CHICKENS COME HOME

1. Dealers in high grade fertilizer
2. Granite 3648
3. 7:00 p.m.
4. Four
5. Mayor

LAUGHING GRAVY

1. 316; Apartment #14

2. $1,000

3. 'The Bohemian Girl' and 'Pardon Us'

4. Charlie Hall

OUR WIFE

1. Flit

2. Dulcy

3. William Gladding

4. Rice and a shoe

5. Dimple Dumplin'

PARDON US

1. $500

2. Stan: "Three times with two leftover"
   Ollie: "There's only one left over"

3. January 14 (which happens to be Hal Roach's birthday)

4. 13 times

5. Beer barons

COME CLEAN

1. "Sorry you're out. If I don't come back, I won't be here." Stan

2. Strawberry, pineapple and vanilla

3. Orange, gooseberry and chocolate

4. Saturday

5. $1,000

6. Buy $1,000 worth of chocolate ice cream

ONE GOOD TURN

1. One Ford, model 1911; one tent, model 1861; one union suit, two shirts and three socks

2. Sells toothpicks

3. $100

4. 1:25 p.m.

5. $100

BEAU HUNKS

1. The Riffians

2. Hollywood 4368

3. Because he feels as if he's traveled all over the world

4. More than the number of hairs on the head of Muhammad

5. Jean Harlow's

HELPMATES

1. Aptoss 8080

2. 1645

3. Noon

4. Chicago visiting her mother

5. To help him clean the house after throwing a wild party

ANY OLD PORT

1. $50

2. Ten to one that Mugsy Long would win

3. A bowl of clam chowder, large porterhouse steak smothered in onions, baked potato, lima beans, buttered beets, combination salad, double portion of apple pie with a large piece of American cream cheese, and a flagon of coffee

4. Ollie is head harpooner on a whaling boat, and Stan is bait

5. Ye Mariner's Rest

THE MUSIC BOX

1. $3.80

2. Laurel and Hardy Transfer Co.

3. 1127 Walnut Avenue

4. M.D., A.D., D.D.S., F.L.D., F.F.F. und F

5. 1931 / 'Tall Oaks From Little Acorns Grow'

6. Medley of Patriotic Songs

7. Susie

THE CHIMP

1. Colonel Fin's Big Show

2. Read, write, and milk a cow

3. Stan got a flea circus; Ollie got Ethel the chimp

4. MGM

5. Destructo, the cannonball king

COUNTY HOSPITAL

1. Room 14

2. Around 11:25 a.m.

3. Room 22

4. Hard-boiled eggs and nuts

5. His right leg

SCRAM

1. One hour to get out of town

2. "Not guilty, Your Highness"

3. Judge & Mrs. Beaumont

4. In appreciation for helping him retrieve his key from a sidewalk grate, Housman offers them lodging for the night.

5. 180 days

PACK UP YOUR TROUBLES

1. He has flat feet
2. Pretend their right arms are amputated
3. Army
4. Three days, one hour and 56 Smiths
5. Corner of 2nd Avenue and 16th Street

THEIR FIRST MISTAKE

1. The Cement Worker's Bazaar; a steam shovel
2. A 'Punch and Judy Show'
3. The alienation of Mr. Hardy's affections
4. Arabella
5. Mr. Jones
6. A baby

TOWED IN A HOLE

1. Joe's Junk Yard
2. Crabs
3. Tic Tac Toe
4. Fish peddlers

TWICE TWO

1. Strawberry

2. Tutti-fruitti

3. The Ambassador

4. Three times

5. Because he spent all his money calling Fanny

ME & MY PAL

1. High noon

2. Train tickets, ring, wedding present (jigsaw puzzle), and a bag of rice

3. Saskatchewan is where he wants to go, but the tickets are for Chicago

4. Two hours

5. Mr. Peter Cucumber ("I don't care if he's Mr. Dill Pickle!")

THE DEVIL'S BROTHER

1. Hanged; shot
2. The Tavern of the Cuckoo
3. 10,000 lire
4. 20,000 lire, dead or alive
5. Chateau Laffae 1728
6. Northern Italy; 18th Century

THE MIDNIGHT PATROL

1. 24 Walnut Avenue
2. 'The Music Box' (1127 Walnut Avenue)
3. 13
4. "Robbing a house without a license"
5. The chief

BUSY BODIES

1. Sawmill workers
2. The Boulder Dam
3. Shaves him with a planer
4. Tiny Sanford
5. With a record player in the engine

DIRTY WORK

1. 20 years

2. A duck

3. Jessup

4. "Jessup? Oh, about 35 miles southeast of Augusta, Georgia."

5. He turns into a chimp after falling into the formula

SONS OF THE DESERT

1. "Auld Lang Syne"
2. Chicago
3. Oasis 13
4. 87
5. Duck hunting
6. Betty
7. Lottie
8. 'The American'
9. Three
10. To the mountains
11. A veterinarian; Dr. Horace Meddick
12. Cannis delirous and it might be double cannis delirous
13. Texas; 97

OLIVER THE EIGHTH

1. 204-J
2. 201 Spring Street, Los Angeles, California
3. Jithers
4. Barbers
5. It was an Oliver that left her on the eve of her wedding

GOING BYE-BYE!

1. Main 489
2. Break off their legs and tie them around their necks
3. "Aren't ya gonna hang him?"
4. Heading east
5. P.S. Those not interested, do not answer.

THEM THAR HILLS

1. Gout
2. Get away, go to the mountains
3. Iron in the water
4. "The Old Spinning Wheel"
5. His right foot

BABES IN TOYLAND

1. Elmer, Willie, and Jiggs
2. $1.48
3. Mid-July
4. Charged with burglary; dunked and exiled to Bogeyland
5. Pignapping
6. Elmer
7. Silas Barnaby

THE LIVE GHOST

1. 8:00 p.m. (and all is swell)
2. Cleaning fish at the fish market
3. Put an egg in their mouths without breaking it
4. Leo Willis

TIT FOR TAT

1. Laurel and Hardy Electrical Company
2. Hall Grocery
3. $1.00
4. It's the Boys' only sequel
5. Alum

THE FIXER UPPERS

1. $50

2. Pierre Gustave

3. 14 Gramercy Place / GR6740

4. Cafe Dos Artistes

5. Two beers (Stan: “I’ll have two beers, too.”)

6. 4:30 p.m.; 11:00 p.m.

THICKER THAN WATER

1. $300

2. $290

3. Vogue

4. F.D. Allen

5. 9:05 a.m.

BONNIE SCOTLAND

1. Miggs
2. Bagpipe and a snuff box
3. A broken heart
4. They stowed away on a cattle boat
5. Their criminal identification cards from New York City
6. Ollie's: 44633; Stan's: 44634 (The same convict numbers as in "Pardon Us")
7. One week
8. The Twiddle Tweed Co.
9. Privates

THE BOHEMIAN GIRL

1. 9:00 p.m.
2. Fingers
3. Arline
4. Devilshoof
5. About 15 minutes to a quarter of an hour
6. Arnheim
7. 12
8. Zither

OUR RELATIONS

1. Mrs. Addelquiste

2. S.S. Periwinkle

3. $74

4. $1

5. Denker's Beer Garden

6. Groagan

7. Lily and Alice

8. Mrs. MacGregor's furnished rooms

9. A and 2 Pawn Shop

10. In the lining of his jacket

11. Judge Polk

12. The Pirates Club

WAY OUT WEST

1. San Francisco

2. Mickey Finn's Palace

3. 10¢

4. Shows his leg

5. August

6. Piece of meat that's as "tough as shoe leather"

7. Take a bath

8. A spittoon

9. Cy

10. Buying the Brooklyn Bridge.
Ollie: "Buying that bridge was no mistake"

11. Three times

12. To the South

13. Slice of opossum and yam

14. Fish and chips

SWISS MISS

1. A sled
2. The Miracle Mouse Trap Co. Limited, Inc., etc. etc.
3. A feather
4. Two weeks and haven't sold a single mousetrap
5. Large slice of apple pie and a demitasse
6. Throws chicken feathers into the air, pretending it's snow and yells for help
7. Maid
8. Skin them alive

BLOCK-HEADS

1. 1313
2. 20 years
3. The Gilberts
4. As a chair
5. Big overstuffed polliwog; an inflated blimp

THE FLYING DEUCES

1. A horse
2. A horse
3. To forget (Georgette)
4. "Shine on Harvest Moon"
5. Six times

A CHUMP AT OXFORD

1. City water department
2. $6
3. Mrs. Vandevere
4. A maid and a butler
5. Farmers and Merchants Bank of Commerce

SAPS AT SEA

1. Sharp and Pierce Horn Mfg. Co.
2. Four
3. G minor horn
4. "Silence while men are working"
5. Hornaphobia and on the verge of hornamania
6. An ocean voyage
7. Slide trombone
8. 'Prickly Heat'
9. Narcissus
10. Nick Grainger
11. Captain McKenzie
12. $5,000
13. #3
14. Nine

GREAT GUNS

1. With scissors
2. Penelope
3. 108
4. A blood transfusion
5. 23
6. Vermont
7. Agatha and Martha
8. In Ollie's pants
9. White

A-HAUNTING WE WILL GO

1. Bums
2. The Inflato
3. $25 per week (But Stan insists on $40 per month)
4. They wanted to go to Florida but ended up in Dayton, Ohio

AIR RAID WARDENS

1. Shave: 15¢; haircut: 35¢; shoe-shine: 10¢

2. Charlie Bogars

3. C. Laurel & Hardy Radio Shop. Eustace Middling ran the radio shop, which was actually a front for a Nazi spy ring, out of their bicycle shop

4. The Taj Mahal

JITTERBUGS

1. Laurel & Hardy, the original zoot suit band, a symphony in a nutshell, we play for victory

2. "Pop goes the Weasel"

3. Butler, valet and general factotum

THE DANCING MASTERS

1. Own and operate a dance school

2. Mary Harlan

3. A flamethrowing machine

4. Through an insurance policy that will pay $10,000 on a broken leg, a policy which Ollie has on Stan

THE BIG NOISE

1. Pajamas, socks, alarm clock, detective hats, hot water bottle, magnifying glass, razor strap, pipe, coats, accordion, top hats, shoes

2. In the accordion

3. Ollie

4. Jones Detective Agency

5. 'Berth Marks' and 'Oliver the Eighth'

NOTHING BUT TROUBLE

1. King Christopher

2. Butler

3. Chef

4. Orlandia

5. His uncle

6. Football

THE BULLFIGHTERS

1. Peoria, Illinois

2. Hattie Blake (Larceny Nell)

3. 418

4. Don Sebastian

ATOLL K

1. Momus

2. Robinson Crusoe

3. Crusoeland

4. Heart with an arrow though it

5. Bramwell, Bramwell, & Bramwell (Notaries covering Madrid, Rome & Tangier)

LOST FILMS

Hats Off & The Rogue Song

TOP 10 LIST

◆ 'Camille' (1927)
◆ 'Cleopatra' (1917)
◆ 'The Divine Woman' (1928)
◆ 'Greed' (1925) 40-reel version
◆ 'The Kaiser, Beast of Berlin' (1918)
◆ 'Little Red Riding Hood' (1922) an early Disney cartoon
◆ 'London After Midnight' (1927)
◆ 'The Rogue Song' (1930) starring Laurel and Hardy
◆ 'That Royle Girl' (1925) starring W.C. Fields
◆ The tenth film, 'Edison's Frankenstein,' has been found

Source: American Film Institute

Out of the 106 total appearances on film, it's actually a miracle that only two — a 1927 short and a 1930 full-length color musical, are lost.

The two-reel comedy "**Hats Off**" was last seen in 1928 and was partially remade four years later as the Oscar-winning "The Music Box."

The 12-reel opera "**The Rogue Song**" was last viewed in the 1950s. Now on the "Most Wanted" film list, one reel has since surfaced but contains no footage of Laurel or Hardy. However, the entire soundtrack to the film still exists. In the 1980s, a three-minute clip from reel 10 was found containing the Boys and a bear, both taking shelter from a severe storm.

The only other partially-missing film that contained Laurel & Hardy, but not together as a team, was the 1927 Charlie Chase comedy "**Now I'll Tell One.**"

Discovered in the 1990s to be the 106th film that contained both of the Boys, the search is now on to find the first reel of this two-reel short.

HATS OFF

Premiere Nov. 5, 1927; two reels; silent

The Cast

Stan Laurel
Oliver Hardy
Store Owner: James Finlayson
Woman at top of stairs: Anita Garvin
Lady at bottom of stairs: Dorothy Coburn

OPENING TITLE:
The story of two boys who figure that the world owes them a living — but is about thirty-five years behind in the payments.

The story of two Boys who figure that the world owes them a living — but is about thirty-five years behind in the payments.

Stan & Ollie are seen being thrown out of a cafe by the manager. He hangs up a card that reads 'Wanted: two dishwashers'.

The Boys get up and put on their hats. They have on the wrong derbys. They swap hats.

Stan looks at the sign in the window, reaches down, and picks up a brick. Just as he is about to throw it, Ollie rushes in and stops him.

> **Oliver:** Curb your terrible passion! – Control your terrible Corsican blood! Break the glass an' you'll go to jail! – Then what will become of me?

Ollie turns and throws the brick through the Cafe's window.

The Boys run off and hide in a nearby doorway. Smiling at each other, they notice a sign hanging in the window.

'Wanted: snappy salesmen to sell washing machines'.

Stan: What does it say?

James Finlayson, the manager of the Kwickway Washing Machine Company, sees the Boys reading the sign and talks to them. He removes the "help wanted" sign, and the Boys examine the product that they are about to peddle door-to-door. Stan removes the washing machine's cover, and water splashes all over their new boss and Ollie.

Oliver: We're sorry, boss – my secretary and I will accept this position.

Stan and Ollie grab one of the washing machines and carry it to the truck.

Finlayson: Be careful! – That machine is worth $175!

The Boys manage to place the washer on the truck without any accidents. They get into their Ford truck and start to pull out just as the washer falls off and onto their boss. The Boys stop and pick up the washing machine and Finlayson.

Finlayson: I warn you again! – Be careful!

They put the washer back onto the truck and start to pull out again – and the washing machine falls off and onto Finlayson again.

The Boys' first stop is a four-plex apartment building. They carry the machine up to the first door, and Stan knocks.

A door on the other side of the apartment opens and closes.

Seeing this, they carry the washer down to that apartment and knock. The door they just left now opens. They see the woman and hurriedly carry the machine back to her door, but she has already gone back inside. They knock on her door again and the center apartment door opens. Seeing her, they now carry the machine to her door. They knock, and the door beside them opens. They haul the washing machine next door. Stan starts to knock, and Ollie stops him and knocks himself.

They then pick up the machine and quickly move it next door, anticipating this woman would come to her door. The woman on whose door they actually knocked opens her door. They try to get back over to her, but she doesn't see them and closes her door.

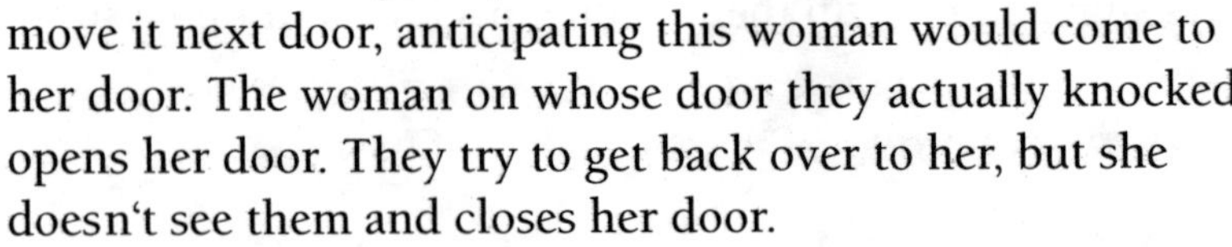

Perplexed, Ollie gets an idea. He tells Stan that they both should knock on the center two doors. As they do, the two end doors open. They run for these doors, but they are closed by the time they get there. They knock on the two end doors, and the two middle apartment doors open. They rush for them, but of course, they are closed by the time

they get there. They start sneaking to the end doors again. They knock on all four doors. They start running to all of the doors as they open, but all are closed before they get to them. Frustrated, the Boys give up and carry the washing machine down the steps, just as the two end doors open. They turn and run, one to each open door. They actually catch the women, and each starts telling them about the machine. They both come back to get the washer to show it to their prospective buyers. They struggle over it and in the meanwhile, both women close their doors.

The Boys throw down their hats in disgust. Ollie yells at Stan and they pick up their hats and put them on. They are wearing each other's hat. They exchange hats and start knocking on doors again. The routine continues as they try knocking on all the doors again. Just then, a cop walks up and watches the Boys. They start kicking the doors, and Stan kicks his open and looks in. Ollie turns around and sees the policeman. Stan turns to tell Ollie that his door is open and also sees the cop. Stan grins at the officer and walks toward the washing machine. Stan and Ollie pick up the washer and start running.

The Boys, driving down the road, see a woman sweeping the sidewalk in front of her house. They stop the truck and approach her, and Stan tells her about their washing machine. Ollie stops him and starts talking to the woman. The annoyed woman turns and slams her door in their faces. Their hats blow off. They turn and pick up their hats, but Ollie immediately realizes they have each other's, and they exchange hats. Ollie starts scolding Stan just as they hear a woman calling them. They look around and Stan points up a very long flight of stairs to where the woman is standing.

Woman: Come on up here.

The Boys start carrying their washing machine up the long flight of stairs. Ollie stumbles, and his hat falls off. It falls all the way down the stairs and rolls into the street.

Oliver: You get it. The slightest exertion and everything goes blank with me.

Stan looks down the long flight of stairs and starts crying. Just as Stan leaves to get the hat, Ollie loses his grip on the washing machine. The washer hits Stan, knocking him down and Ollie comes tumbling into him.

Ollie, embarrassed, grins sheepishly. The Boys pick up their hats and put them on. Wrong hats – and they quickly exchange.

They start carrying the machine back up the stairs and the woman sits down while waiting on them.

The Boys finally make it to the top of the stairs and tip their hats to their prospective client.

Woman: Will you mail this letter?

Ollie takes the letter from the lady.

Oliver: Would you be interested in the world's most synchronistical washing machine?

Woman: I would not — I have my own Chinese.

As the woman exits, Stan and Ollie turn and look at each other, and then go down the long flight of stairs. Each takes a long breath, pick up the machine, and start down.

Carrying the washer down the steps, the Boys stumble,

and their hats fall off. They pick up their hats and put them on their heads. Wrong hats. They exchange and start down the stairs again.

Just as the Boys reach the bottom of the stairs, the woman they just talked to comes running out and yells for them to come back.

Oliver: Maybe the Chinaman sprained his back – you go up an' see.

Stan starts crying. He starts back up the stairs.

Just as Ollie leans on the washer to rest, it rolls out from under him, and he falls. He angrily picks up the washer and leans on it again. It rolls out from under him, and again he falls. Madder than ever, Ollie gets up and kicks the washing machine.

Stan, exhausted, stops to rest. Ollie motions for him to go on. Stan picks up a rock and throws it at Ollie. Stan slowly starts up the steps again. Stan straightens his bow tie as he reaches the top.

Woman: I forgot to put a stamp on my letter.

Stan looks at the woman and then turns and motions for Ollie to come up.

Oliver: Great Kid! – He's made a sale!

Ollie picks up the washing machine and starts up the steps. Struggling by himself, Ollie stumbles and drops the machine. The woman tires of waiting and sits down.

Stan: He's bringing the washer. Imagine a man being that dumb.

Stan sits down and watches Ollie coming up the stairs.

Again he falls and drops the washer. He picks it up and starts carrying it again.

Stan: I wouldn't be surprised if he stopped to demonstrate it.

A tired Ollie sets the washing machine down to rest, and it rolls down the steps. He chases after it.

Stan: He's sure gettin' a lot o' mileage outta that machine.

Ollie, now at the bottom again, starts back up the steps with the washer. This time he manages to make it all the way to the top of the stairs. Ollie starts talking to the woman about her new washer, and Stan shakes his head no.

Stan: She forgot the stamp – and you've got the letter.

A shocked Ollie looks at the stamp the woman offers him, then looks at the stairs and punches Stan in the nose. Stan's hat falls off, and he starts to cry. The woman punches Ollie in the nose. She takes the letter back from Ollie.

Woman: You're the kind of man that always thinks of himself first!

The women exits, and Ollie starts crying. The Boys pick up their washer and start down the stairs.

Stan: I'm growing fond of this thing.

The Boys continue down the stairs.

Oliver: It might be worse. Yes. We might be selling tractors.

They finally reach the bottom of the stairs and set the washer down to rest. A lady approaches them.

Lady: I would love to have a demonstration.
Oliver: Where do you live?

The lady points up the flight of stairs and starts up the steps. Stan kicks her in the fanny. She angrily turns around, thinking Ollie did it, and punches him in the nose. It knocks his hat off. She turns and makes a motion towards Stan, scaring him, and his hat falls off. She turns and storms up the stairs.

Oliver: Thinking of myself again.

They pick up their hats and put them on. Wrong hats again. Ollie takes the hat off and hands it to Stan. Stan, having both hats in his hands, accidentally gives Ollie back the same hat. They start carrying the washer until Ollie sees Stan's hat appears too large for him. Ollie hands him his hat and Stan again accidentally crosses them. Ollie sees where Stan is going wrong and tells him that he wants that hat.

Stan crosses them again, handing Ollie the wrong hat. Ollie, realizing Stan's mistake, throws the hat to the ground and kicks it. Stan throws Ollie's hat to the ground and kicks it. A crowd gathers as the Boys shove each other around. Stan pushes Ollie down, as Ollie sits on Stan's hat. In revenge, Stan turns to kick Ollie's hat, but misses and kicks a street marker. Stan cries and grabs his toes.

The Boys' boss, who happens to be strolling by sees the Boys fighting. He also sees his washing machine sitting in the road. During all the ruckus, a steam roller driving down the road runs over the unattended washing machine. Finlayson turns and sees his washer is destroyed.

Ollie starts laughing and hits Stan on the shoulder. Ollie puts out his hand to Stan to forgive and forget.
Stan gives him a razzberry. Stan knocks Ollie's hat off, and the pushing and shoving starts up again.

Finlayson goes up to the Boys and starts yelling at them. Stan looks at him and knocks his hat off. A man approaches the Boys and speaks to Finlayson.

Man: I saw the whole thing – it was all your fault!

Finlayson knocks the man's hat off. The man knocks Finlayson's hat off. Finlayson stomps on the man's hat and starts to run away. Stan points out a rock to the man, who picks it and throws it at Fin. It hits Finlayson's hat off and he accidentally steps on it.

Another man enters and talks to Ollie and the man.

Man: I saw everything!

Stan knocks the man's hat and Ollie's hat off. Another

man walks up to Stan, and Stan knocks his hat off. That man turns and knocks another man's hat off. Ollie knocks Stan's hat off. A free-for-all ensues.

A policeman enters and sees all the men knocking each other's hats off. The cop turns and talks to Ollie. Stan knocks his hat off. Stan sees a man standing on the corner down the road. Stan runs down to him, knocks his hat off and runs back to the crowd in the street.

The man on the corner bends over, picks up his hat, and puts it back on his head. Another man comes around the corner and knocks his hat off again. He knocks his hat off with his cane.

The police come in and chase everyone away, leaving Stan & Ollie sitting in the center of the road, surrounded by hats. They look at each other and exchange hats.

THE ROGUE SONG

Premiere Jan. 17, 1930; twelve reels; two-color Technicolor

The Rogue Song was directed by *Lionel Barrymore,* better known to audiences today for the perennial Christmas favorite, "It's a Wonderful Life." He played the evil town banker, Mr. Potter, in this 1946 Frank Capra classic.

The Cast

Yegor: Lawrence Tibbett
Princess Vera: Catherine Dale Owen
Princes Alexandra: Nance O'Neil
Countess Tatiana: Judith Vosselli
Prince Serge: Ullrich Haupt
Yegor's mother: Elsa Alsen
Nadja: Florence Lake
Ossman: Lionel Belmore
Hassan: Wallace MacDonald
Petrovna: Kate Price
Frolov: H.A. Morgan
Count Peter: Burr MacIntosh
Azamat: James Bradbury, Jr.
Ali-Bek: Stan Laurel
Murza-Bek: Oliver Hardy

On a snowy mid-summer day in 1910, Yegor and his tribesmen ride up to the Turk's Inn in the Kaishar Mountains in South Russia.

Yegor tells Ali-Bek (Stan) and Murza-Bek (Ollie) to take care of the horses as he and the tribesmen enter the inn.

Oliver looks through the inn doors and then at Stan.

Oliver: He always talks to me like that. That's for the benefit of the other men.

I was with his father before him. In fact, — I saved his father's life once. (Stan reacts) There were lions — mountain lions — four of them. Was I afraid? Hah! No!

Oliver raises his hand and pulls out a dagger.

Oliver: I just finished polishing my saber, not wishing to dirty it . . .

(Stan, now joining in to finish the story he has apparently been told many times)

Oliver & Stan: . . . I slapped them to death.

Oliver glares at Stan. He smiles back at Ollie.

Back inside the inn, Yegor tries to sell Ossman, the inn's owner, a Damascus cloth and bales of gold tissue.

A nervous Ossman explains that an imperial princess and a serene countess are staying at the inn during the snowstorm.

During the negotiating, Petrovna, the princess' servant, informs Yegor that Countess Tatiana should like to meet him. He boldly tells her that the countess can come down if she would like to meet him.

Fearing for her life, Petrovna screams. Princess Vera and Countess Tatiana walk out onto a balcony overlooking the inn to see what had happened.

Yegor, upon seeing the princess and the countess, climbs up the balcony and sings. He introduces himself to the ladies — Son of Prince Yegor, chief of the Kaishar mountain tribesmen. Tatiana asks Yegor if his band are all thieves. He

explains Kaishar means 'Robbing Larks', or bandits who repay their victims with a song.

After learning who he is, Vera wants nothing to do with him; however, Tatiana is intrigued.

She gives him her strand of pearls for making her boring life suddenly exciting. He thanks her and exits the inn.

Outside, Yegor instructs his tribesmen to go ahead, but tells Stan & Ollie to wait there with him. He then scales a balcony toward a window where he overhears the countess telling Ossman to have the Cossacks waiting in the Thieves' Market to catch Yegor disposing of her "stolen" pearls. She instructs that he is to be hung upon his arrest.

Oliver puts his dagger away in its holder. Stan goes inside the inn and closes the door. Oliver opens the door and hits Stan in the nose.

Oliver: Close the door.
Stan: You hit me on the nose.
Oliver: Well, it serves you right. Close it from the outside. Watch me.

Ollie slams the door, causing loose snow on the roof of the inn to topple down on him. Stan points at Oliver and smiles.

Upstairs, Yegor sneaks through a window into the room where Vera and Petrovna are sleeping.Vera awakens and Yegor asks her for her funny hat with a feather she was wearing earlier. He tells her that he knows someone who would like it and she obliges. Yegor then exits by the window. Vera gets up and watches as he mounts his horse and rides off.

As the Boys prepare to ride off, Oliver puts his foot into the stirrup, and it breaks. He tries to fix it but has no luck.

He then tries jumping on the back of the horse which also fails.

> **Stan:** May I suggest something?
> **Oliver:** What?
> **Stan:** Why don't you get on the barrel, then get on to the horse?
> **Oliver:** Thank you.
> **Stan:** You're welcome.
> Oliver climbs on top of the barrel of frozen water.
> **Oliver:** At last you have shown some intelligence.

Just as he goes to step onto the horse, the ice breaks and Ollie falls into the barrel of water. Ollie comes up out of the water and looks at Stan. Stan looks at Oliver and waves at him to follow as Stan rides off.

In the village of the Kaishar tribesmen Yegor, Hassan and Azamat ride into the cheering crowd. At Yegor's house, he is greeted by his mother and he gives her the pearls. His mother is concerned for Nadja, Yegor's younger sister, who has not been not eating, sleeping or smiling since going to the Thieves' Market and dancing on St. Lankas Day. Yegor tries to cheer her up with the princess' hat. She declines his offering, saying all Russian princesses are no good. Yegor thinks she must be in love.

At the Thieves' Market, Ossman is stopped by the captain of the Cossacks. He informs Ossman that the three men of Yegor's tribe that he had pointed out had been hanged, and that he should keep searching for the Singing Bandit.

Yegor, Hassan, Azamat, Laurel and Hardy ride into the market. Yegor dismounts and walks in front of the Boys' horses.

Ollie grins at him. Stan grins, too.

Yegor orders the Boys to stay there and do their job, which is to take care of the horses.

Stanley starts to get off his horse and gets his foot caught in Ollie's coat pocket. Ollie tries to remove it and rips his pocket.

Stan tries to fix it for him, but Oliver slaps his hands.

Oliver: Get your hands off of it.
Stan: You're always picking on me for everything.
Oliver: Well, it serves you right.

Stan pokes Ollie in the eye with his finger. Stanley quickly gets back on his horse, ripping Ollie's coat again.

Princess Vera, Petrovna, and a Cossack guard enter the marketplace. Vera grabs a woman's baby and threatens to keep it unless she tells her if she knows of the tribesman called Yegor. The woman obliges and says she does know him but hasn't seen him. Just then, Vera hears Yegor's singing coming from a nearby wine cellar.

She enters and stares at him as he sings his song. She admits her feelings toward Yegor and warns him that the Cossacks are searching to hang him for stealing the countess' pearls. When questioned on why she came, she said it was unjust to hang a man for something he didn't do. As they look through the nearby window, they see Ossman's carriage going by in search of Yegor. He asks her to wait on the roof of the wine cellar while he tends to some business.

While fixing the horse's saddle, Oliver is goosed with the captain of the guards' cane. He jumps up and looks at the soldier and then at the horse.

Captain of the guards: Say, whose horses are these?
Oliver: I don't know.
Captain: You don't, eh?
Oliver: No, sir.

Stan, standing by the horses, lowers his eyes and looks back at the officer.

Captain: Who is that fellow?

Stan, looking at the captain and Ollie, gives a silly grin.
Oliver: Never saw him before in my life.
Captain: You didn't, eh?

The captain walks over to Stan, who is now petting the neck of his horse and polishing his saddle. Stan starts to get on his horse to ride off.

Captain: Wait a minute. Whose horse is that?
Stan: What horse?
Captain: That horse. Say, who are you with?

Stan looks at Ollie and laughs. The captain laughs along.

Stan: Who — me?

Ollie, looking at the captain and Stan, nervously waves at them.

Captain: Yes, you.
Stan: (Pointing toward Ollie) I'm with him.

Ollie starts to pick his nails while looking at the captain, Stan waves hands.

Stan turns and starts to get on his horse.

Captain: You stay right here.

Soldiers enter, Ollie nervously waves, and Stan starts crying.

Captain: Arrest those men.

As the captain turns to give further instructions to his soldiers, the Boys run off and are chased by the guards.

Yegor returns to the wine cellar roof where Princess Vera has been waiting. He tells her of her beauty and confesses his love for her too.

After eluding the guards, Stan and Ollie sit down to rest. Stan starts to eat a piece of cheese, Ollie takes it away from him and breaks it in two — giving the smallest piece to Stanley. They start to eat it.

Oliver: Just a moment. (Hears buzzing noise)

As Stanley takes a bite of his half of the cheese, he sees its covered with flies. He tries shooing them away and then starts flicking them. He tries hiding the cheese under his coat until the insects leave. Oliver pulls back Stan's coat, and breaks off a small corner and places it on the ground so the flies will be attracted to it and leave their cheese alone. The Boys then go to the corner of the tent, and Stan takes a big bite of cheese.

As he moves the cheese towards his mouth again, a bee buzzes. Stan attempts several times to take another bite but

is stopped each time by a strange buzzing sound.

Oliver: What is that? (buzz, buzz)
Stan: Oh, what's the matter with me? (buzz, buzz)
Stan: Oh, what's — (buzz, buzz)
Stan: Oh, somethings happened (buzz, buzz)
Oooh! Oooh!

The buzzing appears to be coming from Stan's stomach. As he touches his side and the bee buzzes. Stanley starts to cry.

Oliver reaches over and pushes on Stan's stomach. The bee buzzes again. Stan leaps into the air and starts to run around frantically as the buzzing sound continues.

Oliver: What is it? What is it?
Stan: I think I swallowed a bee — or something. (buzz, buzz)
Oliver: A bee! (buzz) Wait – there it is – there it is. I'm holding it.
Stan: Ooh, there – there.
Oliver: There – right there – hold it right there – and I'll get it.
Stan: Oh – oh – oh – (buzz, buzz)
Oliver: Hold it there.

Oliver gets a long stick and tries to hit the bee. He misses and hits Stan on the hand. Ollie swings back again and smacks the mule, who breaks loose from the wagon and starts chasing the Boys.

The captain of the Cossack guards sees Ossman in his carriage. As he attempts to speak to him, the guard realizes

that Ossman has been murdered. He sounds a general alarm throughout the market. Inside the carriage is a letter stating Yegor punishes his betrayers. Just then group of soldiers ride into the market.

Yegor, hearing the alarm, realizes he must leave town, and runs to the edge of the roof, and climbs over. As he and Azamat flee the market, they are spotted and the soldiers give chase. The soldiers shoot at Yegor and he returns fire, killing several. He jumps onto a horse and laughs as he rides away.

Yegor returns home only to find that his sister, Nadja, has stabbed herself and is near death. He pleads for her to explain, but all she is able to utter is a name – Prince Serge – and then dies.

Yegor, vowing revenge, remembers hearing at the market that Countess Tatiana is giving a ball that evening and is certain that the man responsible for his sister's suicide will attend.

That evening at the ball, Yegor sneaks into the room where Countess Tatiana is getting ready. He returns her pearls to her, and she throws them to the floor. He suggests he would like to sing to her guests before being hanged, and she obliges.

As the guests arrive, Vera greets her brother, Prince Serge, and her father, Prince Paul Borisoff.

Yegor enters, singing an ode of his sister's death caused by a vile man, to the guest's astonishment. Prince Serge realizes Yegor is singing about him and quickly retreats upstairs. Yegor follows and grabs the prince by his throat and strangles him. Vera walks in and screams. Yegor tries to explain that the tale in his song was ***his*** sister and ***her*** brother. He explains that Serge, seeing Nadja at the Thieves' Market,

shamed her so that she took her own life.

Vera doesn't understand how Yegor could think that his sister's life was in any way equal to the life of a prince. Her screams are heard by the Cossack soldiers, who rush upstairs only to find an empty room and Prince Serge dead.

Forcing Vera to return to his home with him, Yegor tells his mother that they must move to hills far, far away. He tells the princess that she shall never be found and will work for his family because of her lack of remorse for her brother's actions against his sister.

Yegor's caravan starts outward into the hills.

After making camp that night, Stan prepares to shave Ollie.

Oliver: Whew! Wasn't that a long ride today?

Stan: It sure was.

Oliver: And wasn't that desert hot?

Stan: And sandy, too.

Oliver: Say, you know Yegor was so tired he wouldn't even talk to me.

Stan: I noticed that (Ollie snaps his fingers at Stan who is preparing to lather his face)

Oliver: And don't dip your brush in the soup.

Stan: I thought it was water.

Oliver: Come on and let's get this over with. Now be careful.

As Stan begins to lather Ollie's face, some women walk by and smile at Stan. He smiles back. Stan, more interested in the women than what he is doing, accidentally sticks the lather brush in Ollie's mouth. The Boys struggle with each other; Ollie pushes Stan's hand away. All the hairs of the

brush have come off the handle in Ollie's mouth.

Oliver: Oh! Oh! Oh! Oh! Why don't you shave me?
Stan: Wait a minute — wait a minute.

Stan, looking at the razor, decides it needs sharpened. He picks up a rock and starts to sharpen it. Stan accidentally drops the rock, which lands on Ollie's toes. Ollie screams. Stan picks up another rock which Ollie pushes out of his hands. It also lands on Ollie's foot. Ollie yells.

Stan tests the razor's sharpness, which makes a booming sound. Ollie reacts to the sound. He sharpens a little more and tests it again. Stan looks at Ollie and smiles.

Stan, who put his lather on Ollie's shirt, starts to shave him. Ollie removes the lather just as Stan hooks his fingers under Ollie's nose and lifts. He shaves Ollie's neck and wipes off the lather on the back of his neck.

Oliver: I think you'd better shave the back of my neck.

Stan sits down on a crate and starts shaving the back of his neck (noise of razor scraping). A chicken inside the crate pecks Stan in the seat of his pants. A startled Stan drops his razor down the back of Ollie's shirt.

Oliver: Oh – oh!
Stan: What's the matter?
Oliver: The razor — the razor — Oh!
Stan: Where is it?
Oliver: Down my back. Get it out – get – get – oh! Oh!
Stan: Relax — relax.
Oliver: All right –

Now be careful.
Oliver: Oh!
Stan: Don't move now.
Oliver: I won't.
Stan: Don't get excited –
Oliver: I'm not excited –
Stan: I've found it –
Oliver: Take it easy — take it easy –
(A tearing sound is heard)

Elsewhere in the camp, Yegor's cleaning of his horse is interrupted by the sound of laughter. He looks around to see Vera laughing at him. She informs him that his efforts to make her a robber's trull have failed, for she is happy with the tribe and the scenery. She tells of a road and a lake in the nearby mountains where she played as a child.

Yegor, furious, explains that they will now go by the desert instead of the mountain trail just to make her unhappy. Vera leaves with Hassan. Yegor's mother turns and tells him that no good will come of his actions — for he is in love with the princess. Yegor becomes enraged as he tells his mother of his detest for the princess.

With a storm suddenly approaching, Yegor hunts for Hassan and finds him chatting with Vera. He sends Hassan to the tents to prepare. Yegor pulls Vera aside to tell her he thinks of Hassan as a brother — and not to break his heart. The storm hits the camp with rain, lightning and thunder.

The storm is so intense it blows Stan & Ollie's tent away. Oliver sits up in bed, looks around and then at Stan. The storm's thunder frightens the Boys as they quickly pull their blankets over themselves.

A bear is seen entering a nearby cave. The Boys, seeking

shelter from the rain, enter the cave.

Oliver: Whew! Isn't it dark in here?
Stan: It sure is.
Oliver: I can't see a thing.
Stan: So can I.
Oliver: What do you mean – so can I? Lie down.
Hi-ho! Say, where did you get that fur coat?
Stan: What fur coat?
Oliver: Haven't you got a fur coat on?
Stan: Why I've got no fur coat.
Oliver: Well, it feels like a fur coat.
(The bear growls)
The Boys scream and run from the cave.

With the storm raging all around, Vera collapses into Yegor's arms. He carries her to his tent and closes the flaps. Yegor confesses he still loves her and vows to go toward Kars, to the lake where she played as a child. Vera tells Yegor to do as he pleases. She exits the tent and goes to find Hassan. She finds him saddling horses, and he turns and kisses her hand. She tells him of Yegor's plan to go to Kars and asks if he will still help her. He tells her that he would do anything for her love. In return for his help, she promises him that no harm shall come to Yegor or his men.

Arriving at the lake, Yegor is captured by soldiers that were waiting for him. Vera informs him that this wasn't a remote mountain lake but actually her home. Peter, her uncle, comes out to greet the princess and is thankful for her safe return.

Hassan, seeing that he had been tricked, rushes up to Yegor, apologizes for his mistake, pulls out a knife and kills

himself.

Yegor is dragged to the fortress and flogged. Meanwhile, inside the castle, Vera paces nervously around Petrovna . He sings throughout his lashings until he finally faints. Vera, fearful that he'll be beaten to death, also faints.

Upon regaining consciousness, Yegor finds himself imprisoned in the dungeon.

Vera enters the dungeon and orders her uncle and the guards to leave. Vera confesses her love to Yegor.

Stan and Ollie, sitting nearby in a tree, look toward the castle for Yegor.

Stan: Look —
Oliver: Where? Oh, get off my foot.

At the castle's gate, crowds of people gather to ask the fate of Yegor. The guard informs them that Yegor has died and to move on.

Suddenly, the tree the Boys are in breaks and falls to the ground, throwing Stan and Ollie into the lake.

Vera frees Yegor from the dungeon and orders a guard to bring Yegor his horse. Vera and Yegor kiss. Yegor tells the princess that someday he may return for her when all the barriers between them are gone. Yegor rides away as Vera watches sadly.

Stan and Ollie return the to Kaishar tribesmen camp, thinking their leader is dead.

Man: Any news of Yegor?
Oliver: Yegor is dead.
Man: Did he have anything to say before he died?
Oliver: His last words were: 'Oliver, I want you to

carry on'.

Stan: He never . . .

Oliver: Shh — and if you boys don't mind,
I'm your chief.

Azamat and tribesmen start laughing.

Suddenly, Yegor's singing can be heard coming toward the camp. Hearing Yegor's return, the Boys pick up their shovels and return to their former position with the horses.

Yegor is welcomed back by his men and all join in the singing of his song.

The End

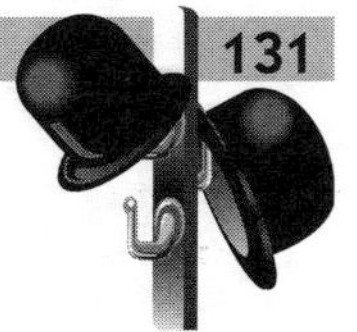

HATS ON

Stan And/Or Ollie's Head Gear

Name the films in which the Boys wore the following hats:

1. ____________
2. ____________
3. ____________
4. ____________
5. ____________
6. ____________ (Ollie)
7. ____________ (Stan)
8. ____________ (Stan)
9. ____________
10. ____________ ____________ (Stan)
11. ____________ ____________
12. ____________

Name the films in which the Boys wore the following hats:

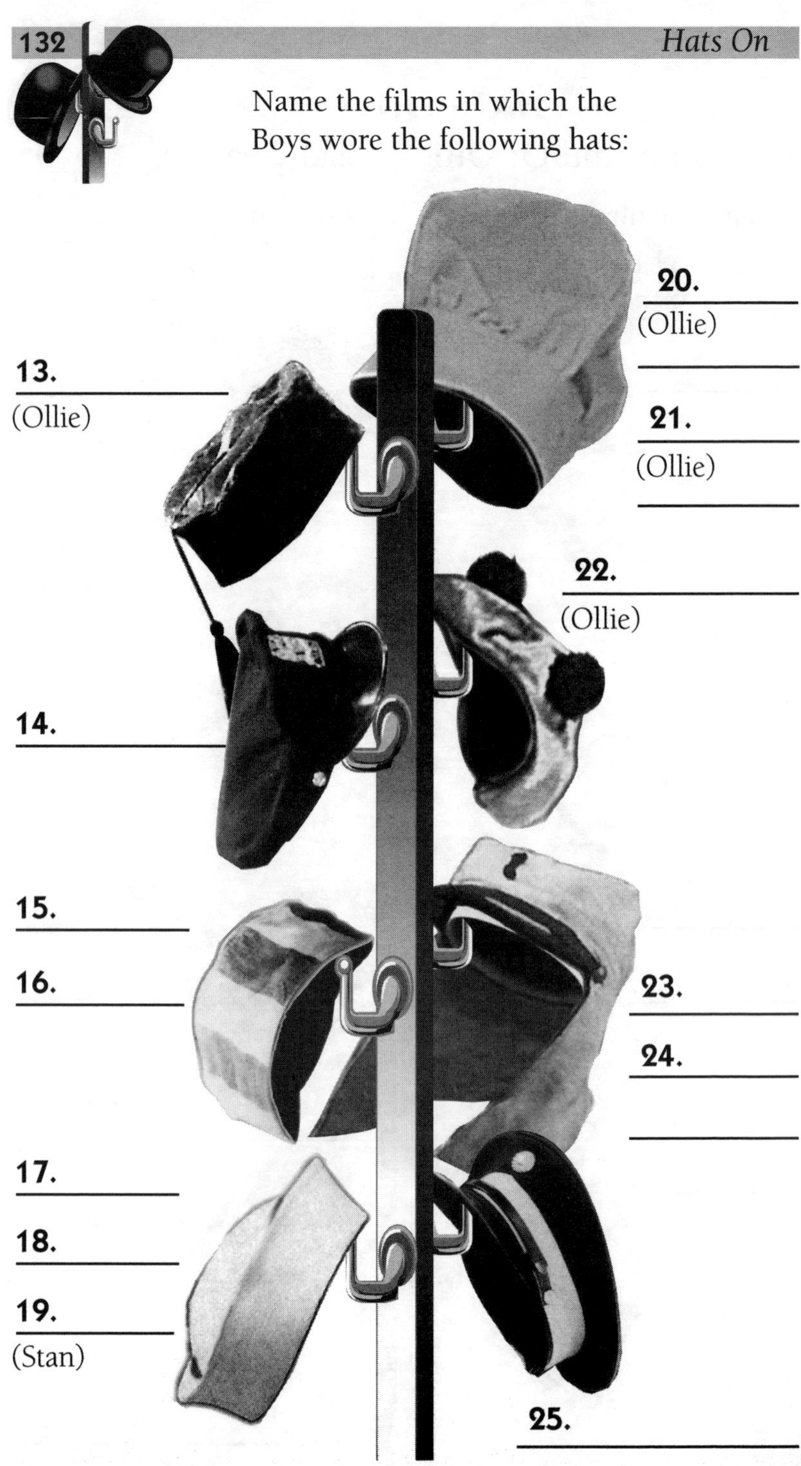

13. ______
(Ollie)

14. ______

15. ______

16. ______

17. ______

18. ______

19. ______
(Stan)

20. ______
(Ollie)
______

21. ______
(Ollie)
______

22. ______
(Ollie)

23. ______

24. ______
______

25. ______

Name the films in which the Boys wore the following hats:

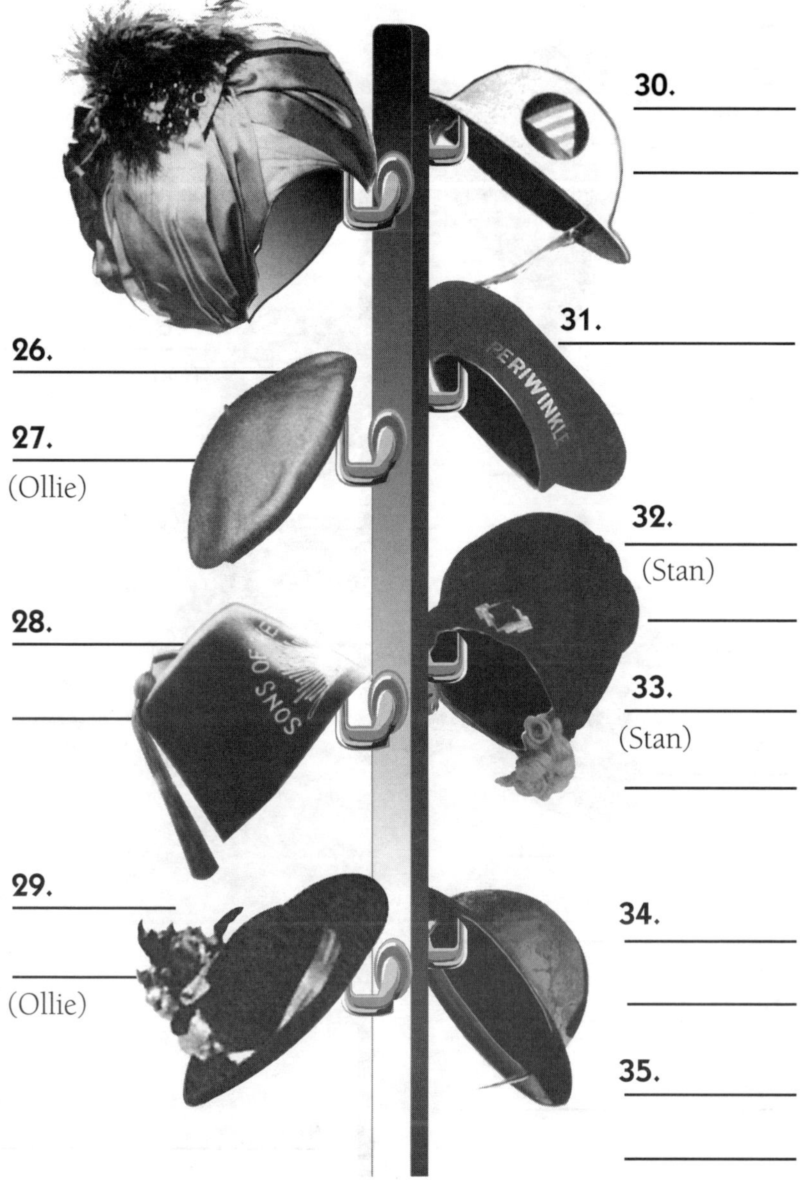

26. ______

27. ______
(Ollie)

28. ______

29. ______
(Ollie)

30. ______

31. ______

32. ______
(Stan)

33. ______
(Stan)

34. ______

35. ______

Name the films in which the Boys wore the following hats:

36. ______
(Stan)
______
______

37. ______

38. ______
(Ollie)

39. ______
(Ollie)
______
______

40. ______
(Ollie)

41. ______
(Ollie)

42. ______
(Ollie)

43. ______
(Stan)

44. ______

45. ______
(Ollie)
______

46. ______
(Ollie)

47. ______
(Stan)
______
______

48. ______

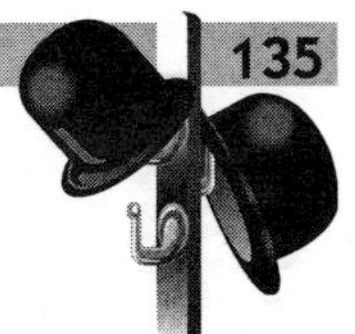

49. What company made the Boys' derbies?

HATS ON
Answers

1. The Chimp
2. A Chump At Oxford
3. Great Guns
4. With Love and Hisses
5. Blotto
6. Putting Pants on Philip
7. Lucky Dog
8. Jitterbugs
9. Early to Bed
10. The Bullfighters
11. Bonnie Scotland
12. The Devil's Brother
13. Another Fine Mess
14. Midnight Patrol
15. The Second Hundred Years
16. Liberty
17. Two Tars
18. Pack Up Your Troubles
19. Saps at Sea
20. Nothing But Trouble
21. Pack Up Your Troubles
22. The Dancing Masters
23. Beau Hunks
24. The Flying Deuces
25. You're Darn Tootin'
26. A-Haunting We Will Go
27. Them Thar Hills
28. Sons of the Desert
29. Swiss Miss
30. Air Raid Wardens
31. Our Relations
32. Why Girls Love Sailors
33. Sugar Daddies
34. Pack Up Your Troubles
35. Block-Heads
36. Babes in Toyland
37. The Second Hundred Years
38. Duck Soup
39. Call of the Cuckoos
40. Early to Bed
41. Our Wife
42. Babes in Toyland
43. Great Guns
44. The Dancing Masters
45. Double Whoopee
46. Atoll K
47. Putting Pants on Philip
48. The Rogue Song
49. The John B. Stetson Company

FINLAYSON'S FUN FILM FACTS
School Is Now In Session

Join Professor Finlayson on his excursion through the hallowed halls of the wacky academy of Laurel & Hardy. His curriculum includes illnesses in the films; proper greeting techiniques; furry co-stars; the Boys' names around the world; suicide; murder; blackmail; wars; weddings; fairy tales and much more! Put on your thinking caps and begin.

INTELLIGENCE TEST

All right students! Those that are here will say 'present' and those that are not here will say 'yes.'

- ♦ **Q.** Who was Columbus?
  A. The mayor of Ohio.
- ♦ **Q.** What did he do?
  A. He died.
- ♦ **Q.** Who killed him?
  A. Cock Robin.
- ♦ **Q.** What is a blizzard?
  A. A blizzard is the inside of a buzzard.
- ♦ **Q.** What is a comet?
  A. A comet is a star with a tail on it.
- ♦ **Q.** Name one.
  A. Rin Tin Tin.

FILM FACTS
106 Times Together

FEATURES

- **24 movies**
- **Longest Laurel & Hardy movie:** 'Atoll K' at 98 minutes.
- **Shortest movie:** 'Block-Heads' at 57 minutes

SHORTS

- **74 shorts**
- **Longest short:** 'Beau Hunks' at four-reels long

SILENT & SOUND

- **Number of silent films:** 32
- **Number of films with sound:** 74

COLOR FILMS

- Only two films had color: **'The Rogue Song'**, which used two-color Technicolor, and the 1943 U.S. Department of Agriculture short, **'A Tree In A Test Tube'**
- In 1983, the first black & white film to have color added via computer was **'Way Out West'**

CAMEO APPEARANCES

Two films, five shorts

- 'The Hollywood Revue Of 1929'
- 'The Stolen Jools'
- 'On The Loose'
- 'Wild Poses'
- 'Hollywood Party'
- 'On The Wrong Trek'
- 'The Tree In A Test Tube'

SMALLEST CASTS

- Two shorts, **'Early to Bed'** and **'Brats,'** contained no other actors beside Stan & Ollie

ILLNESS OR INJURIES

From Broken Bones to Shakedowns

OLLIE'S

- **Bad cold:** 'They Go Boom'
- **Hangover:** 'Helpmates'
- **Broken Leg:** 'County Hospital' & 'The Dancing Masters'
- **Gout:** 'Them Thar Hills'
- **Blood transfusion:** 'Thicker Than Water'
- **Nervous breakdown** : 'Saps At Sea'
- **Faked sickness:** 'Be Big,' 'Sons of the Desert' & 'Bonnie Scotland'
- **Black eye:** 'Sailors Beware'; 'Slipping Wives'; 'Do Detectives Think?'; 'Helpmates'; 'Sons of the Desert'

STAN'S

- **Toothache:** 'Leave 'Em Laughing' & 'Pardon Us' (NOTE: Stan's brother died in the dentist chair in 1933)
- **Black eye:** '45 Minutes From Hollywood'; 'Do Detectives Think?'; 'Towed in a Hole

OTHERS

- **Finlayson's toothache:** 'Flying Elephants'
- **Quarantined for smallpox:** 'Laughing Gravy'
- **Kennedy's gout:** 'Perfect Day'

LESSON #1

Flying Elephants Greeting

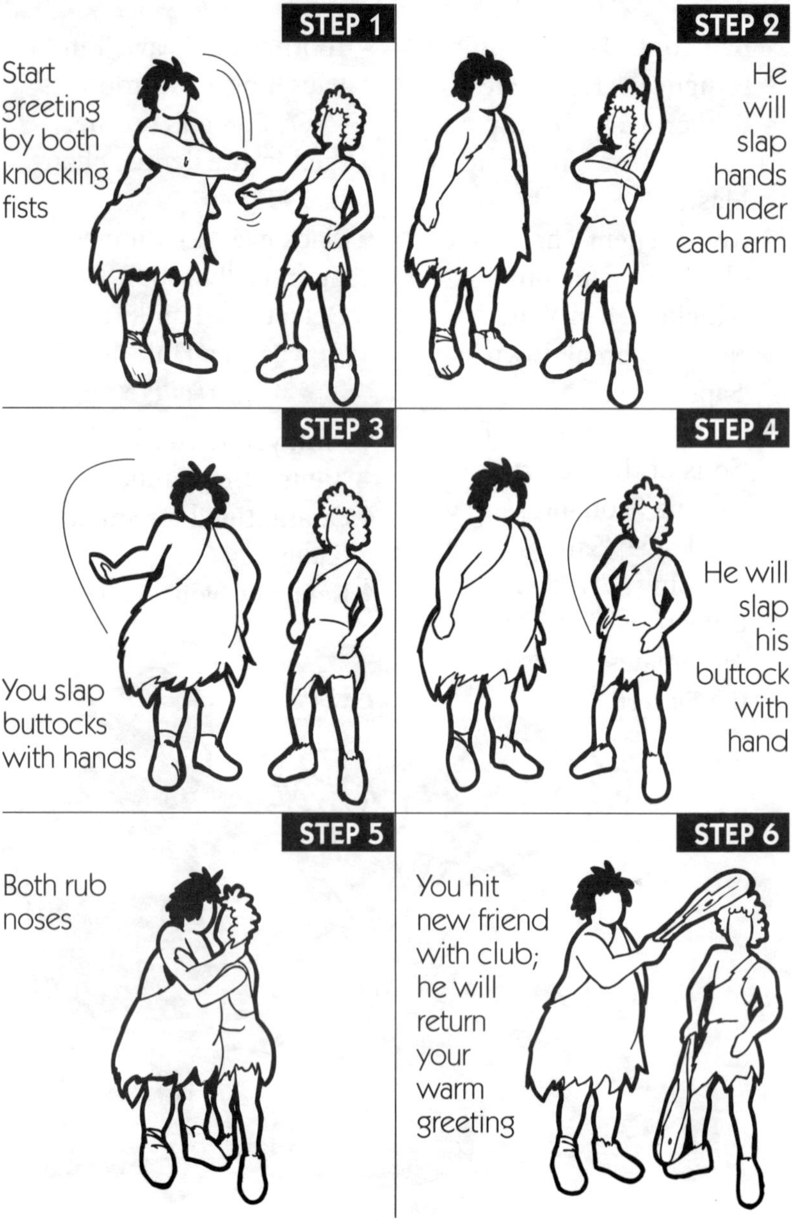

STEP 1

Start greeting by both knocking fists

STEP 2

He will slap hands under each arm

STEP 3

You slap buttocks with hands

STEP 4

He will slap his buttock with hand

STEP 5

Both rub noses

STEP 6

You hit new friend with club; he will return your warm greeting

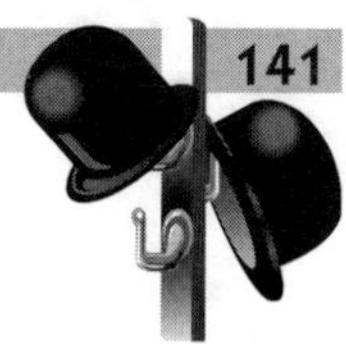

MATCHUP
Around The World

Stan & Ollie are known by many different names around the world. Try to match the proper names to the correct country.

1. Laurel and Hardy	A. Egypt
2. Gog and Cokke	B. Sweden, Norway
3. Xonapoe and Azsnoe	C. In Spanish countries
4. Helan and Halvan	D. Hungary
5. Dick und Doof	E. Denmark
6. El Tikhin Ouel Roufain	F. Turkey
7. Stan es Pan	G. Germany
8. Stan and Bran	H. Poland
9. O Bucha and O Estica	I. Romania
10. Crik and Crok	J. Portugal
11. Hashamen ve Haraze	K. Italy
12. Sisman ve Zaif	L. Greece
13. De Dikke en de Dunne	M. U.S., U.K.
14. Flaco y Gordo	N. Israel
15. Flip i Flap	O. The Netherlands

MATCHUP
Answers

1. Laurel and Hardy	M. U.S., U.K.
2. Gog and Cokke	E. Denmark
3. Xonapoe and Azsnoe	L. Greece
4. Helan and Halvan	B. Sweden, Norway
5. Dick und Doof	G. Germany
6. El Tikhin Ouel Roufain	A. Egypt
7. Stan es Pan	D. Hungary
8. Stan and Bran	I. Romania
9. O Bucha and O Estica	J. Portugal
10. Crik and Crok	K. Italy
11. Hashamen ve Haraze	N. Israel
12. Sisman ve Zaif	F. Turkey
13. De Dikke en de Dunne	O. The Netherlands
14. Flaco y Gordo	C. In Spanish countries
15. Flip i Flap	H. Poland

WARS
The Boys In Battles

♦ The Boys served in the Army, Navy and Foreign Legion several times in their films, but actually saw action in only five films (four wars and one revolution). Name the films in which the Boys fought in wars.

ANSWERS

1. Beau Hunks 2. Pack Up Your Troubles 3. Block-Heads 4. Air Raid Wardens 5. Atoll K

WAR BONDS
The Boys During WWII

◆ Even though their popularity had waned at the box office, Laurel & Hardy remained popular on tour. They sold more war bonds in the 1940s than anyone else, except for sarong-wearing Dorothy Lamour.

WEDDED BLISS
The Boys & Film Weddings

Match the wedding to the appropriate film:

♦ **1.** 'Little Bo Peep' (Stan in disguise) and Barnaby are wed
♦ **2.** Cherie and Jack's marriage
♦ **3.** It's Ollie's wedding anniversary
♦ **4.** Ollie is to be married
♦ **5.** Ollie elopes
♦ **6.** Zerlina and Lorenzo's wedding
♦ **7.** The men are to find wives within 24 hours
♦ **8.** Boys disrupt Grady Sutton's wedding

A. Flying Elephants
B. Our Wife
C. Pack Up Your Troubles
D. Me and My Pal
E. The Devil's Brother
F. Babes in Toyland
G. Block-Heads
H. Atoll K

ANSWERS:

1. F
2. H
3. G
4. D
5. B
6. E
7. A
8. C

FURRY FRIENDS
The Other Co-stars

Stan & Ollie had lots of co-stars over the years, including many four-legged friends. Here are some of the animals that appeared with the Boys.

◆ **1.** Bats appeared in four films. Name them.

◆ **2.** In what film did a giraffe appear?

◆ **3.** Flies appeared in 'The Rogue Song'. Name three other films in which the insects are seen.

◆ **4.** Name two films with bulls.

◆ **5.** A lion appeared in four films. Name them.

♦**6.** The Boys worked with a gorilla or a chimp in four films. Can you name the films?

♦**7.** In what film does Stan have a pet lobster?

♦**8.** In what film does Stan have a pet raven?

♦**9.** Dogs were seen in 15 films. How many can you name?

♦**10.** Name two films with bees in them.

♦**11.** Goats appeared in three films. Name them.

♦**12.** Horses appeared in 14 films & mules in three. How many films with horses & mules can you name?

♦**13.** Name four films with mice.

♦**14.** Cats appeared with the Boys nine times. How many of these films can you name?

FURRY FRIENDS
The Answers

♦ **1.** Habeas Corpus; The Laurel~Hardy Murder Case; Babes in Toyland; Atoll K
♦ **2.** Hollywood Party
♦ **3.** Chickens Come Home; Our Wife; Pack Up Your Troubles
♦ **4.** The Devil's Brother; The Bullfighters
♦ **5.** The Chimp; Hollywood Party; Nothing But Trouble; Atoll K
♦ **6.** The Chimp; Dirty Work; Hollywood Party; Swiss Miss
♦ **7.** Atoll K
♦ **8.** Great Guns
♦ **9.** Lucky Dog; Sugar Daddies; Putting Pants on Philip; From Soup to Nuts; Early to Bed; Perfect Day; Bacon Grabbers; Hog Wild; Laughing Gravy; Pardon Us; Sons of the Desert; Way Out West; Great Guns; Air Raid Wardens; The Dancing Masters
♦ **10.** With Love & Hisses; Bonnie Scotland
♦ **11.** Flying Elephants; Angora Love; Saps at Sea;
A goat's shadow is seen in 'Do Detectives Think?' and the Boys hide under a goat's skin in 'Another Fine Mess'.
♦ **12.** Horses: With Love & Hisses; We Faw Down; Wrong Again; The Rogue Song; Beau Hunks; The Music Box; The Chimp; The Devil's Brother; Hollywood Party; The Bohemian Girl; Way Out West; The Flying Deuces; Great Guns; Air Raid Wardens
Mules: Way Out West; Swiss Miss; Jitterbugs
♦ **13.** Forty-Five Minutes From Hollywood; Brats; Hollywood Party (animated Mickey Mouse); Babes in Toyland (Mickey Mouse). Although Stan & Ollie sell mousetraps in 'Swiss Miss', no mice are seen.
♦ **14.** Forty-Five Minutes From Hollywood; Slipping Wives; Habeas Corpus; Brats; The Laurel~Hardy Murder Case; Pack Up Your Troubles; Babes in Toyland; Pick a Star; Atoll K. In 'Night Owls', the Boys pretend to be cats to trick the police chief.

SUICIDE, MURDER, & BLACKMAIL
Stan & Ollie Are In A Fix

ATTEMPTED MURDER OR MURDER

- **'Lucky Dog'**: Ollie plays a robber who tries to kill Stan.
- **'Do Detectives Think?':** The Tipton Slasher is out for revenge against Judge Finlayson for sentencing him to death.
- **'Wrong Again'**: A cop fires his gun at the Boys after they bring a horse into a millionaire's home.
- **'The Laurel~Hardy Murder Case'**: All the surviving relatives of Ebeneezer Laurel must stay in a scary house overnight, but each of them is being bumped off so he won't get any inheritance.
- **'Be Big'**: Stan and Ollie's wives come after them with shotguns because the Boys lied to them.
- **'The Devil's Brother'**: Fra Diavolo tells Stan to hang Ollie, but, of course, Stan can't even do that right.
- **'The Midnight Patrol'**: The Boys are shot by the chief of police because they accidentally arrested him.
- **'Oliver the Eighth'**: Mae Busch attempts to kill Ollie by cutting his throat with a butcher's knife just because his name is Oliver.
- **'The Fixer-Uppers'**: Mae Busch's husband Pierre catches Ollie with his wife and challenges him to a duel to the death.
- **'Nothing But Trouble'**: An uncle tries to kill his boy king nephew but is stopped by Stan & Ollie.
- **'Atoll K'**: The Boys are almost hanged by the people of Crusoeland.

SUICIDE

♦ **'Laughing Gravy'**: Charlie Hall, Laurel and Hardy's landlord, shoots himself (off camera) after a quarantine notice is posted.

♦ **'Come Clean'**: Mae Busch attempts suicide, but the Boys save her. Busch decides that since they saved her, they have to take care of her, which won't go over well with the wives.

♦ **'Bonnie Scotland'**: According to Stan, his father committed suicide after taking one look at Stan when he was born. Also, the Boys are told to shoot themselves, but Stan misses.

♦ **'The Flying Deuces'**: Ollie wants to attempt suicide and asks Stan to join him because Ollie can't have Georgette.

BLACKMAIL

♦ **'Sugar Daddies'**: Fin's new in-laws are blackmailing him for $5,000.

♦ **'Chickens Come Home'**: Mae Busch is blackmailing the happily married Ollie with a photo of the two of them together.

♦ **'Come Clean'**: Mae Busch blackmails Stan and Ollie after they save her life. She knows they don't want their wives to find out about her, so she blackmails them.

♦ **'Pack Up Your Troubles'**: The Boys are accused of trying to blackmail a man about to be married, but, of course, it's just a misunderstanding.

♦ **'Sons of the Desert'**: Ollie threatens to tell Stan's wife that he's been smoking.

♦ **'Babes in Toyland'**: Barnaby blackmails Little Bo Peep into marrying him.

YOU'RE GUZZLED

Who Drank More In Their Films?

Who drank more in the Laurel & Hardy films, **Stan**, **Ollie**, or **Arthur Housman**? Choose one of the above names and try to match it to the number of times he was pickled in the films.

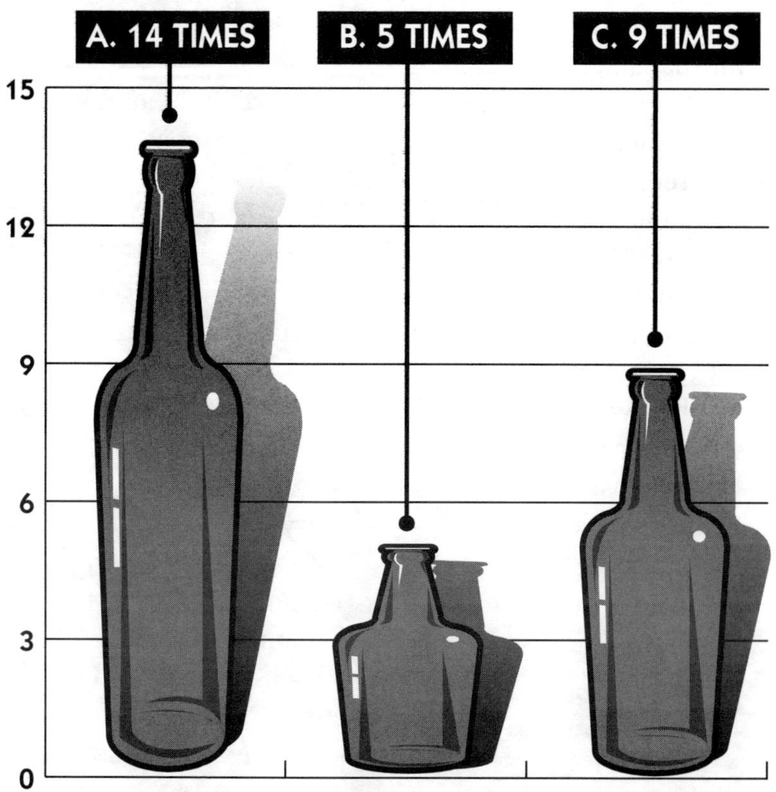

ANSWERS

A. 14 times — Stan Laurel
B. 5 times — Arthur Housman
C. 9 times — Oliver Hardy

LAUGHTER 101
Weird Or Uncontrollable Laughter

Laughter and the varying styles used in the films:

LOONEY

Characters who had unusual laughs in the films:

- **Sir Leopold Plumtree:** 'Another Fine Mess'
- **Foreign Legion Commander:** 'Beau Hunks'
- **William Austin**, Ollie's roommate in the hospital: 'County Hospital'
- **Ollie's wife:** 'Twice Two'
- **Professor Noodle**, the mad scientist: 'Dirty Work'

SIDE-SPLITTING

- The Boys are high on laughing gas: **'Leave 'Em Laughing'**
- The Boys share beer and giggles with their girlfriends: **'We Faw Down'**
- Stan and Ollie get drunk, or so they think: **'Blotto'**
- The Boys get the judge's wife tipsy: **'Scram!'**
- Stan gets drunk while trying to bottle wine: **'The Devil's Brother'**
- Stan and Ollie go to the mountains and drink well water spiked with moonshine: **'Them Thar Hills'**
- To get the deed from Stan, Lola tickles him until he can't take it anymore: **'Way Out West'**

ROOM FOR RENT
The Landlords

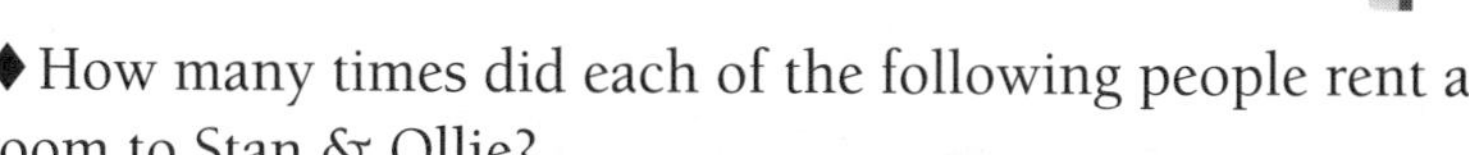

♦ How many times did each of the following people rent a room to Stan & Ollie?

1. Charlie Hall	**A. 5 times**	**B. 3 times**	**C. 1 time**
2. Edgar Kennedy	**A. 5 times**	**B. 3 times**	**C. 1 time**
3. Walter Long	**A. 5 times**	**B. 3 times**	**C. 1 time**
4. Billy Gilbert	**A. 5 times**	**B. 3 times**	**C. 1 time**

♦ Mother Peep ('Babes in Toyland') & Mrs. Bickerdike ('Bonnie Scotland') also rented the Boys rooms.

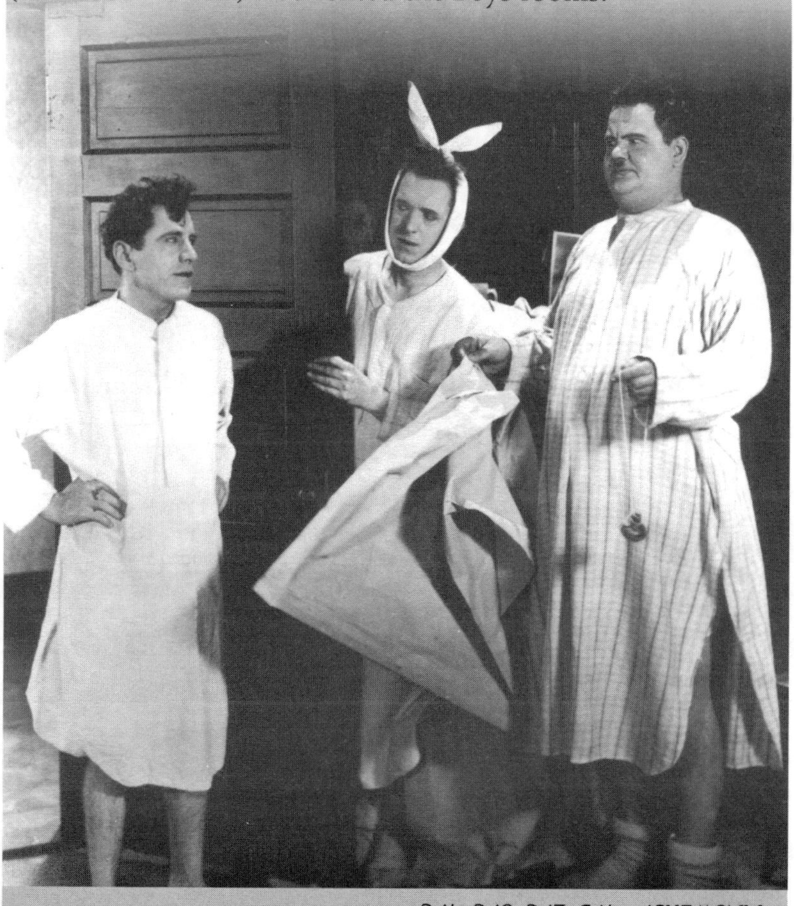

ANSWERS: 1. B 2. C 3. C 4. C

IN OR OUT

Films Containing Break-ins Or Out-ofs

- '**The Second Hundred Years**': Out of prison
- '**Habeas Corpus**': Into a cemetery
- '**Liberty**': Out of prison
- '**The Hoose-Gow**': Attempted escape from prison
- '**Night Owls**': Into the chief of police's home for Officer Kennedy
- '**Another Fine Mess**': Into Colonel Buckshot's home
- '**Pardon Us**': Out of prison
- '**The Music Box**': Into Professor Schwarzenhoffen's home
- '**Scram**': Accidentally went into judge's home
- '**Way Out West**': Into Mickey Finn's Palace
- '**Air Raid Wardens**': Into Nazi headquarters

ARTWORK
Paintings & Portraits

The painting collection includes:

- **'Their Purple Moment':** A painting serves as Stan's hiding place for his money from his wife.

- **'Early To Bed' & 'Wrong Again':** The famous Gainsborough painting 'Blue Boy' appears in both of these films.

- **'The Laurel~Hardy Murder Case':** A skeleton painting is hanging in the bedroom where the Boys are sleeping.

- **'Another Fine Mess':** Ollie is showing Plumtree around the house and pointing out paintings: 'Physic at the Well' and 'A Gondola Going through the Panama Canal in Venice'.

- **'Dirty Work':** As the Boys clean up, they discuss the seascape painting.

- **'The Big Noise':** The painting 'The Height of Spring' by Anthony van Dyke (1599-1641) is seen in this film.

PAINTED PORTRAITS

- **'The Laurel~Hardy Murder Case':** General Grant
- **'Twice Two':** Fanny looks just like portrait of the queen hanging on the wall when a cake falls on her head.
- **'The Fixer Uppers':** Mae Busch
- **'Bonnie Scotland':** Stan's grandfather.
- **'A Chump At Oxford':** A portrait of the 'old buzzard' Dean Williams.
- **'Air Raid Wardens':** Adolf Hitler

TELEGRAMS & MAIL
In The Films

♦ How many times did Stan and Ollie receive mail or telegrams in their films?

A. 12 times
B. 14.times
C. 16 times

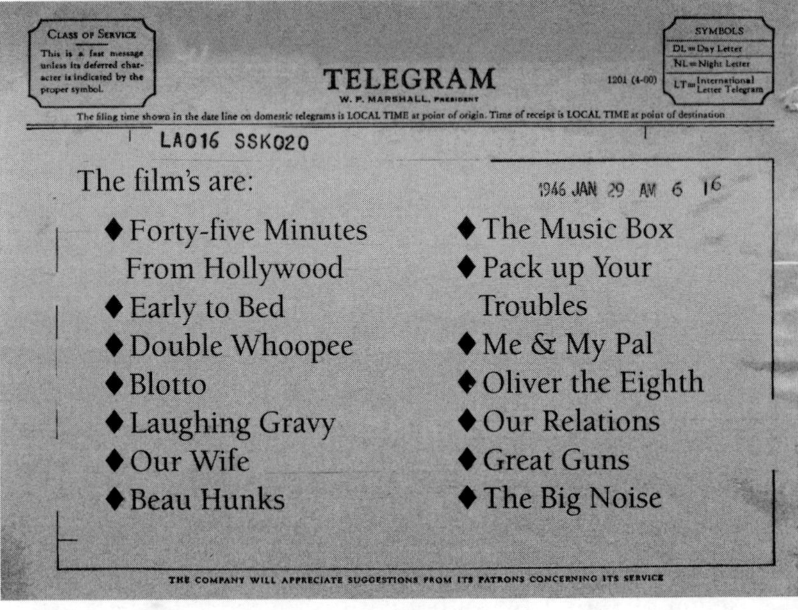

CLASS OF SERVICE
This is a fast message unless its deferred character is indicated by the proper symbol.

TELEGRAM
W. P. MARSHALL, PRESIDENT

1201 (4-60)

SYMBOLS
DL = Day Letter
NL = Night Letter
LT = International Letter Telegram

The filing time shown in the date line on domestic telegrams is LOCAL TIME at point of origin. Time of receipt is LOCAL TIME at point of destination

LA016 SSK020

1946 JAN 29 AM 6 16

The film's are:

- ♦ Forty-five Minutes From Hollywood
- ♦ Early to Bed
- ♦ Double Whoopee
- ♦ Blotto
- ♦ Laughing Gravy
- ♦ Our Wife
- ♦ Beau Hunks
- ♦ The Music Box
- ♦ Pack up Your Troubles
- ♦ Me & My Pal
- ♦ Oliver the Eighth
- ♦ Our Relations
- ♦ Great Guns
- ♦ The Big Noise

THE COMPANY WILL APPRECIATE SUGGESTIONS FROM ITS PATRONS CONCERNING ITS SERVICE

ANSWER

B. 14 times

CHILDREN
Kids In Their Films

Match the child to the film that he or she appeared in:

1. A nanny pushes a baby in stroller
2. Arlene
3. King Christopher
4. Girl with the doll that says "Mama"
5. Tommy "Butch" Bond plays with his football
6. Robert Blake as Bobby Hartley
7. Ollie adopts a baby
8. A child named Sturgeon
9. The Boys play their own children
10. A midget pretending to be a child

A. Sailors Beware
B. You're Darn Tootin'
C. Brats
D. The Music Box
E. Their First Mistake
F. The Bohemian Girl
G. Block-Heads
H. Saps at Sea
I. The Big Noise
J. Nothing But Trouble

ANSWERS:

1. D
2. F
3. J
4. H
5. G
6. I
7. E
8. B
9. C
10. A

ANIMATION & FAIRY TALES
In Their Films

ANIMATED EFFECTS

♦ Stan sees stars	**Lucky Dog**
♦ Flying elephants	**Flying Elephants**
♦ Bird landing on chimney	**The Finishing Touch**
♦ Automobile's clutch	**Perfect Day**
♦ Mouse	**Brats**
♦ Sparks flying	**Hogwild**
♦ Stop-motion of soldiers	**Babes In Toyland**
♦ Ollie's neck being stretched	**Way Out West**
♦ Bees	**Bonnie Scotland**
♦ Recruiting poster talks	**Air Raid Wardens**

FAIRY TALES OR CARTOON CHARACTERS

♦ Little Jack Horner	**Putting Pants On Philip**
♦ Cinderella	**Helpmates**
♦ Goldilocks, Cinderella	**Pack Up Your Troubles**
♦ Little Boy Blue, Mary Quite Contrary, Mickey Mouse, Little Bo Peep, Three Little Pigs, Mother Goose, Little Miss Muffet, Queen of Hearts, Old King Cole, Cat and the Fiddle	**Babes In Toyland**
♦ Old Mother Hubbard	**Saps At Sea**
♦ Mickey Mouse	**Great Guns**
♦ Snow White and the Seven Dwarfs	**Atoll K**

HAPPY HOLIDAYS
Christmas Mentioned In Films

- ♦ **Putting Pants on Philip**: Santa Claus
- ♦ **Big Business**: Selling Christmas trees
- ♦ **The Laurel~Hardy Murder Case**: "The day after Christmas?" (No, the day before, November 15)
- ♦ **Chickens Come Home**: Christmas present delivered
- ♦ **Pack Up Your Troubles**: Want to send baby Christmas gift
- ♦ **Babes in Toyland**: Making toys for Santa
- ♦ **The Fixer Uppers**: Selling Christmas cards
- ♦ **Way Out West**: "Only four more months till Christmas."

LEISURE ACTIVITIES

Sports and Games

POKER AND OTHER GAMES

◆ **A.** Name two films in which Stan & Ollie play checkers.

◆ **B.** Name two films in which Stan & Ollie are playing or going to play poker.

◆ **C.** In what film does Stan play a slot machine and win?

THE BOYS & SPORTS

◆ **1.** Name three films in which Stan boxes.

◆ **2.** What is the name of the short in which Stan & Ollie go golfing?

◆ **3.** In what two shorts do the Boys play billiards?

◆ **4.** In what short does Ollie claim to play croquet, Parcheesi, and billiards?

◆ **5.** In what film do Stan & Ollie 'golf' in the street?

SPORTS ANSWERS:

1. The Battle of the Century, Any Old Port, Brats
2. Should Married Men Go Home?
3. Brats, Any Old Port
4. Another Fine Mess
5. A Chump At Oxford (while cleaning the streets)

GAME ANSWERS:

A. Brats, The Live Ghost
B. Sailors, Beware! We Faw Down
C. Way Out West

DANCING
Light On Their Feet

♦ In how many films did Stan Laurel and/or Oliver Hardy dance?

A. 10 films **B.** 11 films **C.** 13 films

ANSWERS

A. 10 films, which include the following films: Sugar Daddies, Early to Bed, That's My Wife, The Chimp, Scram!, Bonnie Scotland, Way Out West, Swiss Miss, Jitterbugs, The Dancing Masters

FOOT COMEDY
Ticklish Tootsies

- **With Love and Hisses:** Soldiers with foot odor.
- **Habeas Corpus:** Stan hits Ollie's toes with shovel.
- **Liberty:** Stan hangs on to Ollie's foot atop the girders of a building being constructed.
- **Berth Marks:** Stan hops as he gets into train's berth.
- **Perfect Day:** Uncle Ed has gout in his foot.
- **Angora Love:** Ollie rubs Stan's foot instead of his own without realizing it.
- **Night Owls:** Stan drops a bag of tools on Ollie's foot
- **Brats:** The door knob falls on Ollie Jr.'s foot.
- **Be Big:** Stan hits Ollie's foot with hammer. Ollie mistakenly puts on Stan's boot and then can't get it off.
- **Beau Hunks:** Ollie rubs Stan's foot instead of his own without realizing his error. Stan's shoe has sand and a large rock in it.
- **Helpmates:** Stan steps in water bucket.
- **The Music Box:** Ollie steps on a nail
- **Their First Mistake:** Stan cleans his shoes with the bedsheet he's lying on.
- **Towed In A Hole:** While cleaning the boat, Stan mistakenly grabs Ollie's leg instead of the anchor and starts scrubbing it.
- **Oliver The Eighth:** Stan shoots Ollie in the foot.
- **Bonnie Scotland:** Stan jabs Ollie in the foot with stick while picking up trash. Ollie rubs Stan's foot instead of his own
- **Way Out West:** Stan has a hole in his shoe and his toe sticks out. When he steps on a lit cigar, his shoe starts to smolder.
- **Swiss Miss:** Stan drops a package on Ollie's foot.
- **The Flying Deuces:** Ollie rubs Stan's foot instead of his own
- **Saps At Sea:** Stan has a nail in his shoe, unravels his sock and sticks his feet in Ollie's face.
- **Air Raid Wardens:** A bicycle hits Ollie's foot.
- **Atoll K:** Stan's foot gets stuck in a bucket.

WEATHER

When It Rains, It Pours

The Boys endured raging snowstorms, thunderstorms and even a sandstorm, all in the name of comedy.

♦ **1.** It snowed on Stan & Ollie four times out of their 106 films together. One of those films with snow was 'The Rogue Song'. Name the other three.

♦ **2.** Name five films in which it rained on the Boys.

ANSWERS

1. Below Zero, Laughing Gravy, The Fixer Uppers
2. The Laurel~Hardy Murder Case, Helpmates, Scram!, Sons of the Desert, Atoll K

"THROW ME MY HAT!"
Hat Switches

Films in which Stan & Ollie inadvertently switch hats with each other:

- ♦ Hats Off
- ♦ Do Detectives Think?
- ♦ You're Darn Tootin'
- ♦ Habeas Corpus
- ♦ We Faw Down
- ♦ Liberty
- ♦ Wrong Again
- ♦ Berth Marks
- ♦ Beau Hunks
- ♦ The Music Box
- ♦ Air Raid Wardens
- ♦ The Dancing Masters
- ♦ The Big Noise
- ♦ Atoll K

What two films contain the most hat switches:

Answer:
'Hats Off' (eight times) and 'Do Detectives Think?'(six times)

PHONE COMEDY
That's Levity

Telephone comedy is very prominent part of the Laurel and Hardy films. The phone is used as a comical element, such as in **'Helpmates,'** where Stan starts to talk into a statue, or in **'Saps At Sea,'** where Stan grabs a banana instead of the telephone earpiece.

Phone booths are another version of the comical gag, which is used in '**Our Relations**,' where Bert, Alf and Arthur Housman are all crowd into a phone booth. **'Blotto'** also uses the phone booth as a comedy element, but this time only Ollie is in the booth. Everytime Ollie calls, Stan hangs up on him and each time a more frustrated Ollie has to look up the number again in the phone-book. He eventually ends up breaking the glass in the phone booth.

Eavesdropping is used in **'Our Wife'**, **'Twice Two'** and **'Blotto'**. Stan listens in on conversations in **'Our Wife'** and '**Twice Two**'. Mrs. Laurel listens in on Stan and Ollie's conversation in '**Blotto**'.

The gag of funny phone noise is used in **'Blotto'**, **'Chickens Come Home'**, **'Twice Two'** and **'The Flying Deuces'**.

PROP COMEDY
Items Used For A Laugh

DOOR

Approximately 56 of the Boys' films contain door comedy, which includes doorbells, doorknobs, walking into doors, missing the door and walking into the wall, being hit by the door, getting locked out and destroying doors. The door is recognized as a great comic tool by Stan and Ollie and they use it well. Door comedy is a true Laurel and Hardy trademark, appearing in over half of their films.

WATER

Water is another comedy prop used in just about every film the Boys did. From spills to all out water battles, it was always an easy laugh. Hoses, fountains, sinks, leaking pipes, bathtubs, and the infamous Ollie falling into a bottomless pit of water are all part of this water humor, used so brilliantly, it's almost an art form.

CLOTHES

Clothes are a big part of Laurel and Hardy's comedy. The Boys have had arms caught in sleeves and other entanglements, pants falling down, articles of clothing being ripped, and clothing becoming lost as just some of the gags used in the Laurel and Hardy films. The same ideas are reworked each time to make the gag seem fresh, new, and even more hilarious.

DESTROYED ITEMS
Broken By The Boys

Laurel and Hardy broke and/or destroyed at least one item in every film. Sometimes the items were small and simple such as dishes or vases, but other times they were large and complex such as houses or a cars. Other destroyed items have included beds, doorbells, chairs, lamps, records, statues, flower pots, radios, grandfather clocks, windows and/or glass, pianos, boats, entire rooms, hats, musical instruments, chimneys, and many, many other items. The item being destroyed never seems to make any difference in the reaction; the gag is always funny.

OASIS 13

Clubs & Organizations

- **The Laurel~Hardy Murder Case:** Hardy claims he belongs to fraternity Delta Phi Delta
- **Be Big:** Hunting Lodge
- **Sons Of The Desert:** Los Angeles, Oasis 13
- **A-Haunting We Will Go:** Laurel & Hardy say they belong to a lodge
- **Air Raid Wardens:** Boys volunteer as Air Raid Wardens to do their part for the war effort

PLANES, TRAINS & AUTOMOBILES
Modes Of Transportation

AUTOMOBILES
A slightly dilapidated Model T was the Boys' main form of transportation over the years; however, they did travel by the following ways as well:

FILMS WITH BOATS
- Why Girls Love Sailors
- Sailors, Beware!
- Putting Pants on Philip
- Two Tars
- Men O'War
- Any Old Port
- Towed in a Hole
- Sons of the Desert
- The Live Ghost
- Our Relations
- Saps at Sea
- Jitterbugs
- Nothing But Trouble

FILMS WITH TRAINS
- Forty-Five Minutes Hollywood
- With Love And Hisses
- Berth Marks
- Great Guns

FILMS WITH BICYCLES
- Forty-Five Minutes Hollywood
- Duck Soup
- Men O' War
- Another Fine Mess
- Me and My Pal
- A Chump at Oxford
- Air Raid Wardens

FILMS WITH AIRPLANES
- The Flying Deuces
- The Big Noise

BIZARRE CHARACTERS
In Their Films

CAST OF CHARACTERS	
♦ **Sailors, Beware!**	A midget as a baby
♦ **You're Darn Tootin'**	A cross-eyed pedestrian
♦ **Berth Marks**	A midget and the garbled train announcer
♦ **The Hoose-Gow**	Prison cook (mushmouth)
♦ **The Laurel~Hardy Murder Case**	A transvestite and other bizarre relatives of Ebeneezer Laurel
♦ **Our Wife**	Cross-eyed preacher (Ben Turpin)
♦ **Pack Up Your Troubles**	Cross-eyed man and the butler's eyes freak out
♦ **Me and My Pal**	Cross-eyed telegram delivery man
♦ **Dirty Work**	Professor Noodle
♦ **The Bohemian Girl**	Cross-eyed bartendar
♦ **Block-Heads**	Deep-voiced midget
♦ **Saps at Sea**	Cross-eyed plumber (Ben Turpin)

WACKY CHARACTERS
In Their Films

♦ **Call of the Cuckoos**	Max Davidson thinks his neighbors are crazy for romping about in their backyard.
♦ **Do Detectives Think?**	An escaped killer, The Tipton Slasher poses as Fin's butler to get revenge on him.
♦ **Early to Bed**	Ollie thinks Stan is "mad" as he appears to be frothing at the mouth after falling into a frosted cake.
♦ **Habeas Corpus**	A mad scientist sends the Boys to graveyard to snatch a body for him.
♦ **Wrong Again**	Ollie suggests the millionaire owner of 'Blue Boy' is a bit touched.
♦ **The Laurel~Hardy Murder Case**	A transvestite killer and bizarre butler plot to do away with their guests.
♦ **Dirty Work**	Professor Noodle is simply nuts.
♦ **Sons Of The Desert**	Ollie fakes a nervous breakdown to get out of going to the mountains so he can go to the convention.
♦ **Oliver the Eighth**	Mae Busch kills men with the name Oliver while the butler serves invisible food.
♦ **Saps at Sea**	Ollie has a hornophobia breakdown.

BIZARRE ENDINGS
In Their Films

♦ **With Love And Hisses**

The army troop lose their clothes while swimming, so they try to hide their nakedness behind a billboard, but stumble upon a bees nest. At the end you see them marching away with swollen posteriors.

♦ **Liberty**

The Boys are chased by police after they escape from prison and end up on top of a high-rise construction site. Once they finally make it to the elevator to come back down, the Boys land on a police officer and squash him to about three and a half feet high.

♦ **Below Zero**

Stan and Ollie are thrown out of the restaurant where they are eating lunch because they haven't any money. Stan gets thrown into a barrel and ends up drinking all the water that was in it. He emerges extremely bloated and needing to use the facilities.

♦ **Dirty Work**

Stan and Ollie are chimney sweeps at the home of a mad scientist, Professor Noodle. The professor has a rejuvenation formula he wants to try out and Ollie accidentally gets knocked into the vat of formula. He re-emerges as a chimpanzee.

♦ **Going Bye-Bye**

The Boys testify against Butch Long in court and he vows to get even. Of course, Long eventually runs across Stan and Ollie and ties their legs around their necks.

♦ **The Live Ghost**

A sea captain threatens that if anyone mentions the word "ghost" when talking about his ship, that he'll twist their head around so that when they're walking north, they'll be looking south. The Boys accidentally say the dreaded word and end up twisted around.

♦ **Thicker Than Water**

Mrs. Hardy hits Ollie on the head with a frying pan after learning he spent their life savings on a grandfather clock that was accidentally destroyed. Stan takes Ollie to the hospital and a blood transfusion is needed, so Stan volunteers. After the transfusion, Stan and Ollie's identities are switched.

♦ **The Bohemian Girl**

Stan and Ollie are grabbed by Count Arnheim's men after the Boys try to rescue Ollie's daughter, who is in Arnheim's prison. Stan and Ollie are sent to the torture chamber. When they emerge, we see an elongated Ollie and a compressed Stan.

♦ **The Flying Deuces**

The Boys discuss reincarnation early on in the film and Ollie says he'd like to come back as a horse. In the end of the film, the plane the Boys are flying crashes and Ollie doesn't survive, but he does come back as a horse.

♦ **A-Haunting We Will Go**

This one involves a magician and murder. Once the crooks are apprehended at the end, Ollie hears Stan crying from inside a giant egg. The egg hatches and out emerges a two foot tall Stan.

♦ **The Bullfighters**

A man is falsely imprisoned because of the Boys' testimony. Once released from prison, the man goes after them and skins them alive. We see two skeleton bodies and the Boys' heads.

READ BETWEEN THE LINES
Double Meanings & Implied Jokes

On occasion, gags in Laurel & Hardy films leaned towards being suggestive or daringly close to improper, especially for the time period in which the films were made. Yet the material always ended up in comically good taste.

PUTTING PANTS ON PHILIP

♦ Scotsman Stan loses his underwear from under his kilt and then walks over a sidewalk grating. The reaction from the street crowd tells you what they saw.

WITH LOVE AND HISSES

♦ Skinny-dipping soldiers' uniforms catch fire when a cigarette is thrown onto their clothes. The naked soldiers try to make it back to camp without anyone seeing their predicament.

LEAVE 'EM LAUGHING

♦ The Boys are in bed together and Stan has a toothache. Stan is using a hot water bottle for some relief from the pain, but the bottle opens up and leaks onto the bed, soaking Ollie's backside. Ollie's startled expression shows all to well how he thinks the bed became wet.

WE FAW DOWN

♦ In the final scene, a shotgun blast sends many philanderers running without their pants from the apartments.

LIBERTY

♦ Having just escaped from jail, the Boys try to change out of their prison garb and into street clothes. They jump into a cab, and when they emerge from the vehicle, they are pulling up their pants. A couple waiting on the cab are shocked at the site.

THAT'S MY WIFE

♦ Stan is dressed up as Ollie's wife to fool Ollie's rich uncle, but Stan loses his necklace down his dress and needs Ollie's assistance retrieving it. Throughout the restaurant and even on the dance floor, Ollie is seen reaching down Stan's clothes. The uncle thinks that Ollie and his wife are outlandish for their indecent display in public.

MEN O'WAR

♦ The Boys find a pair of lady's bloomers and try to delicately return them to their rightful owner. The woman lost her gloves, though, not her underwear.

THEY GO BOOM

♦ Stan has put a nail through the water pipe above their bed and it starts to leak onto the bed. Ollie's startled expression shows all to well how he thinks the bed became wet.

ANGORA LOVE

♦ Stan and Ollie are being quite loud trying to repair the damage the goat has done to the room. The landlord pounds on their door and yells at the Boys about their excessive noise and explains that this is a respectable hotel. As he is telling this to the Boys, a sailor and girl go romping by the door.

ANOTHER FINE MESS

♦ **Mrs. Plumtree talking to Agnes (Stan):**
"How many maids does the Colonel keep?"
Agnes: "Oh, he never tells me his private affairs."
Mrs. Plumtree: "Private affairs! Why, servants aren't private affairs."
Agnes: "Oh, some of them are."

ANOTHER FINE MESS *(continued)*

♦ When Mrs. Plumtree inquires why the unmarried Colonel Buckshot has a baby nursery, Stan (as Agnes) replys "He has that in case of accidents."

HELPMATES

♦ Stan throws his alarm clock down to make it stop ringing, but when the clock hits the floor, it sounds as if it went into a bedpan. Stan looks down curiously to see what has caused the noise and lifts up a vase that the clock has fallen in to.

THE MUSIC BOX

♦ **The nanny to the police officer about Laurel and Hardy:** "He kicked me! Right in the middle of my daily duties!"

THE CHIMP

♦ **Ollie:** "That settles it. That's the last time I'm going to be in this end of the horse.
Stan: "Well, I can't go in there."
Ollie: "Why?"
Stan: "Well, you look better in that end than I do."
Ollie: "Do you mean to insinuate that I look like a horse's . . ."

♦ Ethel the chimp kisses Ollie on the back of the neck and he thinks Stan did it.

♦ Stan and Ollie yell at Ethel to stop dancing and go to bed. Gilbert thinks his wife, also named Ethel, is in the room with the Boys.

COUNTY HOSPITAL

- Stan goes to visit Ollie in the hospital. The nurse walks out of the room carrying a baby, which Stan thinks is Ollie's room and baby. He has the wrong room.

- An egg falls off the table and onto the floor, but it sounds as if it fell into a bedpan. Stan picks up a pitcher to show what the egg has fallen into.

PACK UP YOUR TROUBLES

- Ollie complains to Stan that he has ironing to do and that Stan could help watch the baby. (They fight like a couple)

THEIR FIRST MISTAKE

- **Stan:** "Well, I'll be seeing ya."
  Ollie: "Where are you going?"
  Stan: "I'm just going down....."
  Ollie: "Well, you can't leave me here with this child."
  Stan: "Why?"
  Ollie: "Why? Why, you're just as much responsible for it as I am."
  Stan: "What have I got to do with it?"
  Ollie: "What have I got to do with it? What have I got to do with it? Why, you were the one who wanted me to have a baby. And now that you've gotten me into this trouble, you want to walk out and leave me flat."
  Stan: "Well, I don't know anything about babies."
  Ollie: "Well, you should have thought of that before we got it."
  Stan: "I don't want to get mixed up in this. I have my future, my career to think of."
  Ollie: "Your career! What about me? What will my friends

THEIR FIRST MISTAKE *(continued)*

say? Why I'll be ostracized."
Stan: "Well, I'm going to lose my hook, line and sinker."
Ollie: "So, you're going to desert me. Just when I need you most."

♦ **Stan (about the baby):** "I wonder what's the matter with it?"
Ollie: "I don't know, maybe it's hungry. Why don't you give it something to eat?"
Stan starts unbuttoning his pajamas as if he's going to breast feed but pulls out the baby's bottle.

SONS OF THE DESERT

♦ **Charley Chase to his sister, Mrs. Hardy:** "And you used to pump the organ, remember? You little organ pumper, you!

BLOCK-HEADS

♦ In the final scene, a shotgun blast sends many philanderers running without their pants from the apartments.

SAPS AT SEA

♦ As Dr. Finlayson examines Ollie to determine his ailment, a baby is calling 'Mama'. All are shocked, until they realize it's a little girl's talking baby doll making the sound.

AIR RAID WARDENS

♦ Stan throws the alarm clock under the bed, making a "clank" sound. Stan looks shocked as if it were a bedpan, but reveals it to be his air raid helmet.

POM-POM

Music and Lyrics

Oliver Hardy was not only a superb comic, but also a tremendous singer. He sang in quite a few of the Laurel and Hardy films, which added a special touch of Babe Hardy to each. The following is a list of songs as well as the lyrics that appeared in their films.

THE MANY SONGS OF OLIVER HARDY

- **On The Trail Of The Lonesome Pine:** Way Out West
- **Let Me Call You Sweetheart:** Swiss Miss
- **Honolulu Baby:** Sons of the Desert
- **Shine On Harvest Moon:** The Flying Deuces
- **You Are The Ideal Of My Dreams:** Beau Hunks
- **We're Going To Go Way Down In Dixie:** Way Out West
- **Sons of the Desert:** Sons of the Desert
- **Lazy Moon:** Pardon Us
- **Go To Sleep My Baby:** Brats
- **Fresh Fish!:** Towed In A Hole
- **Somebody's Coming To My House:** Chickens Come Home
- **Humming The Wedding March:** Our Wife
- **In The Good Ol' Summertime:** Below Zero
- **It's Just An Idea Of My Own:** Swiss Miss
- **I'm Sitting On Top Of The World:** Oliver The Eighth
- **You'll Be Sorry:** Laughing Gravy
- **Good Morning to You:** Pardon Us
- **Pom-Pom (The Old Spinning Wheel):** Them Thar Hills

'The Trail of the Lonesome Pine'

On a mountain in Virginia
Stands a lonesome pine.
Just below, is the cabin home
Of a little girl of mine.
Her name is June and very, very soon
She'll belong to me.
For I know she's waiting there for me
'Neath that lone pine tree.
In the Blue Ridge Mountains of
Virginia,
On the trail of the lonesome pine,
In the pale moonshine, our hearts entwine,
Where she carved her name and I carved mine.
Oh June, oh June, just like the mountains,
I'm blue.
Like the pine I am lonesome for you.
In the Blue Ridge Mountains of Virginia,
On the trail of the lonesome pine.
In the Blue Ridge Mountains.....

At the age of 8, Hardy ran away from home and toured with a troupe called the Coburn's Minstrels.

'Let Me Call You Sweetheart'

Let me call you sweetheart,
I'm in love with you,
Let me call you sweetheart,
I'm in love with you,
Keep the love light burning,
In your eyes so blue.
Let me call you sweetheart,
I'm in love with you.

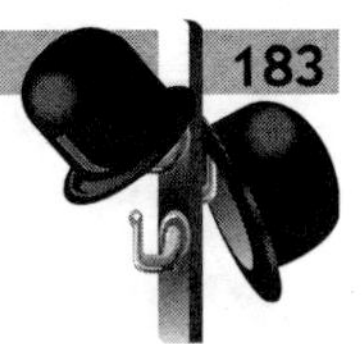

The 'Coo Coo' theme was first heard in the opening credits of what Laurel and Hardy film?

Answer: 'Brats'

'Honolulu Baby'

While down on the South Sea Island,
Underneath the beauty of the stars,
I strayed upon some maidens,
Who were strumming on their guitars,
A hula maid was dancing,
And I knew I'd found my paradise,
So this is what I told her,
As I gazed into her eyes...
Honolulu Baby, where d'ya get those eyes?
And the dark complexion I just idolize.
And those pretty red lips,
And that sunny smile?
When you start to dance,
Your hula hips entrance,
Then you shake it up and down.
You shake a little here,
You shake a little there.
Well, you got the boys going to town.
Honolulu Baby, you know your stuff,
Honolulu Baby, don't call your bluff.

'Shine On Harvest Moon'

Shine on, shine on harvest moon,
Up in the sky.
I ain't had no loving,
Since January, April, June or July.
Snow time, pay no time to stay,
Outdoors and swoon.
Shine on, shine on harvest moon,
For me and my girl.

'You Are The Ideal Of My Dreams'

I love you, I love you, I love you,
You are the ideal of my dreams.
I always knew t'would be someone like you.
I've loved you forever it seems.
For years in my mind's fondest fancy,
A picture of your face I drew,
And I knew you somehow,
When I met you just now,
You are the ideal of my dreams.

'Going Down To Dixie'

We're going to go, we're going to go.
We're going to go way down in Dixie,
Where the hens are doggone glad to lay
Scrambled eggs in the new-morn hay.
We're going to see. We're going to see.
We're going to see my home in Dixie,
You can tell the world we're coming to...
D-I-X-I know how to spell it.
Then we're going. Why we're going.
You know we're going.
To a home in Dixieland.
We're going to go way down in Dixie...

Name the song that makes Stan cry in 'Blotto.'

Answer:
'The Curse of the Aching Heart.'

'Sons of the Desert'

We are the Sons of the Desert,
Having the time of our lives,
Marching along, two thousand strong,
Far from our sweethearts and wives,
God bless them.
Tramp, Tramp, Tramp the boys are marching
And dancing to this melody...
Dah...dah...dah...dah...dah...
Dah...dah...dah...dah...dah...
Sons of the Desert are we.

'Coo Coo' Theme Song

Coo Coo comes in various forms in Laurel and Hardy films. Each version of the theme captures the style of each and lets us know the Boys are about to enter. Here are a few examples of the different Coo Coo theme used in the films:

♦ **Baroque Coo Coo** in The Devil's Brother

♦ **Coo Coo with a twang** in Berth Marks

♦ **Coo Coo with a Gypsy flair** in The Bohemian Girl

♦ **Coo Coo with a western touch** in Way Out West

♦ **Coo Coo with a French twist** in The Flying Deuces

♦ **Coo Coo on an anvil** in Bonnie Scotland

THE HISTORY OF THE 'COO COO'

The Laurel & Hardy signature theme, 'Coo Coo' was written by T. Marvin Hatley. Stan wanted to use the theme in their films. He felt that the tune represented Ollie, since it was like a bugle call and dominant. The Coo Coo part, he thought, represented him, as it was limited to only two notes and his character was always doing something wrong.

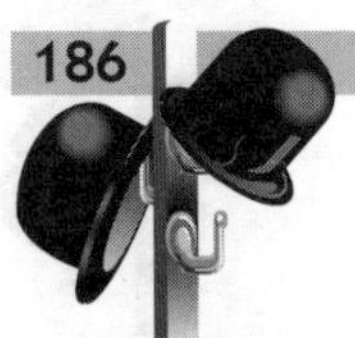

STAN'S SINGING
Stan Chimes In

- **Go To Sleep My Baby:** Brats
- **Good Morning To You:** Pardon Us
- **Stan as a woman humming:** Twice Two
- **Stan's singing drunk:** The Devil's Brother
- **Honolulu Baby:** Sons Of The Desert
- **Pom-Pom:** Them Thar Hills
- **Stan sings like a woman and in a low, deep voice of a man:** The Bohemian Girl and Way Out West
- **On The Trail Of The Lonesome Pine:** Way Out West

THE OPERAS

- The Rogue Song
- The Devil's Brother
- Babes In Toyland
- The Bohemian Girl

MUSICALS OF SORTS

- Hollywood Revue of 1929
- Pardon Us
- Sons Of The Desert
- Bonnie Scotland
- Way Out West
- Swiss Miss
- The Flying Deuces

MUSICAL INSTRUMENTS

"Pianos, I hate and detest pianos!"

Many Laurel and Hardy films include instruments. The plots range from moving an instrument to having a hornophobia breakdown and everything in between.

FILMS WITH PIANOS

- Duck Soup
- We Faw Down
- Wrong Again
- That's My Wife
- Big Business
- Night Owls
- Another Fine Mess
- Chickens Come Home
- Beau Hunks
- The Music Box
- Scram!
- Me and My Pal
- Dirty Work
- The Bohemian Girl
- Way Out West
- Swiss Miss
- Jitterbugs
- The Dancing Masters

FILM WITH BELLS & WHISTLES

Whistles:

- Leave 'Em Laughing
- Two Tars
- Pardon Us
- Pack Up Your Troubles
- Air Raid Wardens
- Big Noise
- Nothing But Trouble
- Atoll K

Bells:

- Their First Mistake
- Oliver the Eighth
- The Live Ghost
- Swiss Miss
- Flying Deuces
- Chump at Oxford
- Atoll K

OTHER INSTRUMENTS
Used In The Films

♦ The Second Hundred Years	**Triangle, gong**
♦ Berth Marks	**Fiddle**
♦ Below Zero	**Organ and double bass violin**
♦ The Music Box	**Harp**
♦ Pack Up Your Troubles	**Harp**
♦ Towed in a Hole	**Saw and nail played by Stan**
♦ The Devil's Brother	**Guitar**
♦ Busy Bodies	**Record player**
♦ Sons of the Desert	**Ukulele**
♦ Them Thar Hills	**Guitar**
♦ Babes in Toyland	**Fiddle**
♦ Bonnie Scotland	**Bagpipe and accordion**
♦ Pick A Star	**Harmonica**
♦ Swiss Miss	**Pipe organ, tuba, bass fiddle, Violin, tambourine**
♦ Flying Deuces	**Bed springs**
♦ A Chump at Oxford	**Xylophone**
♦ Saps at Sea	**Slide trombone**
♦ Jitterbugs	**Trumpet, drum, base, clarinet, sax, tuba**
♦ The Big Noise	**Accordion**
♦ Atoll K	**Bagpipes and ukulele**

LYRICS OF A TRIBUTE

A Song About The Boys

Jan and Dean, the surfing duet of the 1960's, recorded a song entitled 'Laurel and Hardy', which was released in 1968. Below are the lyrics to this nice tribute to the Boys.

'LAUREL AND HARDY'

by Jan and Dean

In a world grown complicated, it comes as quite a surprise
That a couple of simple people are still masters in our eyes
Many a time you've seen them laughing, spreading joy for all to see
Mr. Laurel, Mr. Hardy, I'll tell you what they mean to me.

Roller coasters on the rainbow, running like endless time
With Stan and Ollie in the front, and my heart - each he left behind
Here's the past and they're still here, with a smile that time can't void
And laughter waits throughout the world for their hearts preserved on celluloid.

In a world filled with confusion, I just want to go back when
Life was filled with simple pleasures, will they come again?
They were born to put the world on, slapstick clowns and fancy free
Mr. Laurel, Mr. Hardy, I'll tell you what they mean to me.
Roller coasters on the rainbow, reaching far across the sky
Mr. Laurel, Mr. Hardy never really said goodbye
Many times I've seen them laughing, many times they've made me die
And I know they keep folks happy, in the laughing sky.

LYRICS OF A TRIBUTE
Songs That Mention The Boys

OTHER SONGS

- **'Junior's Farm' by Paul McCartney:** Contains the lyrics "Ollie should'a had more sense"
- **'Damnation's Cellar' by Elvis Costello:** Contains the lyrics "Bring back Liberace or Ollie and Stan"
- **'Nobody Sees Me Like You Do' by Yoko Ono:** Contains the lyrics "In their eyes we were Laurel and Hardy"
- **'Laurel And Hardy' by The Equals**

INTERESTING FACTS

IRVING BERLIN (1888-1989)

Oscar nominated nine times for best song over the span of his sixty-year career. Best known as the composer of such hits as 'Alexander's Ragtime Band' and 'White Christmas'.
Way Out West (1937) Composer; Pardon Us (1931) Composed music and lyrics
Other notable films: Pride of the Yankees (1942), Composed music and lyrics; Alexander's Ragtime Band (1938) Composed music and lyrics

MARVIN HATLEY (1904-1986)

Worked for the Hal Roach Studios from 1930 to 1939. Composer of the 'Coo Coo' song and earned three Oscars nominations for 'Way Out West', 'Block-Heads', and 'There Goes My Heart'.
Chump at Oxford (1940), Composer; Saps at Sea (1940), Composer; Swiss Miss (1938), Music director; Way Out West (1937); Our Relations (1936); Pack up Your Troubles (1932), Composer; Pardon Us (1931), Music and lyrics
Other notable films: Zenobia (1939), Composer; There Goes My Heart (1938), Music director, composer; Pick a Star (1937) Music director, music and lyrics, composer; Topper (1937), music director; General Spanky (1936), composer

THE BOYS
Stan Laurel & Oliver Hardy

This chapter compares the film lives of Stan & Ollie. It looks at their film families and even their run-ins with the law. This section also examines such personal facts as who wore glasses more often and who smoked more in the films. It tallies their occupations, their addresses and phone numbers, and even tries to come to a conclusion on who is dumber – Stan or Ollie.

OUR RELATIVES

Stan's Family Tree

Film family seen or mentioned:

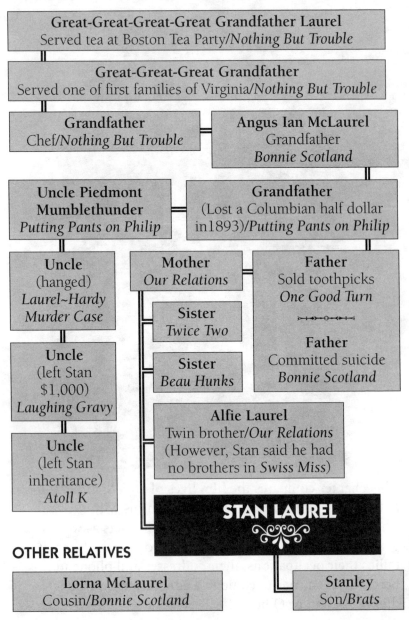

Great-Great-Great-Great Grandfather Laurel
Served tea at Boston Tea Party/*Nothing But Trouble*

Great-Great-Great Grandfather
Served one of first families of Virginia/*Nothing But Trouble*

Grandfather
Chef/*Nothing But Trouble*

Angus Ian McLaurel
Grandfather
Bonnie Scotland

Uncle Piedmont Mumblethunder
Putting Pants on Philip

Grandfather
(Lost a Columbian half dollar in1893)/*Putting Pants on Philip*

Uncle
(hanged)
Laurel~Hardy Murder Case

Uncle
(left Stan $1,000)
Laughing Gravy

Uncle
(left Stan inheritance)
Atoll K

Mother
Our Relations

Father
Sold toothpicks
One Good Turn

Father
Committed suicide
Bonnie Scotland

Sister
Twice Two

Sister
Beau Hunks

Alfie Laurel
Twin brother/*Our Relations*
(However, Stan said he had no brothers in *Swiss Miss*)

STAN LAUREL

Stanley
Son/*Brats*

OTHER RELATIVES

Lorna McLaurel
Cousin/*Bonnie Scotland*

OUR RELATIVES

Ollie's Family Tree

Film family seen or mentioned:

Great-Great-Great-Great Grandfather Hardy
Served tea at Boston Tea Party/*Nothing But Trouble*

Great-Great-Great Grandfather
Served one of first families of Virginia/*Nothing But Trouble*

Grandfather Hardy
Chef/*Nothing But Trouble*

Uncle Bernal
That's My Wife

Uncle
Left Ollie fortune/*Early to Bed*

Mother
Alice/*Our Relations*

Father
Our Relations

OLIVER NORVELL HARDY

Fannie
Sister/*Twice Two*

Louise
Sister/*Putting Pants on Philip*

Bert Hardy
Twin brother/*Our Relations*

Oliver
Son/*Brats*

Adopted Baby
Their First Mistake

Arlene
Daughter
(or so he was told)
The Bohemian Girl

RELATED BY MARRIAGE

Mother-in-law
Helpmates

Charlie Chase
Brother-in-law/*Sons of the Desert*

OTHER RELATIVES

Philip
Nephew/*Putting Pants on Philip*

STICKS & STONES
Nicknames The Boys Were Called

STAN

- **Little Goofy**: The Second Hundred Years
- **The Human Mop**: The Battle of the Century
- **General**: Men O'War
- **Bluebird**: Chickens Come Home
- **Squirt**: Pardon Us
- **Rosebud**: Pardon Us
- **Weasel**: Tit for Tat
- **Wax-eater**: Sons of the Desert
- **Dodo**: Sons of the Desert
- **Woodpecker**: The Bohemian Girl
- **Lover**: Our Relations
- **Desert Rat**: Way Out West
- **A Chump At Oxford**: Little Shrimp
- **Jitterbugs**: Saps at Sea
- **Dopey**: Saps at Sea

OLLIE

- **Big Boy**: We Faw Down
- **Puzzums**: Unaccustomed As We Are
- **Honey-bub**: Be Big
- **Apple-cheeked boy**: Chickens Come Home
- **Wall-eyed pike**: Chickens Come Home
- **Dimple-dumplin**: Chickens Come Home
- **Papa**: Come Clean
- **Big bozo**: One Good Turn
- **Pudgy Wudgy**: Twice Two
- **Fatty**: Me & My Pal
- **Overfed windbag**: The Devil's Brother
- **Puffed-up bullfrog**: The Devil's Brother
- **Tumbleweed**: Thicker Than Water
- **Barnacle**: Sons of the Desert
- **Inflated tadpole**: Sons of the Desert
- **Papa**: Our Relations
- **Desert Rat**: Way Out West
- **Fatty**: Swiss Miss
- **Big, overstuffed pollywog**: Block-Heads
- **Inflated blimp**: Block-Heads
- **Fatty**: A Chump At Oxford
- **Jitterbugs**: Saps at Sea
- **Creampuff**: Saps at Sea
- **Dizzy**: Saps at Sea
- **Blimp**: Great Guns

IN BED

Sharing quarters

The Boys rarely had more than a few cents between them, which often meant splitting or sharing anything and everything they had. One of the more frequently shared items between them in their films was a bed, which always was good for a laugh.

♦ **1.** The Boys appeared in bed 26 times in their career. How many of these films can you name?

♦ **2.** There are six films in which The Boys had separate beds. How many can you think of?

♦ **3.** Name the first film in which Stan & Ollie appear in bed together.

IN BED
The Answers

♦ **1.** Do Detectives Think?; Leave 'Em Laughing; Berth Marks; They Go Boom; Angora Love; Brats; The Laurel-Hardy Murder Case; Be Big; Laughing Gravy; Pardon Us; The Chimp; Pack Up Your Troubles; Their First Mistake; Sons of the Desert; Oliver the Eighth; Babes in Toyland; The Live Ghost; The Fixer Uppers; Bonnie Scotland; Our Relations; A Chump At Oxford; Saps at Sea; Great Guns; Air Raid Wardens; The Big Noise; Atoll K

♦ **2.** Early To Bed; Beau Hunks; The Chimp (in bed together at first, Stan moves to his own bed); Bonnie Scotland (after joining the army); The Flying Deuces (two single beds in room, but never in bed); Great Guns

♦ **3.** Do Detectives Think?

SPECTACLES
Eyewear Of The Boys

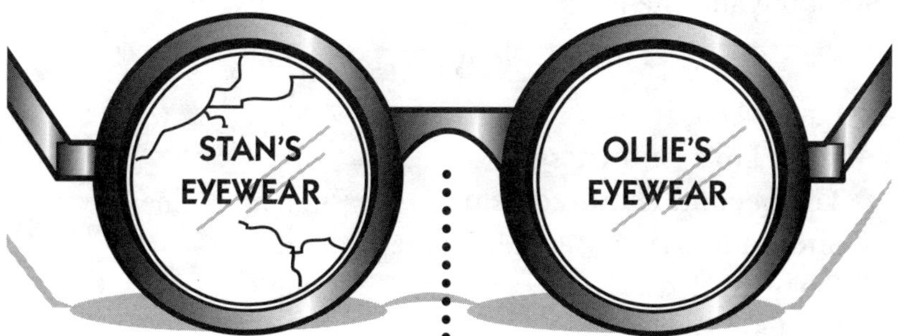

Stan wears glasses in the following films:

- ♦ **Sugar Daddies**
- ♦ **Beau Hunks**
- ♦ **Going Bye-Bye**
- ♦ **Saps At Sea**
- ♦ **Great Guns**
- ♦ **The Tree In A Test Tube**
- ♦ **The Dancing Masters**
- ♦ **Atoll K**

Ollie wears glasses in the following films:

- ♦ **Below Zero**
- ♦ **Another Fine Mess**
- ♦ **Chickens Come Home**
- ♦ **Beau Hunks**
- ♦ **Going Bye-Bye**
- ♦ **Our Relations**

Stan wore a monacle in **'A Chump At Oxford'** and Ollie wore a monacle in **'Duck Soup'**.

DO YOU MIND IF I SMOKE?
Cigarettes, Cigars, Pipes & Tobacco

Smoking and the Boys' films:

CIGARETTES	
♦ **Lucky Dog**	Ollie
♦ **With Love And Hisses**	Ollie
♦ **The Second Hundred Years**	Stan and Ollie
♦ **Should Married Men Go Home?**	Stan
♦ **Early To Bed**	Ollie
♦ **We Faw Down**	Stan
♦ **Another Fine Mess**	Ollie
♦ **Sons Of The Desert**	Stan
♦ **The Tree In A Test Tube**	Stan

CIGARS	
♦ **Duck Soup**	Ollie
♦ **Slipping Wives**	Stan
♦ **Do Detectives Think?**	Stan and Ollie
♦ **Should Married Men Go Home?**	Ollie
♦ **That's My Wife**	Ollie
♦ **Big Business**	Boys give Fin an exploding cigar
♦ **Double Whoopee**	Stan
♦ **Chickens Come Home**	Ollie
♦ **Scram!**	Stan
♦ **Pack Up Your Troubles**	Stan and Ollie
♦ **The Bohemian Girl**	Stan and Ollie
♦ **Our Relations**	Stan and Ollie
♦ **Pick A Star**	Stan and Ollie
♦ **Swiss Miss**	Stan and Ollie
♦ **The Flying Deuces**	Stan and Ollie
♦ **A Chump At Oxford**	Stan and Ollie
♦ **Jitterbugs**	Ollie

PIPES

♦ **Why Girls Love Sailors**	Ollie
♦ **Beau Hunks**	Stan
♦ **Thicker Than Water**	Stan
♦ **Way Out West**	Stan's talent of smoking his thumb as a pipe.
♦ **Block-Heads**	Stan and Ollie
♦ **A Chump At Oxford**	Stan
♦ **The Tree In A Test Tube**	Stan
♦ **Jitterbugs**	Stan
♦ **The Big Noise**	Stan and Ollie

Can you name the two films that contained snuff?

ANSWER: Putting Pants On Philip and Bonnie Scotland

OLLIE'S OCCUPATIONS

Careers Selected Most Often

Military service: **12 times**

Convict: **5 times**

Vagrant: **9 times**

Detective or Cop: **6 times**

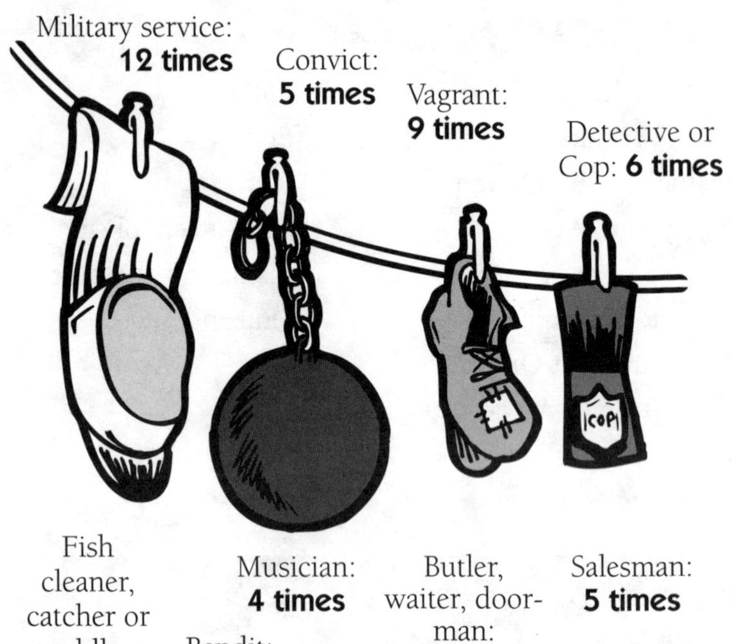

Fish cleaner, catcher or peddler: **3 times**

Bandit: **3 times**

Musician: **4 times**

Butler, waiter, door-man: **4 times**

Salesman: **5 times**

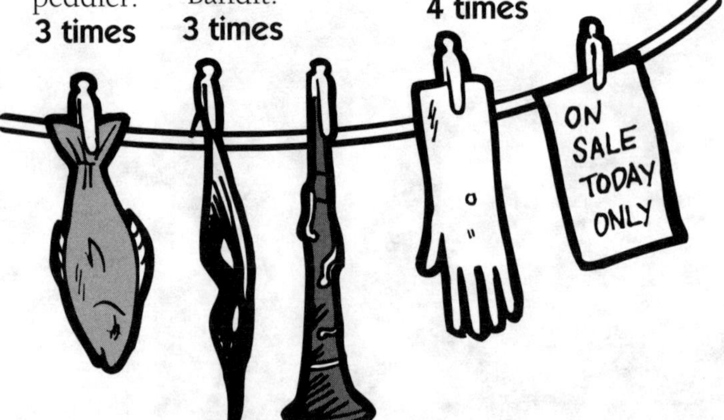

SOME OTHER JOBS HE HELD

- Deliveryman
- Businessman
- Dance Instructor
- Chimney Sweep
- Barber
- Brain Specialist

STAN'S OCCUPATIONS

Careers Selected Most Often

Detective or Cop: **5 times**

Vagrant: **9 times**

Convict: **5 times**

Military service: **10 times**

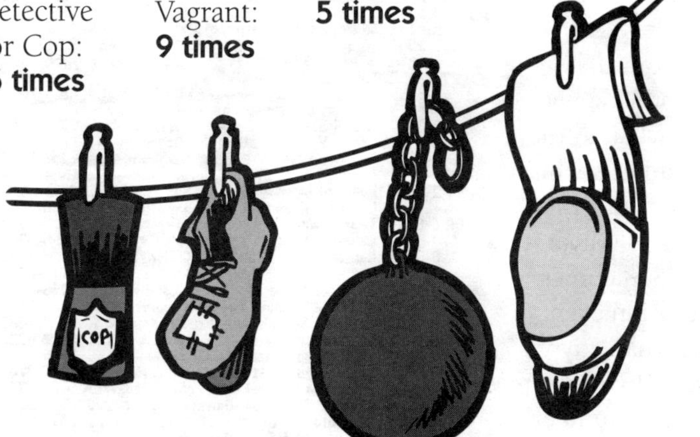

Salesman: **5 times**

Butler, waiter, doorman: **4 times**

Musician: **4 times**

Bandit: **3 times**

Fish cleaner, catcher or peddler: **3 times**

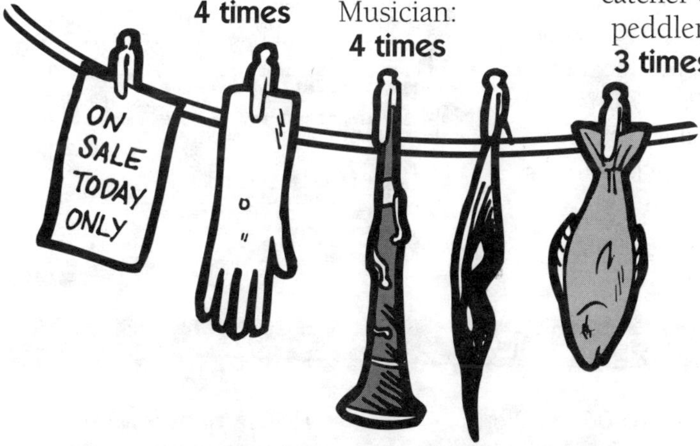

COP

ON SALE TODAY ONLY

SOME OTHER JOBS HE HELD

- Deliveryman
- Businessman
- Dance Instructor
- Chimney Sweep
- Barber
- Boxer

ADDRESSES & PHONE NUMBERS

Stan's On-screen Listings

Ordinary items such as telephones and addresses were great props that could provide big laughs when in the right hands, such as the hands of Stan Laurel and Oliver Hardy. Sometimes, the joke ran even further than anyone realized. In 'Blotto', the phone number Stan gave was his actual number at the time. The address, 49 Colebrook Avenue, that was mentioned in 'Pack Up Your Troubles' was actually his father's home in London. Here are some more numbers.

Laskey—Laven 245

..GL 4-5347	Laurel Music 9128 SunstLA 274-9026
.GR 8-6156	Laurel Music Enterprises Inc
.OL 7-2049	120ElCaminoBH.CR 6-4181
.CR 5-6816	After 5PM call.................656-6550
279-2032	LAUREL PLUMBNG CO
. 4-3289	1468 SRobrtsnLA.CR 5-7547
99-4297	From L A telephones call...........BR 2-4858
? 0-8439	Laurel Stan 849 OceanAvSM ....EX 3-5656
X 4-0401	Laurel Virginia Ruth 413 SDohenyDrBH ..273-8138
397-5298	Laurelle Kathryn 25252WMalibuRdMlbu .456-2655
478-4253	Lauren Edw E 17630TramontoDrPPal ...GL 4-5349
.BR 2-8651	Lauren-Finger Agcy 9229 SunstLA .....CR 3-3550
	Lauren S K 24142WMalibuRdMlbu .....GL 6-2848
A.CR 6-8024	Lauren Ward 27120SeavstaDrMlbu .....GL 7-2949
...478-8604	Laurence Douglas 717NCamdenDrBH ....CR 6-3304
.EX 8-8055	Laurence J A 21251WPacCstHwyMlbu ..GL 6-2685
	Laurence Jami 5834PerryDrCC 839-6816
'L 2-4373	Laurence Lorne 22235WPacCstHwyMlbu ..456-8238
94-8583	Laurence Michael 10446 SeaburyLnWLA ..279-1143
5-8998	Laurence School The 6428WoodmnVN ...ST 0-7085
1850	Laurendeau Guy 12425TexasWLA ......GR 3-0322
-8142	Laurendeau Julien 934HarvrdSM ....EX 5-6362
8-4917	Laurendeau R J 1133 6thSM ....EX 4-8204
98-4586	Laurenson Michael R 2820SepulvedaWLA .473-1843
1-8834	Laurent Melvin 676BdwayVen 396-5602
38-7966	Laurentowski Casimir 1143 9thSM 395-0485
479-0047	Laurenzano A P phy & sur MD
GR 9-8779	436LinclnVen.EX 9-2727
	Lauretano Adolph A 8763½VeniceLA 837-4290
79-6160	Lauri Tota 1124NSherbrneDrLA 652-8890
8-7498	Lauria Angela 929LarrabeeLA ....OL 7-0547
4-0880	Lauria V G 918 15thSM 395-8552
2-9555	Lauria V G Realtor 2012WilshrSM .....EX 4-5915
9-7013	Lauria's Telephone Answering Serv .....OL 2-1133
2-2617	Laurie-Barnett Agcy 214NCanonDrBH ...CR 4-2224
3-5868	Laurie Chas 555KeltnAvWLA 477-4900
478-3176	Laurie Francis J 708MarrVen ....EX 2-1426
'E 9-3527	Laurie Frank D 3950 InglwdBlLA 397-7204
X 1-4782	Laurie Geo 1008 7thSM 395-4441
79-1986	Laurie Jack Laurie-Barnett Agcy
	214NCanonDrBH.CR 4-2224
3-6585	Laurie Kim Corporation 9230WilshrBH ..BR 2-3234
2-1518	Laurie Laurence & Associates Inc
2-4319	224NCanonDrBH.274-0851
4-2530	From L A telephones call...........272-2783
6-1115	LAURIE LEASING CORP
91-3092	1220GlndnWLA 474-3597
R 4-3284	Laurie Martin 11748½CulvrBlLA 397-4316
X 3-8742	Laurie Norton R 3120CorinthAvLA .....EX 1-5733
R 4-3985	...rie Norton R CPA 292 SLaCienegaBH .652-4618
477-6...	... SShenand... OL 2-6014

STAN'S PHONE

- **Oxford 0614:** 'Blotto' This was Stan's real phone number at the time
- **Aptoss 8080:** 'Helpmates'
- **Hollywood 4368:** 'Beau Hunks'

STAN'S ADDRESS

- **House number 316, Apt. 14:** 'Laughing Gravy'
- **Prisoner #44634, Cell 14:** 'Pardon Us'
- **2220 Fairview Ave.:** 'Sons of the Desert'

ADDRESSES & PHONE NUMBERS

Ollie's On-screen Listings

OLLIE'S PHONE

- **Granite 3648:** 'Chickens Come Home'
- **Waterloo 22:** 'Twice Two'
- **Main 489:** 'Going Bye-Bye!'

OLLIE'S LICENSE PLATE

- **1-254-592**
  California 1927:
  'Leave 'Em Laughing'

OLLIE'S ADDRESSES

- **House number 984:** 'Should Married Men Go Home'
- **House number 316, Apt. 14:** 'Laughing Gravy'
- **Prisoner #44633, cell 14:** 'Pardon Us'
- **House number 1645:** 'Helpmates'
- **6311 Old Fashioned Way:** 'Me and My Pal'
- **201 Spring Street, Los Angeles, California:** 'Oliver the Eighth'
- **2222 Fairview Ave.:** 'Sons of the Desert'
- **House number 1313:** 'Block-Heads'

COPS AND THE BOYS

Stan & Ollie In The Slammer

In how many films were the Boys in jail or prison?

- ◆**A.** 6 times
- ◆**B.** 8 times
- ◆**C.** 11 times

ANSWER:

B. 8 times — The Second Hundred Years; Liberty; The Hoose-Gow; Pardon Us; Pack Up Your Troubles; Babes in Toyland; Bonnie Scotland; The Flying Deuces

LAW & DISORDER

Good Guys & Bad Guys

Photo courtesy of Larry Bell

Out of the 106 films, how many times were the Boys in trouble with the law?

♦ **A.** 32 times

♦ **B.** 42 times

♦ **C.** 52 times

ANSWER:

C. Believe it or not, the Boys were at odds against the police in 52 films

There were five films in which the Boys are cops or detectives. How many can you name?

ANSWER:

1. Do Detectives Think?
2. Bacon Grabbes
3. The Midnight Patrol
4. The Big noise
5. The Bullfighters

CO-STAR COPS
The Actors

Co-stars who played law enforcement officials in the films:

- Harry Bernard
- James Morton
- Tiny Sandford
- Edgar Kennedy
- Christian Frank
- Edgar Dearing
- Charles Bachman
- Jack Hill
- Sam Lufkin
- Baldwin Cooke
- Charles McMurphy
- Frank Holliday
- Anders Randolph
- Fred Kelsey
- Bill Knight
- Bob Mumford
- Eddie Baker
- Eddie Dunn
- Billy Bletcher
- Dick Gilbert
- Harry Arras
- Harry Neilman
- Stanley Fields
- James Finlayson
- Stanley Blystone
- Gene Morgan
- Bud Geary
- Jack Greene
- Ed Gargan
- Howard Mitchell
- Steve Darrell
- Jose Dominguez
- Joe Yule, Sr.
- Forbes Murray
- Ray Teal

NUMB AND NUMBER
Stan And Ollie

Ollie thinks himself to be the brighter of the two, but sometimes Stanley is not as dumb as you look (or something like that). When Ollie tries to correct Stan's ignorance, he ends up showing us that he usually knows even less than Stan.

HABEAS CORPUS
Stan sees something move in the dirt (Ollie's foot) and tells Ollie. Ollie takes matters into his own hands and whacks his own foot with a shovel.

BELOW ZERO
The Boys are playing "In The Good Old Summertime" in the middle of winter and in front of a deaf and dumb institute.

THE LAUREL-HARDY MURDER CASE
Stan to Ollie: "Three million dollars. Is that as much as a thousand?"
Ollie: "Why, man alive, it's twice as much."

PARDON US
Fin: "How many times does three go into nine?"
Stan: "Three times...with two left over."
Fin to Ollie: "What are you laughing at?"
Ollie: "There's only one left over."

THE MUSIC BOX
Once the mailman (Charlie Hall) explains to Stan and Ollie that they could have driven the piano up to the house instead of carrying it up all those stairs, they pick up the piano and carry it back down so they can drive it up to the house.

THE CHIMP

Billy Gilbert: "No monkeys in my hotel. Get it out of here."
Ollie: "Well, we can't leave it outside."
Stan: "No, it might get cold and die of ammonia."
Ollie: "Not ammonia, he means pammonia."

THE LIVE GHOST

Stan: "I heard the ocean's infatuated with sharks."
Ollie: "Not infatuated! He means infuriated."

THE FIXER UPPERS

Stan answers the pay phone:
Stan: "Hello. It sure is." (He hangs up phone)
Ollie: "Who was it?"
Stan: "Oh, some fella having a joke."
Ollie: "Well, what'd he say?"
Stan: "Well, I said hello and the fella said it's a long distance from Atlanta, Georgia and I said it sure is."
Ollie: "I wish there was some way to put a stop to those practical jokers."

THICKER THAN WATER

The Boys inadvertently bid against each other at an auction.

BLOCK-HEADS

Ollie finds Stan sitting in a wheelchair (who actually has his leg tucked under him) and assumes Stan lost his leg during the war. Ollie carries Stan until finally realizing his mistake. However, Ollie forgets and keeps picking Stan up and carrying him.

THE DANCING MASTERS

The Boys bid against each other for a clock at an auction.

STANLEY
The Facts On Mr. Laurel

This chapter examines the genius behind the characterization of Stan Laurel.

HEAD SCRATCHES
Career Total

Stan's character was very complex on the simplest level. The same is to be said about his head scratching. Sometimes it conveyed joy and self-content, sometimes pure fear.
He did a total of **256** head scratches in their 106 films.

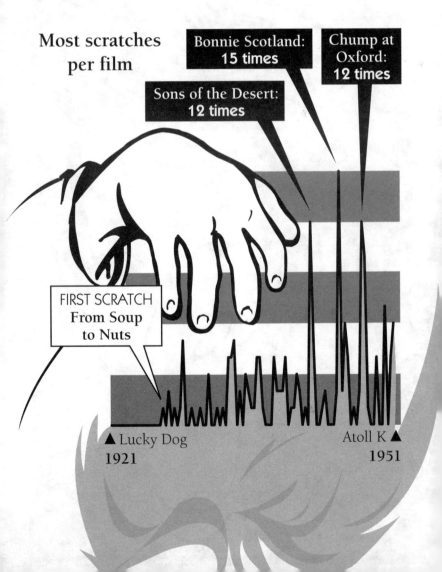

CRYING
Stanley Weeps

Further proving his character to be quite child-like, Stanley openly weeps at the slightest provocation. This was his character's only mannerism which Stan Laurel didn't like. He kept it, however, because it worked and was popular with fans of their films.

- ♦ **First Short In Which Stanley Cries:** 'Forty-Five Minutes From Hollywood'
- ♦ **Most Crying In A Short:** Nine times in both 'Their Purple Moment' and 'The Live Ghost'
- ♦ **Feature Film With The Most Crying:** 'Pardon Us' with 10 cries.
- ♦ **Career-Total Cries:** He cried 306 times in 90 films
- ♦ **Ollie Cries:** On rare occasion, Ollie would burst into tears as well. He cried only five times, once in each of these films: 'Big Business,' 'The Devil's Brother,' 'Blotto,' 'The Fixer Uppers' and 'Great Guns'

WHITE MAGIC
And Stan's Others Talents

Films in which Stan made the impossible possible:

- Stan lays one spoon on top of another and hits the bottom spoon, causing the top spoon to flip into a glass a water / **Their Purple Moment**
- Has the ability to wiggle his ears / **Blotto, Any Old Port, A Chump at Oxford, A-Haunting We Will Go**
- Hides object in hands and makes Ollie guess in which hand it is hidden / **Pardon Us**
- His hat seems to rise by itself when he puts his finger in his mouth and blows/ **Towed in a Hole, Bonnie Scotland**
- The Finger-Wiggle : With fingers interlocked, he twists his hands and wiggles his center fingers / **The Devil's Brother, Babes in Toyland, A Chump at Oxford**
- Kneesey, Earsy, Nosey: One of Stan's mind games which starts with patting of knees and one arm crosses over the other while reaching for the nose and ear / **The Devil's Brother, Babes in Toyland**
- Trick Punches: Throws a punch under his other arm or punches with the opposite hand / **Busy Bodies, Block-Heads**
- Pee Wees: Stan hits a little piece of wood with a stick / **Babes in Toyland**
- Finger Game I: Simultaneously putting out fingers, if the same number comes up, Ollie wins; Stan cheats by lowering his hand below the table top and brings up a winning number of fingers / **The Bohemian Girl**
- Finger Game II: On his index finger, Stan bends back the first two joints and places his thumb from the opposite hand in front, to make it appear as if his finger separates at the joint / **The Bohemian Girl**

- ♦ Sing High, Sing Low: Stan's voice magically changes (from very deep to a very high woman's voice) while singing / **The Bohemian Girl, Way Out West, Swiss Miss**
- ♦ Stan's ability to light his thumbs on fire like a lighter / **Way Out West**
- ♦ Has the ability to close window blinds, even though they are just shadows cast on the walls / **Block-Heads**
- ♦ Smokes a 'pipe' that is actually his hand and uses thumb as the pipe stem / **Way Out West**
- ♦ Ability to play bed springs like a harp / **The Flying Deuces**
- ♦ Unscrews a light bulb from the lamp, yet it stays lit / **Great Guns**
- ♦ Carries a board (very, very long) on both ends / **The Finishing Touch, Great Guns**
- ♦ Uses fingers as a tuning fork / **A-Haunting We Will Go**
- ♦ Pop-Top: Hat pops off head / **The Tree in a Test Tube**
- ♦ Pours oil on troubled water to calm a stormy sea / **Atoll K**

AGNES & FRIENDS

Stan's A Woman

1. How many times did Stan dress as a woman in their films?
2. How many times did he sing like a woman?
3. In 'The Bohemian Girl,' what actress dubbed Stan's female singing voice?
4. In which film did he wear a tutu?
5. Name the two times Stan played a woman named 'Agnes'.

ANSWERS:
1. Nine times: Duck Soup, Why Girls Love Sailors, Sugar Daddies, That's My Wife, Another Fine Mess, Twice Two, Babes in Toyland, A Chump At Oxford, Jitterbugs
2. Twice: The Bohemian Girl & Way Out West
3. Rosina Lawrence
4. The Dancing Masters
5. Another Fine Mess, A Chump At Oxford

FAST FEET
Stanley Leaps

At times, Stan seems to be lighter than air. His leaping ability combined with his agility is great for anything from girl chasing to boxing.

- ♦ **First Time Stan Leaps In A Short:** 'Why Girls Love Sailors'
- ♦ **Most Leaps In Short:** Nine times in both 'Putting Pants On Philip' & 'Flying Elephants'.
- ♦ **Most Leaps In A Film:** Three times in 'The Bohemian Girl'.
- ♦ **Other Films In Which Stan Leaps:**
  'The Battle of the Century'
  'From Soup to Nuts'
  'Early to Bed'
  'Habeas Corpus'
  'Angora Love'
  'Pardon Us'
  'One Good Turn'
  'Any Old Port'
  'The Dancing Masters'
- ♦ **Career-Total Leaps:** 40 times in 13 films.

FLOPPY SOCKS

Stan's Feet

The Boys are known by the clothes they wear, and their bed clothes are also just predictable. Both wear night shirts, usually under their clothes. Ollie sometimes will wear a cap, and Stan always wears a pair of floppy socks.

Films In Which Stan Wore Floppy Socks:

- Forty-Five Minutes From Hollywood
- Leave 'Em Laughing
- From Soup To Nuts
- Early To Bed
- They Go Boom
- Angora Love
- Laurel~Hardy Murder Case
- Laughing Gravy
- Beau Hunks
- Helpmates
- The Chimp
- Pack Up Your Troubles
- Their First Mistake
- Sons Of The Desert
- The Live Ghost
- A Chump At Oxford
- Saps At Sea
- Air Raid Wardens
- **Total:** 18 times worn

STUMBLES & FALLS
Stan Faws Down

When you think of Laurel & Hardy taking a fall for a laugh, it's usually the vision of Ollie plunging off a roof or ladder. However, Stan took just a many falls as did his partner.

- **First Fall:** Was in 'Lucky Dog'. And he got lots of practice with nine falls in this film.
- **Most Falls In Short:** Ten times on gum balls in 'Two Tars'.
- **Feature Film With The Most Falls:** Believe it or not, Stan took eight falls in their last feature film 'Atoll K'. Although he was quite ill during the production of this film, he still took his spills like a real pro.
- **Career-Total Falls:** 195 times in 67 films

HITS ON THE HEAD

Stan's Bumps

Stan has had everything from bricks to shovels bounced off his noggin. Luckily, the damage was minor — just a little dent in the shovel.

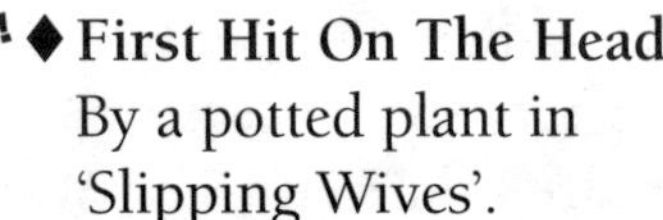

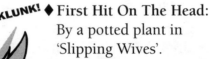

- **First Hit On The Head:** By a potted plant in 'Slipping Wives'.
- **Most Times Hit On The Head In A Short:** Four times each in 'Berth Marks' and in 'Dirty Work'.
- **Feature Film With The Most Hits On The Head:** 'The Dancing Masters' with 10 hits.
- **Hits On The Head Career-Total :** 96 times in 51 films

WHERE'S STAN?

Films in which Stan attempts to hide

In the world of Stan Laurel, his beliefs are as strong and yet as simple of that of an innocent child. He feels 'I can't see you, therefore, you can no longer see me . . .'

- ♦ **'Unaccustomed As We Are'**: Tries to hide Mrs. Kennedy (Thelma Todd) in a trunk
- ♦ **'Be Big'**: Tries to hide a broken bootjack behind his back
- ♦ **'Chickens Come Home'**: Tries to hide a crazed Mae Busch from Ollie's wife
- ♦ **'Laughing Gravy'**: Puts the dog up the chimney
- ♦ **'Come Clean**: Tries to hide in a tub full of water
- ♦ **'The Chimp'**: Hides Ethel
- ♦ **'Pack Up Your Troubles'**: Stan hides with Eddie Smith's baby in a trunk and in a bucket
- ♦ **'Towed in a Hole'**: Hides and peeks at Ollie around boat
- ♦ **'Twice Two'**: Rips Ollie's pants and hides from him
- ♦ **'Way Out West'**: Puts pail over Ollie's head to hide him and also hides inside of piano
- ♦ **'Block-Heads'**: Mrs. Gilbert pretends to be a chair that Stan keeps sitting in
- ♦ **'The Dancing Masters'**: Hides under bed

BOYS WILL BE BOYS

Stan Fights With Ollie

The Boys are essentially children in adult bodies. Their innocence and charm have one other childlike characteristic: they fight with each other as kids do. Here are the times Stan started a fight with Ollie.

- ♦ **First Meeting, First Fight:** Stan, who was being robbed by Ollie, kicks him in the middle of his daily duties in 'Lucky Dog'.
- ♦ **Most Times Stan Fought With Ollie In A Short:** Nine times in both 'You're Darn Tootin' and 'Brats'.
- ♦ **Most Times Stan Fought With Ollie In A Feature Film:** Four times in 'The Devil's Brother"
- ♦ **Stan Fights With Ollie Career-Total** : 104 times in 44 films, yet they always remained best friends.

STAN FINISHES THE FIGHT

Ollie usually bullied Stan throughout their friendship – however, even Stan had his breaking point. Here are the times Stanley retaliated against Oliver:

- ♦ **First Retaliation:** After several hat switches, Stan starts a hat battle with Ollie in 'Hats Off'
- ♦ **Most Times Stan Fought Back Against Ollie In A Short:** Seven times in 'You're Darn Tootin'
- ♦ **Most Times Stan Fought Back In Against Ollie In A Feature Film:** Four times in 'The Devil's Brother'
- ♦ **Stan Fights Back Against Ollie Career-Total** : 69 times in 37 films, yet they always remained friends.

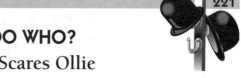

BOO WHO?
Stan Scares Ollie

Oliver Hardy is always the backbone of stability, never allowing Stan to see his weaknesses ... well, unless Stan accidentally scares him.

- **First Time Stan Scared Ollie In A Film:** Four times in 'Do Detectives Think?'
- **Most Scares In Short:** Five times in both 'Night Owls' & 'The Laurel~Hardy Murder Case'
- **Other Films In Which Stan Scares Ollie:** Habeas Corpus; Liberty; Perfect Day; Hog Wild; Another Fine Mess; One Good Turn; Beau Hunks; The Music Box; The Chimp; County Hospital; Dirty Work; Hollywood Party; Babes in Toyland; The Live Ghost; A Chump at Oxford; Great Guns; Air Raid Wardens
- **Total Times Stan Scared Ollie:** 37 times in 20 films

OCEANA
Stan Laurel's Apartment

Photos courtesy of Larry Bell

Photos from Stan's apartment at The Oceana in Santa Monica, California. He lived here from from the late 1950's until his death in 1965. Della Lind, star of 'Swiss Miss', also lived in the complex during that time.

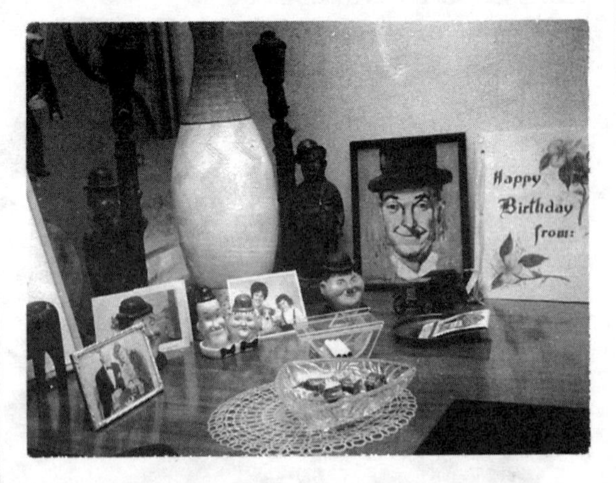

Above, left: Stan's marionettes hang as wall decorations in his apartment.
Above, right: Stan Laurel circa 1960's
Bottom: Stan's own collection of Laurel & Hardy memorabilia.

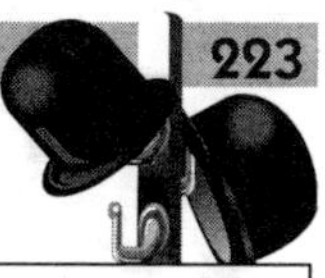

Photos courtesy of Larry Bell

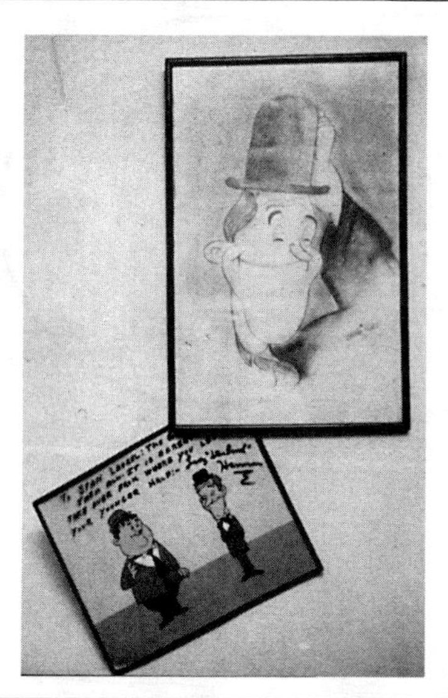

Above, right: Stan and his Oscar in 1961.
Above, left: Drawings that hung on the walls of Stan's apartment.
Bottom: Stan at his writing desk, used for answering all fan letters.

TELL ME THAT AGAIN!
Stan's Moments of Genius

Every once in a while every man has a clear and complete thought. In Stan's case, when his dim bulb would light, it was very bright — but always was very short-lived.

THE SECOND HUNDRED YEARS

Stan comes up with the idea to turn their prison uniforms inside out and pretend to be painters.

BE BIG

Stan tells Ollie to take the rocker bottom off the chair so it won't rock as Ollie is sitting in the chair. Stan can then try to get a good grip on Ollie's boot to pull it off.

CHICKENS COME HOME

Stan takes the blackmail photo of Mae Busch and Ollie from Busch's apartment so she won't have any proof of the supposed illicit affair.

PARDON US

To keep his tooth from buzzing, Stan sticks a piece of gum in it.

SCRAM

Arthur Housman's key has fallen into a street grating, and Stan uses an umbrella with a piece of gum on the end to stick the key to the gum and pull it up out of the grating.

THEIR FIRST MISTAKE

Stan: "You know what the trouble is."
Ollie: "What?"
Stan: "What you need is a baby in your house."
Ollie: "Well, what's that got to do with it?"
Stan: "Well, if...if you had a baby, it would keep your wife's mind occupied, and you could go out nights with me, and she'd never think anything about it. All your troubles would be over."

TOWED IN A HOLE

Stan: "You know, Ollie, I've been thinking."

Ollie: "What about?"

Stan: "I know how we could make a lot more money."

Ollie: "How?"

Stan: "If we caught our own fish, we wouldn't have to pay for it and then whoever we sold it to, it would be clear profit."

Ollie: "Tell me that again."

Stan: "Well, if you caught a fish and whoever you sold it to, they would have to pay for it and the profits, they would go to the fish."

THE DEVIL'S BROTHER

Ollie: "Why don't we start from the top. What do you mean?"

Stan: "Why don't we become bandits? Then we wouldn't have to work hard anymore. Let's get it the easy way. We could rob the rich and give 'em to the poor."

Ollie: "That's the first time that you've shown any intelligence."

Stan: "Well, it's the first time you listened to me. You know, if you listened to me every once in a while, you'd be a lot better off. "

Ollie: "I guess you're right. Tell me that plan again."

Stan: "All of it?"

Ollie: "Certainly...certainly."

Stan: "Well, if we became rich and robbed the poor and we gave 'em to the bandits and we start at the top and we get to the bottom without working hard anymore. We can't go wrong. It's the law of conversation.

Ollie: "What do you mean?"

Stan: "Well, as ye cast your bread upon the water, so shall ye reap."

Ollie: "That's very well thought out."

BUSY BODIES

Pretending to be his pal, Stan gives Charlie Hall a cigar and then calls over the foreman and points to the "no smoking" sign.

SONS OF THE DESERT

Stan referring to Ollie's plan to sleep in the attic for the night then sneak downstairs in the morning and their wives will never be any the wiser:

Stan: "I've certainly got to hand it to you."

Ollie: "For what?"

Stan: "Well, for the meticulous care with which you have executed your finely formulated machinations in extricating us from this devastating dilemma."

OLIVER THE EIGHTH

Stan, referring to woman in ad:

Stan: "Well, after all, beauty's only skin deep. I'd take some of the money, and I'd have her face lifted. Then I could settle down, and I wouldn't have to scrape chins anymore. I wouldn't have to work hard anymore.

Ollie: "Tell me that again."

Stan: "Well, if beauty is only knee....skin deep. I could take some of the money and I could have her skinned and then she'd be able to look at a clock without having to work hard anymore. Then we could settle down and I could scrape her chin and congenial ... if ...if I didn't have to work hard anymore."

Ollie: "That's a good idea."

GOING BYE-BYE

Stan: "Why don't we advertise for somebody to go with us."

Ollie: "Why do we want somebody to go with us for?"

Stan: "Help drive and share expenses. Just like when we came out here, remember?"

Ollie: "At last you're using my brain."

THE FIXER UPPERS

Stan offers advice to a neglected wife.

Stan: "She got a fella to make love to her in front of her husband and it made the husband jealous."

Ollie: "Then what happened?"

Stan: "Well, uh?"

Ollie: "So what?"

Stan: "Well, when the husband got jealous, his wife knew that he was in love with her just because he was jealous. You see if he hadn't been jealous, then he wouldn't a paid any attention to the fella that...that made him jealous. See?"

Ollie: "Well, what'd the husband do? Take a gun and go out and shoot the other fellow?"

Stan: "No, when the husband found out, he was so pleased that he was jealous, he took his wife in his arms and he kissed her and they went out again and they got married all over. And then he kissed her again...."

Ollie: "Now just a minute. What happened to the other fellow?"

Stan: "Well, when the husband found out he was jealous, he was so pleased that the other fellow had made him jealous, he gave the other fellow a lot of money because it made him jealous and they all lived happily ever after."

Ollie: "That's a splendid idea. Why don't you do that?" (to Mae Busch)

THICKER THAN WATER

Stan: "How much money have you and your wife got in the bank?"

Ollie: "Well, if it's any of your business, we have a joint account of $300. Why?"

Stan: "Why don't you draw the money out of the bank, pay off the furniture and own it outright. You wouldn't have any interest to pay and you wouldn't have any hounds in your fireplace."

Ollie, of course, thinks this is

a good idea even if the wife says that they'll do nothing of the kind.

BONNIE SCOTLAND

Stan: "You know what we could do...we could go way, way out west where they'd never find us."

Ollie: "Out west where?"

Stan: "Old Philadelphia, Jersey City, any of those places where they have no exposition laws."

Ollie: "What do you mean, no exposition laws?"

Stan: "Well, if the police found out where we were, they could come and get us if we didn't want them to..."

Ollie: "That's a very, very, very good idea."

A CHUMP AT OXFORD

Ollie: "I wonder what's the matter with us? We're just as good as other people yet we don't seem to advance ourselves. We never get anyplace."

Stan: "Ya know what the trouble is, don't ya? We've never had no education. That's what's the matter. See, we're not illiterate enough."

Ollie: "I guess you're right."

Stan: "Sure I'm right. See, if we went to school like other people, we would learn our three "R's" and today there'd be no job too small for us. Believe me."

Ollie: "What'ya mean three "R's"?"

Stan: "Well, reading...writing...and ...and figurin'"

Ollie: "Figurin'?"

Stan: "Sure, 2 and 2 makes something and 4 and 4 makes something. It's different than the first."

Ollie: "You mean rithmetic."

SAPS AT SEA

Stan: "I just thought of something. We don't have to go way out in the ocean to get sea air.

Ollie: "What do you mean?"

Stan: "Well, we could rent a boat, we could live on it and we don't even have to leave the dock. Get all the sea air we want."

Photo courtesy of Larry Bell

STANISMS
Stan's Infamous Quotes

BIG BUSINESS

♦ ***The Boys sell Christmas trees door-to-door.***

Ollie: "Wouldn't you like to buy a Christmas tree?

Woman: "No."

Ollie: "Wouldn't your husband like to buy one?"

Woman: "I have no husband."

Stan: "If you had a husband, would he buy one?"

MEN O' WAR

♦ ***Stan and Ollie meet up with two ladies while at the park. They take the women to the soda fountain, but have only enough money for three drinks. Stan and Ollie decide to share their drink.***

Fin: "What flavor please?"

Girl 1: "Cherry"

Fin: "And yours?"

Girl 2: "Chocolate"

Ollie: "Sassafras." (Stan nudges at Ollie) "What is it now?"

Stan: "I don't like Frassasass."

♦ (Stan drinks the whole glass) Ollie: "Do you know what you've done? What made you do it?"

Stan: "I couldn't help it."

Ollie: "Why?"

Stan: "My half was on the bottom."

BRATS

♦ ***Stan and Ollie are babysitting their children.***

Ollie: "If you don't keep quiet, you'll have to go to bed."

Stan: "Yes, we'll have to go to bed."

Ollie: "Not we! The kids!"

♦ Ollie: "Boys will be boys."

Stan: "Blood's thicker than water."

♦ ***Stan tells Ollie not to talk to the kids badly. If you treat them kindly, you'll get more out of them.***

Stan: "Remember the old adage. You can lead a horse to water, but a pencil must be le(a)d."

BELOW ZERO

♦ ***The Boys find a wallet and are then pursued by a thug until an officer helps them out. So they decide to treat the kind officer to lunch with the money they found in the wallet. (Did I mention the wallet belongs to the officer?)***

Ollie: "Garcon! Bring me a parfait."

Stan: "Put one on my steak, too."

Ollie: "You don't put parfaits on steak. Just cancel the parfaits, but bring me a small demitasse."

Stan: "Oh Gaston, bring me one too in a big cup."

Ollie: "A big cup! Where were you brung up?"

THE LAUREL-HARDY MURDER CASE

♦ ***Ollie is reading a newspaper article about Ebeneezer Laurel's will and his estate that is to be divided amongst any relatives.***

Ollie: "Say, was your father and mother's name Laurel?"

Stan: "Sure, why?"

Ollie: "Did you ever have any relatives? Where were you born?"

Stan: "I don't know."

Ollie: "Fancy not knowing where you were born."

Stan: "Well, I was too young to remember. How do I know where I was born?"

Ollie: "Didn't you once tell me that you had an uncle?"

Stan: "Sure, I've got an uncle, why?"

Ollie: "Now we're getting some place. Is he living?"

Stan: "No, he fell through a trap door and he broke his neck."

Ollie: "Was he building a house?"

Stan: "No, they were hanging him. Poor old Unc."

♦ ***The Boys find out Ebeneezer Laurel was murdered, which now makes them suspects since they claim Stan is a relative.***

Ollie: "Here's another nice

mess you've gotten me into."
Stan: "What do you mean, I got you into?"
Ollie: "Well, your name is Laurel, isn't it?"
Stan: "Only on my mother's side, you see it was like this..."
Ollie: "Mother's side!"

♦ ***The detective investigating the murder is questioning Stan.***
Detective: "Where were you November 15?"
Stan: "November 15?"
Detective: "Yes."
Stan: "The day before Christmas?"
Detective: "No, the day after Christmas. November 15.
Stan: "November. Septober, Octember, Nowonder 15?"

ANOTHER FINE MESS
♦ ***Stan and Ollie hide out in a mansion from the cops and are mistaken as the owner who is seeking to rent the house. So Ollie pretends to be the owner and Stan plays both the butler and the maid. As Agnes, the maid, Stan is being questioned by the wife of the potential renter.***
Mrs. Plumtree: "I'd like to find out a few details regarding the house."
Stan: "Yes, ma'am."
Mrs. Plumtree: "How long have you been here?"
Stan: "About half an hour. How silly of me. I'm so nervous. I mean half a year. To be exact three months."
Mrs. Plumtree: "How many bedrooms are there?"
Stan: "I haven't looked yet."
Mrs. Plumtree: "You haven't looked yet?"
Stan: "Oh, I'm still nervous. Of course, there must be bedrooms. Fancy a house without bedrooms. Let's see now. There's mine and the master's and the master's and mine, that's four. Not forgetting the couch in the hall."
Mrs. Plumtree: "No,no, no, no. There's the master's and

yours. That's two."

Stan: "Oh, then there's the nursery."

Mrs. Plumtree: "The nursery? I didn't understand that the Colonel was married."

Stan: "Oh, no, no, he has that in case of accidents."

Mrs. Plumtree: "Accidents?"

Stan: "Oh, no, no you misunderstood me, didn't you, silly? He has that in case of accidents to any of the help around the house. A sort of a kind of a hospital."

Mrs. Plumtree: "How noble of him!"

Stan: "Isn't it?"

♦ **Ollie:** "Oh, Agnes, call me a cab."

Stan: "Huh?"

Ollie: "Call me a cab!"

Stan: "You're a cab."

Ollie: "On the telephone!"

CHICKENS COME HOME

♦ ***Mrs. Hardy comes to her husband's office where Stan also works.***

Mrs. Hardy: "How's Mrs. Laurel?"

Stan: "Fine, thank you."

Mrs. Hardy: "I'd like to meet her some time."

Stan: "Neither do I, too."

PARDON US

♦ **Stan to Ollie:** "The harder they fall, the bigger I am."

♦ ***The Boys are in jail and must attend Fin's school. Fin is questioning the class.***

Fin: "What is a blizzard?"

Stan: "A blizzard? A blizzard is inside of a buzzard."

ONE GOOD TURN

♦ ***Stan and Ollie are victims of the depression. They are going door-to-door for handouts.***

Ollie: "Pardon the intrusion, lady, but my friend and I are victims of the Depression. We haven't tasted food for three whole days."

Old Lady: "Fancy not eating for three whole days."

Stan: "Yes, ma'am. Yesterday, today and tomorrow."

♦ Stan suggests they cut wood for the old lady in appreciation for the food.
Ollie: "Well, you suggested it, now you cut it."
Stan: "I don't know anything about cutting wood."
Ollie: "Well, you ought to. You once told me your father was in the lumber business."
Stan: "Why, I know he was, but it was only in a small way."
Ollie: "What do you mean a small way?"
Stan: "Well, he used to sell toothpicks."

BEAU HUNKS

♦ Ollie: "I'm going to be married."
Stan: "You don't believe me."
Ollie: "Yes, I don't believe.... what do you mean?"
Stan: "Who?"
Ollie: "A woman, of course. Did you ever hear of anyone marrying a man?"
Stan: "Sure."
Ollie: "Who?"
Stan: "My sister."
Ollie: "This is no time for levity."

♦ A knock at the door, Stan picks up the phone:
"Hello."
Ollie: "What are you doing?"
Stan: "Somebody's knocking on the phone."
Ollie: "That's levity."
Stan: "Hello, Mr. Levity."

HELPMATES

♦ Ollie on the phone to Stan.
Ollie: "Where have you been?"
Stan: "I was here with me."
Ollie: "Why weren't you over to the party last night?"
Stan: "I couldn't make it. I was bitten by a dog.
Ollie: "You were what?"
Stan: "A dog bit me."
Ollie: "I can't understand you. Spell it."
Stan: "A dog bit me. B - i -it me. Bit me."
Ollie: "Where?"

Stan: (rolls up sleeve to show Ollie) "There. They took me to the hospital. The doctor said it was hydrophosphates."
Ollie: "Hydrophosphates, you mean hydrophobia."

ANY OLD PORT

♦ ***The Boys have just docked and are looking for a room.***

Ollie: "We'd like to see your floor plan, please."
Walter Long: "Floor plan?"
Stan: "Yes, sir, we'd like a room with a southern explosion."
Ollie: "Not explosion, exposion."

♦ **Stan:** "Can you beat that?"
Ollie: "What?"
Stan: "What a terrible catsafterme."

THE MUSIC BOX

♦ **Stan to cop:** "Don't you think you're bounding over your steps?"

THE CHIMP

♦ **Stan:** "Let's get a room with twin beds."
Ollie: "Why twin beds?"
Stan: "One for me."
Ollie: "Well, I can't sleep with a monkey."
Stan talking to Ethel the chimp: "Oh, she won't mind. You don't mind sleeping with Ollie, do ya? No, she doesn't."

COUNTY HOSPITAL

♦ ***Stan goes to visit Ollie in the hospital.***

Stan: "Could you tell me where room 14 is, please?"
Nurse: "Right down to the end of the hall."
Stan: "Is that the room next to the aquarium?"
Nurse: "Aquarium? Oh, you mean the solarium."

PACK UP YOUR TROUBLES

♦ ***The sergeant is looking to recruit soldiers, but the Boys pretend to have one arm amputated.***

Ollie: "We're incapacitated."

Sergeant: "Incapacitated?"
Stan: "There's a lot of it going around lately."

THEIR FIRST MISTAKE

♦ ***Stan comes up with the idea that Ollie and his wife should adopt a baby, but conveying this idea gets a little cloudy.***

Stan: "You know it's a well known fact that all the happiness in a home when you have a baby and there's a wife and you and the, the baby, it's a well known fact. I know I've read about that."
Ollie: "I'm beginning to think that you're right."
Stan: "You bet your life I'm right. You know I'm not as dumb as you look."
Ollie: "You bet your life you're not. Anybody that could think.... what do you mean you're not as dumb as I look!?"

♦ ***As the Boys are getting ready to go to bed, Stan turns off the light.***

Ollie: "What did you strike that match for?"
Stan: "I wanted to make sure the light was off."

TWICE TWO

♦ ***The Laurels and the Hardys are making plans to have dinner together.***

Stan on the phone: "That's a good idea. Let's go down to Foo Youngs and get some Sucki Yaki."

♦ **Stan on the phone:** "Is that you, Fanny?" (Yes) "Say, listen, Ollie wants to take us out tonight to celebrate our university."

♦ **Ollie:** "Who were you talking to?"
Stan: "I was just talking to Fanny."
Ollie: "What'd she say?"
Stan: "She said that we can't go out tonight, that we have to go right home."
Ollie: "Why?"
Stan: "She's got a surprise for you."

Ollie: "What else did she say?"
Stan: "She told me not to tell ya that she had the surprise."
Ollie: "Well, don't tell me."
Stan: "I won't. I can keep a secret."

ME AND MY PAL

♦ **Ollie:** "You know what a magnate is don't you?"
Stan: "Sure, a thing that eats cheese."

THE DEVIL'S BROTHER

♦ **Ollio:** "There it goes after all we went through to get it."
Stanlio: "Oh, well, come easy, go easy, that's my motto."

♦ Stanlio: "Ollio, after you're gone, do you want to be buried or shall I have you stuffed?"
Ollio: "What do you mean stuffed?"
Stanlio: "I thought it would be nice to keep you in the living room."

THE MIDNIGHT PATROL

♦ ***The Boys arrest a criminal and bring him to the station.***
Cop: "What's the charges?"
Stan: "Robbing a house without a license."

SONS OF THE DESERT

♦ **Stan:** "Life isn't short enough."

♦ **Stan:** "Never heard of such goings off...on."

♦ Stan sneaks waxed fruit from the Hardy's fruit bowl and eats it, unaware it isn't real fruit.

OLIVER THE EIGHTH

♦ ***Stan is explaining to Ollie that he thinks they should send letters to the woman looking for a husband. When Ollie suggests she may be unattractive, Stan has these words of wisdom:***
Stan: "Well, after all, beauty's only skin deep. I'd take

some of the money and I'd have her face lifted. Then I could settle down and I wouldn't have to scrape chins anymore. I wouldn't have to work hard anymore. Well, if beauty is only knee....skin deep. I could take some of the money and have her skinned and then she'd be able to look at a clock without having to work hard anymore. Then we could settle down and I could scrape her chin and congenial, if...if I didn't have to work hard anymore."

GOING BYE-BYE

♦ ***A newspaper ad by Stan:*** Two young gentlemen who are making a motor trip east would like for someone to drive and also pay expenses. Like when we came out here. Phone Main 489. Sincerely yours, Mr. Laurel and Mr. Hardy
P.S. Those not interested, do not answer.

THEM THAR HILLS

♦ Stan: "One month up here (referring to the mountains) and we wouldn't know each other."

BABES IN TOYLAND

♦ ***Ollie has been charged with a crime and is being dunked for punishment. When the rope breaks that is dunking Ollie, he gets trapped under water and everyone is scurrying around to help get him out.***

Stan: "Hurry! He'll die of ammonia!"

THE LIVE GHOST

♦ ***Walter Long asks the Boys to be a part of the crew on his ship, but Stan is not too keen on the idea.***

Stan: "I heard the ocean's infatuated with sharks."

Ollie: "Not infatuated. He means infuriated."

THE FIXER UPPERS

♦ ***Mae Busch explains how her husband doesn't pay attention to her anymore, so Stan offers her advice. He tells her to make her husband jealous by being caught with another man. As Stan tries to explain his idea, it gets lost in the translation.***

Stan: (to Ollie and Mae Busch) "Well, when the husband found out that the other fella was jealous, he took him in his arms he gave his wife a lot of money and he kissed the other fella because he made him jealous and went out and they all lived happily ever after."

♦ **Stan:** (on the phone to Pierre) "Hello. This is me. Say listen, if you had a face like mine, you'd punch me right in the nose and I'm just the fella that can do it."

THE BOHEMIAN GIRL

♦ **Stan:** "Well, Oliver, I hope you grow up to be as good a mother as your father."

OUR RELATIONS

♦ **Stan:** "See ya before you go!"

♦ ***Ollie tells Stan to answer the door because it's probably Mrs. Addlequist for his wife.***

Stan: "It wasn't Mrs. Twiddlepast."

Ollie: "Not Twiddlepast … Paddletwist … Addlequist!"

♦ **Stan:** "We'll give enough rope so we can hang ourselves."

WAY OUT WEST

♦ ***Stan and Ollie are giving the gold mine deed to Lola, who is pretending to be Mary Roberts.***

Lola: "Tell me, tell me about my dear, dear daddy. Is it true that he's dead?"

Stan: "Well, we hope he is,

they buried him.
Lola: "Oh, it can't be. What did he die of?"
Stan: "I think he died of a Tuesday or was it Wednesday?

♦ **Stan to Fin:** "That's right. Any bird can build a nest, but it isn't everyone that can lay an egg."

♦ **Stan to Lola:** "Now that you've got the mine, I bet you'll be a swell gold digger."

♦ **Ollie:** "You said that if we didn't get the deed that you'd eat my hat."
Stan: "Oh, now you're taking me illiterally."

BLOCK-HEADS

♦ ***Stan and Ollie haven't seen each other in 20 years.***
Ollie: "You haven't changed a bit."
Stan: "Neither have you, too. You know if I hadn't seen ya, I never would have known ya. Do you remember how dumb I used to be?"
Ollie: "Yeah."
Stan: "Well, I'm better now."
Ollie: "Well, I'm certainly glad to hear it."

♦ **Stan:** "You want me to go. I'll stay as long as you want."

JITTERBUGS

♦ **Stan:** "My name is Pots. P-o-ots. Pots."

THE DANCING MASTERS

♦ ***The Boys run their own dance school and Stan is stretching with his foot up on the banister.***
Ollie: "What's a matter now?"
Stan: "I think I've got Charlie's horse.

THE BIG NOISE

♦ ***The phone rings and Stan answers the door:***
Stan: "Come in."
Ollie: "It's the telephone."

♦ **Servant:** "Demitasse?"

Ollie: "Thank you."
Stan: "Could I have mine in a mug?"
Servant: "I beg your pardon?"
Stan: "A mug. M - u -ug. Mug."

◆ **Stan:** "And you know what else the old man said. Every time she walks in her sleep, that's the tip top."
Ollie: "Not tip top, tip off."

NOTHING BUT TROUBLE

◆ **Ollie:** "You're always showing your ignorance."
Stan: "Well, I have as much right to be ignorant as you have; in fact, more."
Ollie: "Much more!"

ATOLL K

◆ ***Ollie, explaining how to use the life raft to Stan.***
Ollie: "When you release the valve, it fills up large enough to carry four people."
Stan: "What about me?"

OLIVER
The Facts On Mr. Hardy

This chapter examines the genius behind the characterization of Oliver Hardy

TIE TWIDDLES
The Look

As if waving a peace flag, Ollie coyly waves his necktie at the inadvertently wronged parties. However, his tie twiddles also can be a way of overcoming his shy ways when flirting with the opposite sex.

- **First Tie Twiddle:** You're Darn Tootin' (Although Oliver Hardy claimed the first tie twiddle was in 'Why Girls Love Sailors', it doesn't appear in the film)
- **Most Tie Twiddles In A Short:** 'Beau Hunks' and 'The Music Box' tied with three tie-twiddles each.
- **Feature Film With The Most Tie Twiddles:** 'Pack Up Your Troubles' & 'The Flying Deuces' tied with four each.
- **Short In Which Stan Gives A Tie Twiddle:** 'Thicker Than Water', after receiving some of Ollie's blood in a transfusion
- **Career-Total Tie Twiddles:** 46

CAMERA GLANCES
The Look

By simply looking into the camera, Ollie is able to convey so many different feelings, all brought on by Stan. The feelings vary from frustration to sadness, or even seem to say "Do you believe this?" Because of multiple glances and the varying filming styles from close-up to long shots, determining an accurate total of glances is impossible. These totals are a rough estimate based only on glances brought on by Stan Laurel.

- ♦ **First Camera Glance:** Appears in the short 'Forty-five Minutes From Holly-wood'
- ♦ **Short With The Most:** 'The Chimp' & 'The Laurel~Hardy Murder Case' tied with 18 camera glances each
- ♦ **Feature Film With The Most:** 'The Devil's Brother' with 37 camera glances
- ♦ **Short In Which Stan Gives Two Camera Glances:** 'Thicker Than Water', after receiving some of Ollie's blood in a transfusion
- ♦ **Career-Total Camera Glances:** Over 700

BOTTOMLESS PITS
Ollie Falls Into A Hole

In the world of Laurel & Hardy, even a mere mud puddle can hold surprises. Just ask Oliver Hardy. He plunged to new depths **9 times** in their films.

Film	Plunges per film
♦ Putting Pants on Philip	**1**
♦ Leave 'Em Laughing	**1**
♦ Should Married Men Go Home?	**1**
♦ Habeas Corpus	**1**
♦ Perfect Day	**1**
♦ Angora Love	**1**
♦ Way Out West	**3**

In the short 'You're Darn Tootin',
Ollie fell head first into a open manhole

ALMOST RUN OVER

Maniac Drivers

Although Ollie took several hundred falls in their films, a fall onto a road always brought the same result — a speeding car that nearly runs over Ollie. Films in which he was nearly run over:

Film

- ♦ You're Darn Tootin'
- ♦ Bacon Grabbers
- ♦ Perfect Day
- ♦ Below Zero
- ♦ Hog Wild
- ♦ Any Old Port
- ♦ Thicker Than Water
- ♦ Block-Heads
- ♦ Jitterbugs

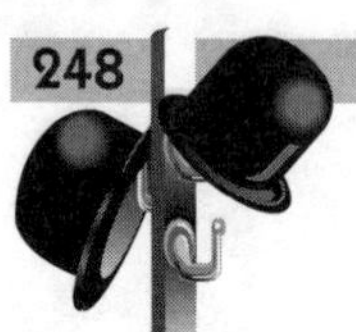

SLIPS & FALLS
Ollie Faws Down

If one had to choose a slapstick comedy element that remained in the Boys' comedies throughout their careers, it would have to be the "accidental fall." Ollie took many tumbles in his career, usually caused by his inept friend, Stan Laurel.
He fell from roofs, down stairs, into water — you name it, he fell or slipped on it.

- **First Fall In A Laurel & Hardy Film:** 'Forty-Five Minutes From Hollywood'
- **Most Falls Ollie Took In A Short:** According to the cutting continuity, Ollie falls nine times in 'Hats Off'. The next highest short for falls would be 'The Finishing Touch' with eight falls.
- **Most Falls Ollie Took In A Feature Film:** A tie with six falls in both 'Pack Up Your Troubles and 'The Devil's Brother".
- **Last Fall In A Laurel & Hardy Film:** Three times in 'Atoll K'
- **Ollie's Career-Total Falls:** He took a grand total of 204 nasty spills in 76 films.

CAPE VS. COAT
Ollie's Outfits

Ollie's appearance was always stylish and eloquent even when he played a vagabond. He usually wore a plain coat jacket, but on occasion, he wore a jacket with an attached cape. Films in which he wore his cape:

- From Soup To Nuts
- Early To Bed
- Double Whoopee
- Berth Marks
- Our Wife
- Going Bye-Bye!
- Bonnie Scotland
- A Chump At Oxford
- Air Raid Wardens
- The Big Noise
- The Bullfighters
- Atoll K

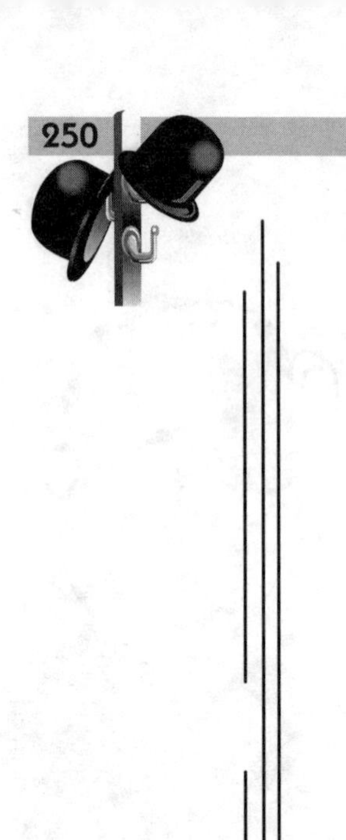

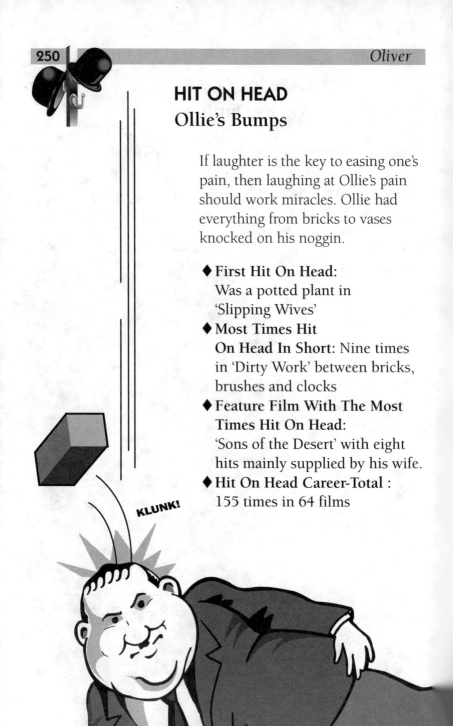

HIT ON HEAD
Ollie's Bumps

If laughter is the key to easing one's pain, then laughing at Ollie's pain should work miracles. Ollie had everything from bricks to vases knocked on his noggin.

- **First Hit On Head:** Was a potted plant in 'Slipping Wives'
- **Most Times Hit On Head In Short:** Nine times in 'Dirty Work' between bricks, brushes and clocks
- **Feature Film With The Most Times Hit On Head:** 'Sons of the Desert' with eight hits mainly supplied by his wife.
- **Hit On Head Career-Total :** 155 times in 64 films

BOYS WILL BE BOYS
Ollie Fights With Stan

The Boys are essentially children in adult bodies. Their innocence and charm have one other childlike characteristic: They fight with each other as kids do. Ollie yells and hits Stanley; yet if someone else starts picking on Stan, Ollie steps up immediately and fights for him.

♦ **First Meeting, First Fight:** Ollie was roughing up Stan in 'Lucky Dog' as he robbed him.

♦ **Most Times Ollie Fought With Stan In A Short:** 16 times in 'Perfect Day'

♦ **Most Times Ollie Fought With Stan In A Feature Film:** 11 times in 'The Devil's Brother"

♦ **Ollie Fights With Stan Career-Total:** 312 times in 76 films, yet they always remained best friends in the end.

OLLIEISMS
Ollie's Faux Pas

THE BATTLE OF THE CENTURY

♦ ***Stan is boxing and Ollie is betting on him.***

Ollie: "If we win, we get $100. If we lose, we get $5. That's a difference of $1,500."

THEY GO BOOM

♦ **Ollie:** "I'm liable to die of ammonia!"

ANGORA LOVE

♦ Ollie rubs Stan's foot instead of his own.

BLOTTO

♦ ***The Boys think they sneak out without Mrs. Laurel catching on to their plan, but she's way ahead of them. She overhears Stan telling Ollie that he is going to take his wife's bottle of liquor. Mrs. Laurel proceeds to dump the bottle and to fill it with a concoction of tea, tabasco and other unknown ingredients.***

Ollie: "You can certainly tell good liquor when you taste it." (after taking a drink of Mrs. Laurel's tea concoction.)

ANOTHER FINE MESS

♦ ***Ollie is impersonating a wealthy plantation owner for a gentleman interested in renting the house he thinks Ollie owns.***

Leopold Plumtree: "Oh, by the way Colonel, do you have any horses?"

Ollie: "I've just shipped all my horses to my plantation in Kentucky."

Plumtree: "What part of Kentucky do you come from?"

Ollie: "Omaha, dear old Omaha."

Stan: "I thought Omaha was in Wisconsin."

BE BIG

♦ Ollie takes a shower with his hat on because he doesn't want to get his hair wet.

♦ "Don't stand there looking like a sphinx."

CHICKENS COME HOME

♦ ***Ollie is being blackmailed by an old ex-girlfriend who comes to visit him at his office.***

Ollie: "Oh, Gabriel, blow your horn!"
He leans on officer buzzer and the entire office comes running in to Ollie's office to catch Mae Busch on Ollie's lap.

BEAU HUNKS

♦ **Stan:** "What's levity mean?"
Ollie: "Levity is a synonymum. You know what a synonymum is? Synonymum is cinnamon…"

♦ ***Stan and Ollie just get back from a long hike and they both take off their shoes. Ollie reaches down to massage his foot, but grabs Stan's instead and begins rubbing the wrong persons foot.***

Stan: After Ollie has been rubbing Stan's foot for a few minutes he says to Ollie: "Scratch my back."
Ollie: "Scratch your own back." Ollie realizes he's got the wrong person's foot.

SCRAM!

♦ ***Stan and Ollie are caught sleeping on a park bench and are taken before the judge.***

Judge: "You're charged with vagrancy. Are you guilty or not guilty?"
Ollie: "Not guilty, your highness."
Judge: "On what grounds?"
Stan: "We weren't on the ground, we were sleeping on a park bench."

PACK UP YOUR TROUBLES

♦ **Ollie to a recruiting sergeant:** "Good morning captain…general."

DIRTY WORK

♦ ***The Boys are chimney sweeps at the home of a mad scientist, Professor Noodle and his butler Jessup.***

Professor Noodle: "Jessup! Jessup! Where is Jessup?"

Ollie: "Jessup? Oh, about 35 miles southeast of Augusta, Georgia."

SONS OF THE DESERT

◆ ***The Boys come back from the convention and neither of their wives are home to greet them. Stan suggests that they must have gone out.***

Ollie: "I know she went out, but what I'd like to know is where did she went."

THE BOHEMIAN GIRL

◆ **Ollie to a lord:** "Yes, Madam."

OUR RELATIONS

◆ Ollie can't read the telegram because his eyes are so bad. Stan accidentally breaks Ollie's lens while cleaning his glasses. Ollie puts his glasses back on without knowing the lenses are broken out. He then reads perfectly.

THE BIG NOISE

◆ **Ollie:** "You want to be a detective, don't you?"

Stan: "Sure, but I don't think I'll make it."

Ollie: "Why not?"

Stan: "Well, you see I don't know what that word means."

Ollie: "Habeas corpus? Why habeas corpus is a name of a town in Texas."

DUCKY LOVER

The On-Screen Girlfriends of The Boys

Every man has a past – with some little 'indiscretion' he would like to bury – Mr. Laurel and Mr. Hardy have 30 or 40 they would like to cremate.

STAN'S GIRLFRIENDS

- **Why Girls Love Sailors** (Delamar): Anna May Wong
- **Their Purple Moment:** Kay Deslys
- **Should Married Men Go Home:** Edna Marian
- **Two Tars:** Thelma Hill
- **We Faw Down:** Kay Deslys
- **Men O'War:** Anne Cornwall
- **The Chimp:** Ethel the Chimp
- **Scram!** (Mrs. Beaumont): Vivian Oakland (mistake)
- **The Fixer Uppers** (Mrs. Gustave): Mae Busch (pretend)
- **Our Relations** (Alice): Iris Adrian (Alfie Laurel's)
- **Way Out West:** Vivian Oakland (mistake)

OLLIE'S GIRLFRIENDS

- **Their Purple Moment:** Anita Garvin
- **Should Married Men Go Home:** Viola Richard
- Two Tars: Ruby Blaine
- **We Faw Down:** Vera White
- **Unaccustomed As We Are:** Thelma Todd (mistake)
- **Men O'War:** Gloria Greer
- **Chickens Come Home:** Mae Busch (ex-girlfriend)
- **Our Wife** (Dulcy): Jean 'Babe' London
- **Beau Hunks** (Jeanie Weenie): Picture of Jean Harlow
- **Scram!** (Mrs. Beaumont): Vivian Oakland (mistake)
- **Me and My Pal** (Miss Cucumber): Marion Bardell
- **Oliver the Eighth:** Mae Busch
- **The Fixer Uppers** (Mrs. Gustave): Mae Busch (pretend)
- **Our Relations** (Lily): Lona Andre (Bert Hardy's)
- **Way Out West:** Vivian Oakland (mistake)
- **Swiss Miss** (Anna Hoepfel Albert): Della Lind (mistake)
- **Block-Heads** (Lulu): Patsy Moran (ex-girlfriend)
- **Block-Heads** (Fifi, Camille, Fannie): Mentioned, not seen
- **Flying Deuces** (Georgette): Jean Parker (mistake)

AIN'T SHE A PIP
The On-Screen Wives of Oliver Hardy

MOVIE	Wife's name	Nagging	Weapon
45 Minutes from Hollywood	Em	Yes	
Their Purple Moment	Mrs.	Yes	
Should Married Men Go Home?	Mrs. Hardy	Yes	
We Faw Down	Mrs.	Yes	Shotgun
That's My Wife	Mrs.	Yes	
Unaccustomed As We Are	Mrs.	Yes	
Perfect Day	Mrs.		
Brats	Mrs.	Unseen	
Hog Wild	Mrs.	Yes	Pan
Be Big	Mrs.		Shotgun
Chickens Come Home	Mrs.		
Our Wife	Dulcy*		
Come Clean	Mrs.	Yes	
Helpmates	Mrs.	Yes	
Their First Mistake	Arabella	Yes	Broom
Twice Two	Mrs.	Yes	
Me and My Pal	*		
Sons Of The Desert	Lottie	Yes	Knife
Thicker Than Water	Mrs.	Yes	
The Bohemian Girl	Mrs.	Yes	
Our Relations	Daphne	Yes	
Block-Heads	Mrs.	Yes	

*Getting married

Doing time

Actresses who played Ollie's wife the most:

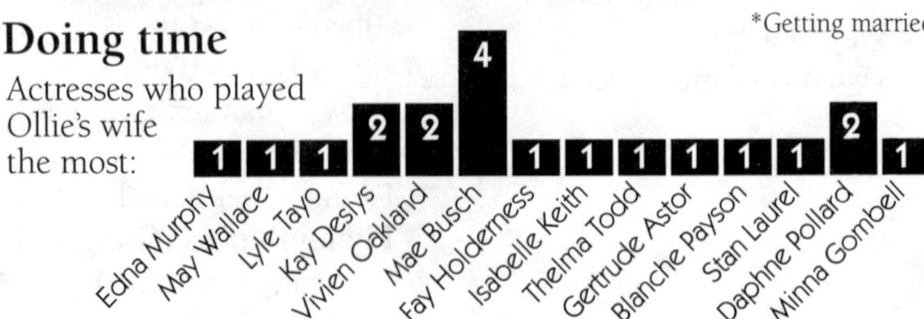

AIN'T SHE A PIP

The On-Screen Wives of Stan Laurel

MOVIE	Wife's name	Nagging	Weapon
Love 'Em And Weep	Mrs.		
Why Girls Love Sailors	Delamar*		
Their Purple Moment	Mrs. Pincher	Yes	
We Faw Down	Mrs.	Yes	
Perfect Day	Mrs.		
Brats	Mrs.	Unseen	
Be Big	Mrs.	Yes	Shotgun
Chickens Come Home	Mrs.		Hatchet
Come Clean	Mrs.	Yes	
Twice Two	Mrs.	Yes	
Sons Of The Desert	Betty	Yes	Shotgun
Babes in Toyland (Stan dressed as bride)	Barnaby		
Our Relations	Betty	Yes	

*Fiancee

Doing time

Actresses who played Stan's wife the most:

Vivien Oakland	1
Fay Holderness	1
Bess Flowers	1
Isabelle Keith	1
Anita Garvin	2
Elizabeth Forrester	1
Linda Loredo	1
Oliver Hardy	1
Dorothy Christie	1
Betty Healy	1

"Mr. Hardy holds that every husband should tell his wife the whole truth - Mr. Laurel is crazy too."

HOLLYWOOD WAX MUSEUM

"You Wax-Eater"

Photo courtesy of Larry Bell

LAUGHING GREATLY

The Boys & Other Comedians

Charlie Chase, who also worked for Hal Roach, worked with Laurel & Hardy on four occasions:
♦ 'Now I'll Tell One'
♦ 'Call of the Cuckoos'
♦ 'Sons of the Desert'
♦ 'On the Wrong Trek.'
However, his brother, James Parrott, directed many of the Boys' early films, such as 'Brats,' 'Two Tars' and 'Hog Wild.'

ABBOTT & COSTELLO

♦ A young Lou Costello can be seen as a spectator in the crowd in the Laurel & Hardy short 'Battle of the Century.'
♦ 'The Abbott & Costello Show,' their syndicated TV show from 1952 & '53, was filmed at the Hal Roach Studios.
♦ When Stan died in 1965, a newspaper reporter telephoned Bud Abbott (surviving partner from the *other* famous comedy team) to inquire whether he might have any comment for publication on the demise of his teammate. An angry Abbott explained that he and Stan never worked together. It had been only 10 to 15 years since either comedy team shot their last film, but the memory of these distinctly different comedy teams was already beginning to fade or blend together.

CHARLIE CHAPLIN

♦ Chaplin and Stan were roommates when they came to the United States in 1910. Stan was Chaplin's understudy.

BUSTER KEATON

♦ Keaton, whose career faded greatly by the 1930's, started gag-writing for MGM, including the Boys' film "Nothing But Trouble."
♦ Keaton's 1951 TV show called 'Life With Buster Keaton' was shot at the Hal Roach Studios in Culver City.

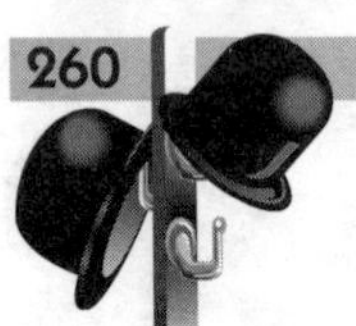

JERRY LEWIS

♦ In the 1960's, Jerry Lewis offered Stan a position as comedy consultant for his films. Stan declined his offer.

THE MARX BROS.

♦ Chico Marx and Ollie were good friends, and both loved to bet on the horses.

THE THREE STOOGES

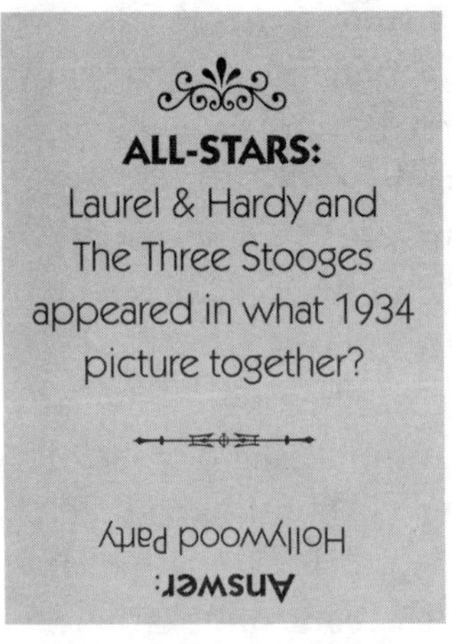

ALL-STARS:
Laurel & Hardy and The Three Stooges appeared in what 1934 picture together?
Answer:
Hollywood Party

♦ The other Babe: Jerome "Curly" Howard was the youngest of five children born to Jennie and Solomon Horwitz. His brothers were Jack, Irving, Moses and Samuel, the latter two better known as Moe and Shemp. Moe gave his younger brother Curly the nickname "Babe."
Moe once said "Babe" had a beautiful singing voice.

♦ The Three Stooges remade a few Laurel & Hardy films.

In 1945, Moe, Larry and Curly filmed '**Booby Dupes**,' with the Stooges as three fish peddlers who decide to cut out the middleman by catching their own fish. They trade their car and $300 for a "new" boat, which soon falls apart and sinks in the middle of the ocean. The plot was obviously borrowed from Stan & Ollie's 1933 short, '**Towed in a Hole**.'

Another film the Stooges remade was the '**The Laurel-Hardy Murder Case**.' Curly learns that he is named in his rich uncle's will in their 1945 short '**If a Body Meets a Body**.'

They go to the uncle's spooky mansion on a dark and stormy night, only to find that the lawyer who was to have read the will has been murdered, and his body and the will have disappeared.

Harry Langdon, famous silent comedian known for his child-like persona, also worked as a writer for The Boys.

Langdon had a string of hit films in 1926 & 1927.

By 1931, his career plummeted, his marriage ended, and he was bankrupt. He became a gag-writer on several of their films, including 'Block-heads' and 'A Chump at Oxford.'

Langdon also starred opposite Hardy in 1939's 'Zenobia.'

Everyone must spend the night while the police investigate.

Fred Kelsey, who played the detective in the 1930 original short, was back again in the same role as the detective.

The Stooges are given the bedroom where the uncle was murdered. Chaos ensues, including a walking skull and the appearance of the uncle's body, which keeps turning up in strange places.

The Stooges unmask the butler and maid as the killers and recover the will.

Upon reading the will, they learn that Curly has been left only 67¢.

W.C. FIELDS

♦ Carlotta Monti, Fields' companion, friend, and practical nurse from 1932 until his death in 1946, appeared with Laurel and Hardy in '**Bonnie Scotland**.' She was one of Jhan Mir Jutra's dancing girls.

HAROLD LLOYD

♦ Even though both worked at the Hal Roach Studios, neither Laurel nor Hardy ever worked with Lloyd. However, Stan's last wife, Ida Kitaeva, did. She appeared in Lloyd's last film in 1947, '**The Sins of Harold Diddlebock.**' It also co-starred one of the Boys' favorite foils, Edgar Kennedy.

TIME LINE

Events in the lives of Stan & Ollie

1887

♦ Co-star Harry Bernard is born in San Francisco, California

♦ **August 27**: James Finlayson is born in Falkirk, Scotland

1888

♦ Co-star Baldwin Cooke is born in New York

1890

♦ **April 26**: Edgar Kennedy is born in Monterey, California

♦ **June 16**: Arthur Stanley Jefferson (Stan Laurel) is born in Ulverston, Lancashire, England

♦ **October 10**: Arthur Housman is born in New York City

1891

♦ **June 18**: Mae Busch is born in Melborne, Australia

1892

♦ **January 14**: Hal Roach is born in Elmira, New York

♦ **January 18**: Norvell Hardy is born in Harlem, Georgia. He later changed his name to Oliver Norvell Hardy

♦ **May 8**: Co-star Sam Lufkin is born in Utah

♦ **November 22**: Oliver Hardy Sr., Ollie's father, dies at age of 50

1893

♦ **October 20**: Charley Chase is born in Baltimore, Maryland

1894

♦ **February 26**: Stanley J. (Tiny) Sandford is born in Oasge, Iowa

♦ **September 12**: William Gilbert Baron (Billy Gilbert) is born in Louisville, Kentucky

1899

♦ **August 19**: Charlie Hall is born in Birmingham, England

1906

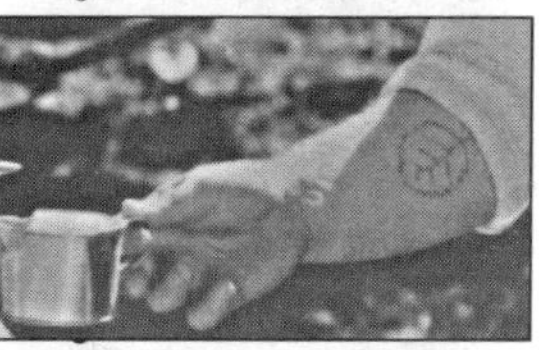

♦ Ollie gets a tattoo of a maple leaf on his inner forearm at age 14. Miss Emmie, as Oliver called his mother, finds out and takes a horsewhip to the the tattooer

♦ Stan makes his his comic stage debut

♦ February 11: Anita Garvin is born in New York

Years 1906 to 1923

♦ Ollie briefly attends the Atlanta Conservatory of Music

♦ **1906-7**: Ollie attends the Georgia Military College in Milledgeville, Georgia

1908

♦ **December:** Stan's mother, Madge Jefferson, dies at age 50

1909

♦ **September:** Stan appears on stage in 'Alone in the World'

1910

♦ **September 22:** Stan leaves Southampton for America as part of the Fred Karno troupe. He is Charlie Chaplin's understudy. They arrive on October 3

1913

♦ Babe goes to Jacksonville, Florida after a friend tells him of the growing film industry

♦ Ollie marries Madelyn Saloshin. He is 21 years old. The marriage lasts 7 years

♦ Karno's troupe breaks up when Chaplin signs a film contract

1914

♦ Ollie becomes known as 'Babe' after his barber calls him "Nice a babe-e-e"

1917

♦ **April 12:** Babe makes his first film, 'Outwitting Dad'

♦ Stan makes his first film, 'Nuts in May'

1918

January 5: Stan begins working at the Hal Roach Studios

♦ Stan enters into a common law marriage with Mae Dahlberg. They remained together from 1918 to 1925

1920

♦ November: Babe and Madelyn divorce

1921

♦ **October:** Stan makes the film 'The Lucky Dog' with Ollie. It is the first time they worked together

♦ **November 24:** Babe marries Myrtle Lee Reeves on Thanksgiving Day in the Church of Christi in Hollywood

1923

♦ Stan meets James Finlayson in the Roach series of one and two reel comedies

Years 1924 to 1927

1924

♦ **February 10:** Stan writes the script 'Big Business' for the Hal Roach Our Gang series

1925

♦ **May:** Stan gives up acting and works as a writer and director at Roach Studios

♦ **June 27:** Babe plays the tin man in the silent feature, 'The Wizard of Oz'

♦ **July 12:** 'Yes, Yes Nanette' is released by Roach. James Finlayson stars with Babe and is directed by Stan. It was his first director's credit with Roach

♦ Stan signed a contract with Joe Rock for 5 years, with a provision that Mae couldn't work with him

♦ Mae Laurel returns to Australia. The day she leaves, Joe Rock introduces Stan to Lois Neilson

1926

♦ **February 6:** Babe signs a contract with Hal Roach to play supporting roles in Charley Chase and Mabel Norman comedies

♦ Myrtle Hardy begins to show signs of a drinking problem, the start of a long battle

♦ **Summer:** Stan returns to acting to replace Babe in a film after he burned his arm cooking a leg of lamb

♦ Joe Rock files suit against Stan, and Stan countersues, charging that Rock was preventing him from working. Rock advises Roach that he has no future claim on Stan's services and releases him from his contract

♦ **August:** Stan marries actress Lois Neilson. The marriage lasts until 1935

♦ **December:** '45 Minutes from Hollywood' is released

1927

♦ **March:** 'Duck Soup' is released. This short is lost for years until a print turns up in Europe in 1974

♦ **April:** 'Slipping Wives' is released

♦ **June:** 'Love 'Em and Weep' is released

♦ **July:** 'Why Girls Love Sailors' is released

♦ **August:** 'With Love and Hisses' is released

Years 1927 to 1929

♦ **September**: 'Sugar Daddies' and 'Sailors, Beware!' are released

♦ **October**: 'The Second Hundred Years,' 'Call of the Cuckoos' and 'Hats Off' are released

♦ **October 5**: Stan & Ollie both appear, but not together, in the Charlie Chase comedy 'Now I'll Tell One'

♦ **November**: 'Do Detectives Think' is released

♦ **December**: 'Putting Pants on Philip' and 'Battle of the Century' are released

♦ **December 10**: Stan's daughter Lois is born

1928

♦ **February**: 'Flying Elephants' and 'The Finishing Touch' are released

♦ **March**: 'From Soup to Nuts' is released

♦ **April**: 'You're Darn Tootin' is released

♦ **April 7**: Babe appears as a startled drunk in Our Gang's 'Barnum & Ringling, Inc.'

♦ **May**: 'Their Purple Moment' is released

♦ **September**: 'Should Married Men Go Home?' is released

♦ **October**: 'Early to Bed' is released

♦ **November**: 'Two Tars' is released

♦ Roach begins to experiment with synchronized music & sound effects

♦ **December**: 'Habeas Corpus' and 'We Faw Down' are released

♦ **December**: Leo McCarey, director for Hal Roach and the Laurel & Hardy series, leaves Roach. For a while, Stan will take over directing the films

1929

♦ **January**: 'Liberty' is released

♦ **February**: 'Wrong Again' is released

♦ **March**: 'That's My Wife' is released

♦ **April**: 'Big Business' is released

♦ **May**: 'Double Whoopee' is released. 'Unaccustomed As We Are' is released as the first Laurel & Hardy talking picture

♦ **June**: 'Berth Marks' is released

Years 1929 to 1931

♦**June**: 'Men O'War' is released

♦**July 25**: Myrtle Hardy files for divorce but reconsiders

♦**August**: 'Perfect Day' is released

♦**September**: 'They Go Boom' is released

♦**October**: 'Bacon Grabbers' is released

♦**November**: 'The Hollywood Review of 1929' and 'The Hoose-Gow' are released

♦**December**: 'Angora Love' is the Boys' last silent film

1930

♦**January 17**: 'The Rogue Song' is released. The boys do a live radio broadcast from Grauman's Chinese Theatre for its premiere

♦**January**: 'Night Owls' is released

♦**February**: 'Blotto' is released

♦**March**: 'Brats' is released

♦**April**: 'Below Zero' is released

♦**May**: 'Hog Wild' is released

♦**May 7**: Stan's wife Lois gives birth two months premature to the couple's second child. The baby, Stanley Robert Jefferson, dies nine days later

♦**August**: 'Pardon Us' is released

♦**September**: 'The Laurel-Hardy Murder Case' is released. Henry "Bardy" Tante, Babe's half-brother, appears in a non-speaking role in this film

♦**November**: 'Another Fine Mess' is released

1931

♦**February**: 'Be Big' and 'Chickens Come Home' are released

♦**March 27**: Myrtle Hardy is taken to Rosemead Lodge Sanitarium for a nervous breakdown

♦**April**: 'The Stolen Jools' and 'Laughing Gravy' are released. Stan has his name legally changed to Stan Laurel

♦**May**: 'Our Wife' is released

♦**June**: Ollie's half-brother, Henry Tante, changes his last name to 'Hardy'

♦**July 31**: Myrtle Hardy pulled over for drunk driving

♦**September**: 'Come Clean' is released

Years 1931 to 1933

♦ **October**: 'One Good Turn' is released

♦ **December**: 'Beau Hunks' and 'On the Loose' are released

1932

♦ Babe and Viola Morse become 'close companions' for the next 8 years. Stan also finds a close companion in Alice Ardell for the next 10 years

♦ **January**: 'Helpmates' is released

♦ **March**: 'Any Old Port' is released

♦ **April**: 'The Music Box' is released

♦ **May**: 'The Chimp' is released

♦ **June**: 'County Hospital' is released

♦ **July**: Stan and Babe make a whirlwind publicity tour in England between London and Glasgow. Lois does not join Stan. When the Hardys return home, Myrtle begins drinking heavily again

♦ **September**: 'Pack Up Your Troubles' and 'Scram!' are released

♦ **November**: 'Their First Mistake' is released

♦ **November 18**: 'The Music Box' wins Best Short Subject Oscar

♦ **December**: 'Towed in a Hole' is released

1933

♦ **February**: 'Twice Two' is released

♦ **April**: 'Me and My Pal' is released

♦ **April**: The Boys' marriages have seen better days. Myrtle Hardy's heavy drinking leads Ollie to vacation in South America alone. Stan and Lois attempt reconciling by taking a four-week vacation to Victoria, British Columbia. Upon their return, Lois files for divorce. Three weeks later, Babe and Myrtle separate

♦ **May**: 'The Devil's Brother' (Fra Diavolo) is released

♦ **August**: 'The Midnight Patrol' is released

♦ **October**: 'Busy Bodies' is released

♦ **October**: Boys make a cameo in the Our Gang short 'Wild Poses'

♦ **November**: 'Dirty Work' is released

Years 1933 to 1936

♦ **December 7:** The Hal Roach Studio celebrates its 20th anniversary. A radio show honoring the event was aired by NBC

♦ **December:** 'Sons of the Desert' is released

1934

♦ **February:** 'Oliver the Eighth' is released

♦ **April:** Stan marries Virginia Ruth Rogers; however, the ceremony was not valid because Stan was not legally divorced from Lois yet

♦ **June:** 'Hollywood Party' and 'Going Bye-Bye!' are released

♦ **July:** 'Them Thar Hills' is released

♦ **November:** 'Babes in Toyland' is released

♦ **December:** 'The Live Ghost' is released

1935

♦ **January:** 'Tit For Tat' is released. The short is nominated for an Oscar, but does not win

♦ **February:** 'The Fixer-Uppers' is released

♦ **1935:** Hal Roach fires Stan and announces a new series, 'The Hardy Family', with Babe, Patsy Kelly and Spanky McFarland. One week later, they reconcile their differences

♦ **July 5:** Babe co-stars with Charley Chase in 'Isn't Life Terrible'

♦ **August:** 'Bonnie Scotland' and 'Thicker Than Water,' their last short, is released

♦ **September 10:** Stan and Lois divorce

♦ **September 28:** Stan legally marries Ruth

1936

♦ **February:** 'The Bohemian Girl' is released

♦ **April:** 'Way Out West' is released

♦ **June:** 'On the

Years 1936 to 1940

Wrong Trek', starring Charley Chase, with a cameo by the Boys, is released

♦ **October**: 'Our Relations' is released

♦ **December**: Mae Laurel sues Stan for property rights. Case settled for undisclosed amount. Ruth divorces Stan

1937

♦ **May**: Babe and Myrtle divorce. 'Pick a Star' is released

1938

♦ **January 1**: Stan marries Vera Ivanova Shuvalova (Illiana). They later repeat their vows in a Russian Orthodox ceremony

♦ **May**: 'Swiss Miss' is released

♦ **August**: 'Blockheads' is released

♦ **August 17**: Harry Langdon signs contract to replace Stan as Ollie's partner due to a contract dispute

♦ **December**: Stan sues Hal Roach for $700,000 for breach of contract

1939

♦ **April 8**: Stan settles dispute with Hal and signs a one-year contract

♦ **April 13**: At her alimony hearing, Stan's estranged wife Illiana claims he threatened to bury her alive in their backyard. She also claims he invited his first wife on their honeymoon

♦ **May**: 'Saps at Sea' is released

♦ **May**: Babe appears with Langdon in "Zenobia.' Stan divorces Illiana. Due to her heavy drinking, she later dies in her early 40's

♦ **October**: 'The Flying Deuces' is released. Babe meets Lucille Jones, his future wife, who is working as a script girl on the film

♦ **December**: Stan and Babe form their own production company, Laurel and Hardy Feature Productions, Inc.

1940

♦ Harry Bernard dies of cancer at age 62

♦ **February**: 'A Chump at Oxford' is released

March 7: Babe marries Lucille

Years 1940 to 1946

Jones. They remain happily married until his death. Viola Morse, Babe's friend and companion for the past 10 years did not take the news well. She took 13 sleeping pills and crashed into three cars. She later left Los Angeles

♦ **April 5**: Boys' contracts expire; they leave Hal Roach Studios

♦ **June**: Babe's half-sister Emily dies

♦ **September**: Boys go on tour with 'The Laurel and Hardy Revue'

1941

♦ **January 17**: Stan remarries Ruth for a third time

♦ **April 30**: Laurel and Hardy Productions signs contact with 20th Century Fox

♦ **October**: 'Great Guns' is released

♦ Babe is sued by the IRS twice for back taxes and twice by Myrtle for back alimony

♦ Margaret Roach, Hal's wife, dies at age 41

1942

♦ **August**: 'A-Haunting We Will Go' is released

♦ **April 7**: Arthur Housman dies of pneumonia at age 51

♦ Anita Garvin retires

1943

♦ **March**: 'Tree in a Test Tube' is released

♦ **April**: 'Air Raid Wardens' is released

♦ **June**: 'Jitterbugs' is released

♦ **November**: The Dancing Masters' is released

1944

♦ **September**: 'The Big Noise' is released

1945

♦ **March**: 'Nothing But Trouble' is released

♦ **May**: 'The Bullfighters' is released

1946

♦ **April**: Charley Chase dies at the age of 46. Stan and Ruth divorce for the second time (although they did have three wedding ceremonies, the first wasn't valid)

♦ **April 19**: Mae Busch dies at age 54 after a long illness

♦ **May**: Stan mar-

Years 1946 to 1953

ries Ida Kitaeva, his fifth wife

1947

♦ **February**: Stan & Babe begin their British Music Hall tour

1948

♦ **January**: The boys return to the United States. Stan learns he has diabetes

♦ **November 9**: Edgar Kennedy dies at the age of 58 of throat cancer

♦ **November 16**: Ollie's mother, Emily Hardy, dies at age 88. She is in a mausoleum in Westview . Cemetery in Atlanta, Georgia

1949

♦ Stan's father, A.J. Jefferson, dies at age 87. He is buried in the village of Barkston near Grantham, Lincolnshire

♦ **October**: 'The Fighting Kentuckian' is released with John Wayne and Babe

1950

♦ **April**: Babe appears in Frank Capra's 'Riding High' with Bing Crosby. This is Ollie's last movie appearance

1951

♦ Stan appears in the Erskine Johnson's Hollywood Reel series entitled 'Close Ups and Long Shots'. He officiates at a children's swim meet for the Brentwood Bantam Club in Brentwood, California

♦ **November**: 'Atoll K' is released in Europe. This was to be the team's last film

♦ The Boys' popularity resurges after Roach releases their films to television

1952

♦ The boys start their second British tour with the sketch 'A Spot of Trouble'

♦ **February 19**: Sam Lufkin dies at age 59 of uremia

♦ **December**: While on tour in England, the Boys stay at the Bull Inn, which is owned by Bill & Olga Healey (Stan's sister)

1953

♦ Baldwin Cooke dies at age 65

♦ **October 9**: James Finlayson dies at the age of 66 of a heart attack

♦ **October**: The Boys' final British

Years 1953 to 1962

tour begins with the sketch 'Birds of a Feather'

1954

♦ **May:** Babe has a mild heart attack while on tour in England. He returns to the U.S.

♦ **December:** 'Atoll K' is released in the United States under the title 'Utopia'

♦ **December 1:** Stan and Ollie are featured on the NBC television program 'This is Your Life'

1955

♦ Boys prepare to do a TV series for Hal Roach Jr. entitled 'Laurel and Hardy's Fabulous Fables'. Stan completes the outline for the first show, 'Babes in the Woods'. Other tentative titles include 'Cinderella', 'Little Red Riding Hood', 'Jack and the Beanstalk', 'Dick Whittington', 'Beauty and the Beast', 'Hop-o'-my Thumb', 'Aladdin', 'Puss-in-Boots', 'The Three Bears' and 'The Three Wishes'

♦ **April 25:** Stan suffers a stroke. The TV series is placed on hold

1956

♦ **Sept. 12:** Babe suffers a stroke

1957

♦ **August 7:** Oliver Hardy dies at the age of 65. He is cremated and buried in the Masonic section of the Garden of Vahalla Memorial Park in North Hollywood

1959

♦ **December 7:** Charlie Hall dies at the age of 60

♦ **September 2:** Hal Roach Studios, now being run by Hal Roach Jr., is in deep financial trouble. He accepts a loan from an industrialist, Alexander Guterma, who has with ties to organized crime. Guterma is indicted for securities violations and Hal Jr. takes over direction of the F.L. Jacobs Co. Within a year, the studio files bankruptcy

1961

♦ Stan receives a special Oscar at the 33rd Academy Awards ceremony. Due to failing health, Danny Kaye accepts on his behalf

♦ October 29: Tiny Sandford dies at age 67

Years 1962 to 1988

"MAIN STREET" of a movie studio - piles of equipment line the sidewalks ready for auction

Your opportunity to see . . . without charge . . .

EVERYTHING INSIDE A FAMOUS MAJOR MOVIE STUDIO LOT!

NO LIMIT - NO RESERVE AUCTION Piece Meal to High Bidders

HAL ROACH MOVIE STUDIO

8822 WEST WASHINGTON BOULEVARD

1 Block West of National; East of Robertson Boulevard

CULVER CITY (L.A.), CALIF.

A Collection of Nearly Half a Century of Major Studio Paraphernalia and Props

4 DAY AUCTION
THURS. - FRI. - SAT. - SUN.
AUG. 1-2-3-4
Starting 10 A.M. Daily

Sound and Film Equipment
Spotlights and Stage Equipment
Woodworking and Machine Shops
Drapery Department - Draperies
Theatres - Still Departments
Paint Booths - Breakaway Dept.
Cafeteria and Kitchen Equipment
Booms - Dollies - Editing Equip.
Complete Special Effects Dept.

Costumes - Wardrobes
Art Objects - Antiques
Still Pictures - Books
Furnishings of every Period and Type
Millions of Props
Fire Engine - Trucks
Executive & Office Furn.
Dismantled Buildings to be moved!

PUBLIC PREVIEW Wed., Thurs., Fri., Mon., Tues., Wed. JULY 24 - 25 - 26 - 29 - 30 - 31 10 A.M.-4 P.M.
Sunday, JULY 28, NOON to 4:00 P.M.
(NO Admission Charge

Demolition of Studio starts after conclusion of the auction by
LIPSETT DIVISION OF LURIA BROS. COMPANY

"DEATH KNELL" of one of HOLLYWOODS most famous studios - Auction notice in paper.

♦ **December 20**: The Hal Roach Studio is sold at auction to a real estate developer. The following year the studio is demolished

1964

♦ **February 11**: Stan is presented the Screen Actors Guild Award for "Outstanding Achievement in Fostering the Finest Ideas of the Acting Profession"

♦ The 'Sons of the Desert,' an appreciation society to the work of Stan and Ollie, is formed in New York with Stan's blessings

♦ Hal Roach's daughter, Margaret, dies at age 43

1965

♦ **February 23**: Stan Laurel suffers a heart attack and dies at age 74. He is cremated and buried at Hollywood Hills Forest Lawn Cemetery. His plaque reads: 'A Master of Comedy: His genius in the art of humor brought gladness to the world he loved'

1969

♦ Mae Laurel, Stan's first wife, dies

1971

♦ **March 29**: Hal Roach Jr., one-time movie and television film producer, dies in a Santa Monica hospital from complications of pneumonia. He was 53

♦ **September 23**: Billy Gilbert dies at the age of 78

Years 1976 to 1994

1976

♦ Virginia Ruth Rogers Laurel, Stan's third wife, dies

1980

♦ **January 26**: Ida Laurel dies

♦ A park is dedicated at the site of the former Hal Roach Studios, in Culver City, California

1981

♦ **January 18**: Myrtle Hardy, Babe's second wife, dies at age 86

1983

♦ Hal Roach receives a special Oscar at the annual Academy Awards

1987

♦ Lucille Hardy Price, Babe's third wife, dies

1988

♦ **December 20**: Laurel & Hardy memorabilia are auctioned off at Christies in London. A pair of the Boys' derbies sells for 10,000 pounds

1990

♦ **February**: A British stamp is issued featuring Stan Laurel's smile

♦ Lois (Neilson) Laurel, Stan's first wife, dies

1991

♦ **September 13**: An American stamp featuring a caricature of the Boys is drawn by Al Hirshfeld

1992

♦ **January 14**: Hal Roach celebrates his 100th birthday at the old MGM Studios

♦ Hal Roach receives a special Oscar at the Academy Awards

♦ **November 2**: Hal Roach dies from pneumonia at the age of 100

1994

♦ **April**: Hallmark Cards Inc. buys RHI Entertainment Inc., which includes the Hal Roach film library, for $365 million

♦ **July 7**: Anita Garvin dies at age 88

♦ A derby of Stan Laurel's sells for 2,000 pounds at a Bonhams of London auction

AND THE OSCAR GOES TO....

Oscar Nominations And Winners

- **Stan Laurel:** Oscar for his 'creative pioneering in the field of comedy'.
- **Roy W. Seawright:** Won for Special Effects, 'Saps At Sea', 'Pick A Star', 'Way Out West' and 'Our Relations'. Nominated for Best Visual Effects, 'Zenobia.'
- **Marvin Hatley:** Nominated Best Score, 'Block-Heads' and 'Way Out West.'
- **Lawrence Tibbett:** Nominated Best Actor, 'The Rogue Song'.
- **Cedric Gibbons:** Nominated Best Art Direction, 'Hollywood Revue of 1929'; also known for designing the Oscar statue.

THE CO-STARS
Supporting Players & Their Careers

There is no denying that Stan and Ollie are the greatest comedy team of all time, but it also must be noted that the Boys had a little help. They share this honor with their venerable cast of co-stars. What would the world of Laurel and Hardy have been without the likes of James Finlayson, Charlie Hall, Tiny Sandford, Mae Busch, Anita Garvin, Billy Gilbert, Edgar Kennedy, Walter Long or Arthur Housman?
This chapter is dedicated to all the co-stars who helped make Laurel and Hardy what they are — screen legends.

Ever wonder what became of some of the co-stars after their days at the Hal Roach Studios were through?
You will be surprised. Some went on to co-star in classic movies, some worked with numerous other comedians and some even went on to direct or write films.

This chapter examines the careers from Iris Adrian, who worked with the Boys in 'Our Relations' to Joe Yule, who worked with Stan and Ollie in 'Nothing But Trouble.'

106 films
47/Charlie Hall
39/Sam Lufkin
34/Jack Hill
33/James Finlayson
30/Baldwin Cooke
26/Harry Bernard
23/Tiny Sandford
13/Mae Busch
11/Anita Garvin
11/Dorothy Coburn
11/Billy Gilbert
10/Chet Brandenburg
9/Edgar Kennedy
9/James C. Morton
8/Bobby Burns

6/Elinor Van Der Veer
6/Thelma Todd
6/Vivian Oakland
5/Walter Long
5/Noah Young
5/Kay Deslys
4/Daphne Pollard
4/Arthur Housman
4/Rychard Cramer
4/Charles Middleton
3/Rosina Lawrence
3/Dorothy Granger
3/Blanche Payson
3/Jean Harlow
2/Ben Turpin

The Supporting Cast played a significant role in all of the Laurel and Hardy films. Many of the co-stars made reoccurring appearances, which made them become as well-known as the Boys themselves. The unique charisma that they all shared, created classic comedy films, which will be enjoyed by all forever.

THE CO-STARS
Their Career Highlights

IRIS ADRIAN (1913-1994)

Our Relations (1936): Alice, the beer garden girl

Other notable films: Freaky Friday (1976) with Jodie Foster; The Apple Dumpling Gang (1975) with Don Knotts, Tim Conway; The Barefoot Executive (1971) Kurt Russell, Joe Flynn; The Love Bug (1968) with Dean Jones, Buddy Hackett; The Odd Couple (1968) with Jack Lemmon, Walter Matthau; That Darn Cat (1965) with Dean Jones, Hayley Mills; Blue Hawaii (1962) with Elvis Presley; The Errand Boy (1961) with Jerry Lewis; My Favorite Spy (1951) and The Paleface (1948) both with Bob Hope; Mighty Joe Young (1949); Wistful Widow of Wagon Gap (1947) with Abbott and Costello; Road to Zanzibar (1941) with Bob Hope, Bing Crosby

ERNIE ALEXANDER

Saps at Sea (1940): Newsboy; Our Relations (1936); Hollywood Party (1934): Servant at the party; Sons of the Desert (1933)

Other notable films: Mr. and Mrs. Smith (1941) directed by Alfred Hitchcock; Test Pilot (1938) with Clark Gable; O'Shaughnessey's Boy (1935) with Jackie Cooper, Spanky McFarland; The Cat's Paw (1934) with Harold Lloyd

LONA ANDRE (1915-1992)

Our Relations (1936): Lily, the other cafe girl

Other notable films: International House (1933) with W.C. Fields

HENRY ARMETTA (1888-1945)

The Devil's Brother (1933): Matteo, the innkeeper trying to emulate Laurel's "kneesie-earsie-nosie" game

Other notable films: Anchors Aweigh (1945) with Frank Sinatra, Gene Kelly; Ghost Catchers (1944) with Olsen and Johnson; Stage Door Canteen (1943) with Katharine Hepburn, Harpo Marx, Ray Bolger; The Big Store (1941) with the Marx Bros.; Rio (1939) with Bob Cummings; The Black Cat (1934) with Boris Karloff, Bela Lugosi, Jacqueline Wells; The Cat and the Fiddle (1934); Imitation of Life (1934) with Claudette Colbert, Alan Hale, Sr.; The Merry Widow (1934) with Maurice Chevalier; Viva Villa (1934) with Wallace Beery; So This Is Africa (1933) with Wheeler & Woolsey; Farewell to Arms (1932) with Gary Cooper; Speak Easily (1932) with Jacquie Lyn, Jerry Tucker, Buster Keaton, Thelma Todd; Scarface (1931); Street Angel (1928) with Janet Gaynor; Seventh Heaven (1927) with Janet Gaynor

CHARLES ARNT (1908-1990)

Great Guns (1941): Doctor

Other notable films: My Favorite Brunette (1947) with Bob Hope; Christmas in Connecticut (1945) with Barbara Stanwyck; Up in Arms (1944) with Danny Kaye

HARRY ARRAS (1881-1942)

Our Relations (1936)

Other notable films: The Gold Rush (1925) with Charlie Chaplin

JOHNNY ARTHUR (1883-1951)

Pick A Star (1937): Ernie; Our Relations (1936)

Other notable films: Road to Singapore (1940) with Bob Hope, Bing Crosby; Our Gang shorts including Feed 'em and Weep (1938) as Darla's father, Night 'Gales (1937) as Darla's father and Anniversary Trouble (1935) as Spanky's father

SAM ASH (1883-1951)

The Dancing Masters (1943): Pianist

Other notable films: The Secret Life of Walter Mitty (1947) with Danny Kaye; San Francisco (1936) with Clark Gable

GERTRUDE ASTOR (1887-1977)

Our Relations (1936); Come Clean (1931): Mrs. Hardy

Other notable films: The Man Who Shot Liberty Valance (1962) directed by John Ford; Sunset Boulevard (1950) with William Holden, Gloria Swanson, directed by Billy Wilder; The Milky Way (1936) with Harold Lloyd; San Francisco (1936) with Clark Gable; Dante's Inferno (1935) with Spencer Tracy; The Strong Man (1926) the first Frank Capra film, the second Harry Langdon film

JIMMY AUBREY

Sons of the Desert (1933): Conventioneer; That's My Wife (1929): Inebriate in soup altercation; Their Purple Moment (1928): Cook

Other notable films: Invisible Man Returns (1940); Waterloo Bridge (1940); Charge of the Light Brigade (1936) with Errol Flynn, David Niven;

JIMMY AUBREY *(continued)*

Love on the Run (1936) with Clark Gable, Joan Crawford; A Tale of Two Cities (1935)

FRANK AUSTIN (1877-1954)

Babes in Toyland (1934): Justice of the Peace; Pardon Us (1931): Prisoner with sore tooth; The Laurel-Hardy Murder Case (1930): Butler

Other notable films: The State of the Union (1948) with Spencer Tracy, Katharine Hepburn; Sea of Grass (1947) with Spencer Tracy; Never Give a Sucker an Even Break (1941) with W.C. Fields; The Devil and Daniel Webster (1941) with Edward Arnold, John Huston; Meet John Doe (1941) with Gary Cooper, directed by Frank Capra; Mr. Smith Goes to Washington (1939) with Gary Cooper, directed by Frank Capra; You Can't Take It With You (1938) with James Stewart, directed by Frank Capra; Dante's Inferno (1935) with Spencer Tracy

WILLIAM AUSTIN (1884-1975)

One of Hollywood's favorite 'silly ass' Englishmen, usually armed with monocle and high-pitched laugh. His son, Laurence Austin, owned and operated in Los Angeles, the world's only theatre devoted solely to continuous showings of silent films, until his murder in January 1997.

County Hospital (1932): English roommate in hospital; Duck Soup (1927): Englishman seeking to rent mansion

Other notable films: National Velvet (1944) with Mickey Rooney, Elizabeth Taylor; Charley's Aunt (1941) with Jack Benny; The Adventures of Sherlock Holmes (1939) with Basil Rathbone; The Gay Divorcee (1934) with Fred

WILLIAM AUSTIN *(continued)*

Astaire, Ginger Rogers, nominated for best picture; Alice in Wonderland (1933) with Cary Grant, W.C. Fields; The Private Life of Henry VIII (1933) with Charles Laughton, nominated for best picture

AVALON BOYS QUARTET

Way Out West (1937): Themselves

Other notable films: It's a Gift (1934) with W.C. Fields

CHARLES A. BACHMAN

Saps at Sea (1940); Pick a Star (1937); Our Relations (1936); Pardon Us (1931); Habeas Corpus (1928); Putting Pants on Philip (1927); Do Detectives Think? (1927); The Second Hundred Years

Other notable films: The Circus (1928) with Charlie Chaplin; A Pleasant Journey (1923) an Our Gang short

IRVING BACON (1893-1965)

Great Guns (1941): Postman

Other notable films: Ma and Pa Kettle at Home (1954) with Marjorie Main; Percy Kilbride; A Star Is Born (1954) with Judy Garland; Riding High (1950) with Oliver Hardy, Bing Crosby; Dear Wife (1949) with William Holden, Joan Caulfield; State of the Union (1948) with Spencer Tracy, Katharine Hepburn; The Bachelor and the Bobby-Soxer (1947) with Cary Grant, Myrna Loy; Dear Ruth (1947) with William Holden, Joan Caulfield; Monsieur Verdoux (1947) with Charlie Chaplin; Spellbound (1945) with Gregory Peck, directed by Alfred Hitchcock; A Guy Named Joe (1944) with Spencer Tracy; Shadow of a Doubt (1943)

IRVING BACON *(continued)*

with Joseph Cotten, directed by Alfred Hitchcock; Holiday Inn (1942) with Bing Crosby, Fred Astaire; Pardon My Sarong (1942) with Abbott & Costello; The Spoilers (1942) with John Wayne; Caught in the Draft (1941) with Bob Hope, Dorothy Lamour; Meet John Doe (1941) with Gary Cooper, directed by Frank Capra; Never Give a Sucker an Even Break (1941) with W.C. Fields; Tobacco Road (1941) with Charles Grapewin; The Grapes of Wrath (1940) with Henry Fonda; Gone with the Wind (1939) with Clark Gable, Vivien Leigh; You Can't Cheat an Honest Man (1939) with W.C. Fields; You Can't Take It with You (1938) with James Stewart, directed by Frank Capra; A Star is Born (1937) with Fredric March, Janet Gaynor; Mr. Deeds Goes to Town (1936) with Gary Cooper; San Francisco (1936) with Clark Gable; It Happened One Night (1934) with Clark Gable, Claudette Colbert; Six of A Kind (1934), If I Had a Million (1932), and Million Dollar Legs (1932) all with W.C. Fields

ROBERT BAILEY (1912-1983)

The Dancing Masters (1943): Grant Lawrence; Jitterbugs (1943)

Other notable films: The Eve of St. Mark (1944) with Vincent Price; Ladies of Washington (1944) with Trudy Marshall; Wing and a Prayer (1944) with Don Ameche, Chet Brandenberg

EDDIE BAKER (1897-1968)

Babes in Toyland (1934); Them Thar Hills (1934); Sons of the Desert (1933): Coterie; Me And My Pal (1933); Any Old Port (1932): Police chief; Pardon Us (1931): Plantation

EDDIE BAKER *(continued)*

overseer; Come Clean (1931): Detective; Another Fine Mess (1930): Meadows, the butler; Bacon Grabbers (1929): Sheriff

Other notable films: Giant (1956) with Rock Hudson, James Dean, directed by George Stevens; It's a Gift (1934) with W.C. Fields; The Lemon Drop Kid (1934); You're Telling Me (1934) with W.C. Fields; Tillie and Gus (1933) with W.C. Fields; If I Had a Million (1932) with W.C. Fields; Million Dollar Legs (1932) with W.C. Fields; Monkey Business (1931) with the Marx Bros.; City Lights (1931) with Charlie Chaplin

FRANK BAKER (1893-1980)

A Chump At Oxford (1940): Dean's Sergeant

Other notable films: My Fair Lady (1964) with Rex Harrison, Audrey Hepburn; Donovan's Reef (1963) with John Wayne, Lee Marvin; The Quiet Man (1952) with John Wayne, Maureen O' Sullivan; Mrs. Miniver (1942) with Greer Garson, Best Picture winner

MONICA BANNISTER

The Flying Deuces (1939): Georgette's Girlfriend

Other notable films: Nothing Sacred (1937) with Fredric March, Carole Lombard; Gold Diggers of 1933 (1933)

LIONEL BARRYMORE (1878-1954)

Hollywood Revue of 1929 (1929); The Rogue Song (1930): Producer, Director

Other notable films: Key Largo (1948) with Humphrey Bogart; Duel in the Sun (1946) with Jennifer Jones, Gregory Peck; It's a Wonderful Life (1946) with James

LIONEL BARRYMORE *(continued)*
Stewart, directed by Frank Capra; A Guy Named Joe (1944) with Spencer Tracy; You Can't Take It With You (1938) with James Stewart, directed by Frank Capra; Captains Courageous (1937) with Spencer Tracy; A Family Affair (1937) with Mickey Rooney; Saratoga (1937) with Clark Gable, Jean Harlow; Ah, Wilderness (1935) with Wallace Beery; David Copperfield (1935); Treasure Island (1934) with Wallace Beery, Jackie Cooper; Grand Hotel (1932) with Greta Garbo; A Free Soul (1931) with Clark Gable; Madame X (1929), Director

JAY BELASCO
Our Relations (1936)
Other notable films: The Milky Way (1936) with Harold Lloyd

LIONEL BELMORE (1867-1953)
The Rogue Song (1930): Ossman
Other notable films: The Adventures of Robin Hood (1938) with Errol Flynn; The Prince and the Pauper (1937) with Errol Flynn; The Toast of New York (1937) with Cary Grant; Last of the Mohicans (1936) with Randolph Scott; Little Lord Fauntleroy (1936) with Freddie Bartholomew; Mutiny on the Bounty (1935) with Clark Gable, Charles Laughton; Frankenstein (1931) with Boris Karloff

BILLY BENEDICT (1917-)
Great Guns (1941) Recruit at corral
Other notable films: The Sting (1973) with Robert

BILLY BENEDICT *(continued)*

Redford, Paul Newman; The Hallelujah Trail (1965) with Burt Lancaster; Road to Utopia (1946) with Bob Hope, Bing Crosby; The Ox-Bow Incident (1943) with Henry Fonda; My Little Chickadee (1940) with Mae West, W.C. Fields; Bringing Up Baby (1938) with Cary Grant, Katharine Hepburn; Libeled Lady (1936) with Spencer Tracy, Myrna Loy

HARRY BERNARD (1917-1940)

Saps at Sea (1940): Harbor patrol captain; A Chump at Oxford (1940): Officer; Way Out West (1937); Our Relations (1936); The Bohemian Girl (1936): Town crier; The Live Ghost (1934): Bartender; Sons of the Desert (1933);The Midnight Patrol (1933): Jail visitor; The Devil's Brother (1933): Bandit/drunk; Any Old Port (1932); Pardon Us (1931): Desk Sergeant; Laughing Gravy (1931): Policeman; Another Fine Mess (1930): Policeman; The Rogue Song (1930); Night Owls (1930): Policeman; Angora Love (1929): Policeman; Bacon Grabbers (1929); Perfect Day (1929): Friendly neighbor; Men O'War (1929): Policeman; Berth Marks (1929): Train passenger; That's My Wife (1929): Waiter; Wrong Again(1929): Policeman; Liberty (1929); Two Tars (1928): Truck driver

Other notable films: On the Wrong Trek (1937), Life Hesitates at 40 (1936) and Neighborhood House (1936) all with Charlie Chase;The Milky Way (1936) with Harold Lloyd; Ruggles of Red Gap (1935) with Charlie Ruggles; Manhattan Monkey Business (1935) and The Pip from Pittsburgh (1931) both with Charley Chase

WILLIE BEST (1916-1962)

A-Haunting We Will Go (1942): Waiter

Other notable films: Hold That Blonde (1945); High Sierra (1941) with Humphrey Bogart; Nothing But the Truth (1941) with Bob Hope; Ghost Breakers (1940) with Bob Hope; General Spanky (1936) with Rosina Lawrence, Spanky McFarland; The Nitwits (1935) and Kentucky Kernels (1934) both with Wheeler & Woolsey, Spanky McFarland; Little Miss Marker (1934) with Shirley Temple

MAURICE BLACK (1890-1938)

Bonnie Scotland (1935): Mir Jutra

Other notable films: Tillie and Gus (1933) with W.C. Fields; Scarface (1931) with Boris Karloff; Little Caesar (1930) with Edward G. Robinson

VIVIAN BLAINE (1921-1995)

Jitterbugs (1943): Susan Cowan

Other notable films: Guys and Dolls (1955) with Marlon Brando, Frank Sinatra; State Fair (1945)

ROBERT BLAKE (1933-)

Born Michael Gubitosi. Appeared in the Our Gang comedies from 1939-1944. Played Little Beaver in the Red Ryder westerns. Starred in the mid-70's TV series Baretta.

The Big Noise (1944): Egbert

Other notable films: The Horn Blows at Midnight (1945) with Jack Benny

BILLY BLETCHER

Block-Heads (1938): Voice of midget; Hollywood Party (1934): Voice of Big Bad Wolf; Babes in Toyland (1934): Chief of police; The Midnight Patrol (1933): Radio dispatcher; Me and My Pal (1933) Police dispatcher; Beau Hunks (1931): New recruit #11

Other notable films: The Patsy (1964) with Jerry Lewis; The Secret Life of Walter Mitty (1947)and Kid from Brooklyn (1946) both with Danny Kaye; Mrs. Parkington (1944); True to Like (1943) with Dick Powell; I Married a Witch (1942) with Veronica Lake, Fredrick March, Joel McCrea; Sullivan's Travels (1941) with Franklin Pangborn, directed by Preston Sturges; Destry Rides Again (1939) with James Stewart, Marlene Dietrich; The Wizard of Oz (1939) voice of the mayor; Professor Beware (1938) with Harold Lloyd; High, Wide and Handsome (1937) with Irene Dunne, Randolph Scott, Alan Hale, Sr.; Man on the Flying Trapeze (1935) with W.C. Fields, Grady Sutton; Old-Fashioned Way (1934) with W.C. Fields; The Cat's Paw (1934) with Harold Lloyd; Punch Drunks (1934) with the Three Stooges; Diplomaniacs (1933) with Wheeler & Woolsey; The Dentist (1932) with W.C. Fields

ERIC BLORE (1887-1959)

Swiss Miss (1938): Edward Morton

Other notable films: Fancy Pants (1950) with Bob Hope; Love Happy (1950) with the Marx Bros., Marilyn Monroe; The Adventures of Ichabod & Mr. Toad (1949), the voice of Mr. Toad in Walt Disney cartoon; Road To Zanzibar (1941) with Bob Hope, Bing Crosby; Sullivan's Travels (1941) with Joel McCrea, directed by Preston Sturges

STANLEY BLYSTONE (1895-1956)

A Chump at Oxford (1940): Officer; Sons of the Desert (1933)

Other notable films: Pardners (1956),You're Never Too Young (1955), and Living It Up (1954), all with Dean Martin and Jerry Lewis; My Favorite Spy (1951) and The Paleface (1948) both with Bob Hope; Samson and Delilah (1950) directed by Cecil B. DeMille; Road to Rio (1947) with Bob Hope, Bing Crosby; Bringing Up Baby (1938) with Cary Grant, Katharine Hepburn; The Toast of New York (1937) with Cary Grant; Modern Times (1936) with Charlie Chaplin; We're Not Dressing (1934) with Burns and Allen

MARY BOLAND (1880-1965)

Nothing But Trouble (1944): Mrs. Elvira Hawkley

Other notable films: One Night in the Tropics (1940) with Abbott and Costello; College Holiday (1936) with Jack Benny, George Burns, Gracie Allen; Early to Bed (1936) with Charlie Ruggles; Ruggles of Red Gap (1935) with Charlie Ruggles; Six of a Kind (1934) with W.C. Fields; If I Had a Million (1932) with W.C. Fields

JOE BORDEAUX (1893-1950)

Our Relations (1936)

Other notable films: You Can't Take It With You (1938) with James Stewart, directed by Frank Capra; Tillie's Punctured Romance (1914) with Charlie Chaplin, Milton Berle

EDDIE BORDEN (1887-1955)

A Chump at Oxford (1940): Ghost; Saps at Sea (1940): Berserk victim; The Flying Deuces (1939); Way Out West (1937); The Bohemian Girl (1936): Foppish nobleman

Other notable films: The Time of Your Life (1948) with James Cagney; A Guy Named Joe (1944) with Spencer Tracy; Early to Bed (1936) with Charlie Ruggles, written by Lucien Littlefield; Belle of the Nineties (1934) with Mae West; Battling Butler (1926) with Buster Keaton

VEDA ANN BORG (1915-1973)

The Big Noise (1944): Mayme

Other notable films: The Alamo (1960); Guys and Dolls (1924) with Vivian Blaine, Frank Sinatra, Marlon Brando; The Bachelor and the Bobby-Soxer (1947) with Cary Grant, Myrna Loy, Shirley Temple

AGOSTINO BORGATO (1870-1939)

Swiss Miss (1938): Man with mule-drawn cart

Other notable films: Farewell to Arms (1932) with Gary Cooper; The Maltese Falcon (1931) with Humphrey Bogart

MATTHEW BOULTON (1892-1962)

Nothing But Trouble (1944): Prince Prentiloff of Marshovia

Other notable films: My Favorite Blonde (1942) with Bob Hope; Sabotage (1936) directed by Alfred Hitchcock

ED BRADY

Saps At Sea (1940): Extra

Other notable films: In Old California (1942) with John Wayne, Patsy Kline; When the Daltons Rode (1940); Stagecoach (1939) with John Wayne, directed by John Ford; In Old Chicago (1938) with Tyrone Power; The Fury (1936) with Spencer Tracy; Tillie and Gus (1933) with W.C. Fields

CHET BRANDENBERG

Pack up Your Troubles (1932); Sons of the Desert (1933); Great Guns (1941); Be Big (1931): Cab driver; The Hoose-Gow (1929): Prisoner; Two Tars (1928): Motorist; Should Married Men Go Home (1928); You're Darn Tootin' (1928) Manhole worker; Putting Pants on Philip (1927); Hats Off (1927); With Love and Hisses (1927)

Other notable films: Love Me or Leave Me (1955) with Doris Day and James Cagney

HENRY BRANDON (1912-1990)

Babes in Toyland (1934): Barnaby

Other notable films: To Be or Not to Be (1983) with Mel Brooks; Auntie Mame (1958) with Rosalind Russell; The Searchers (1956) with John Wayne, Natalie Wood; The Ten Commandments (1956) with Charlton Heston, Edward G. Robinson; Lady Godiva (1955) with Clint Eastwood, Maureen O'Hara; Casanova's Big Night (1954) with Bob Hope; The Caddy (1953) and Scared Stiff (1953) both with Dean Martin and Jerry Lewis; War of the Worlds (1953) with Gene Barry; Wake of the Red Witch (1949) with John Wayne; The Paleface (1948) with Bob Hope; Shepherd of

HENRY BRANDON *(continued)*

the Hills (1941) with John Wayne, Charles Middleton; Beau Geste (1939) with Gary Cooper, Ray Milland; If I Were King (1938), directed Preston Sturges; Three Comrades (1938) with Robert Young; The Trail of the Lonesome Pine (1936) with Henry Fonda, Fred MacMurray, Spanky McFarland

EDDIE BRIAN

Swiss Miss (1938)

Other notable films: Angels With Dirty Faces (1938) with Humphrey Bogart, James Cagney

MATT BRIGGS (1882-1962)

The Dancing Masters (1943): Wentworth Harlan

Other notable films: The Ox-Bow Incident (1943) with Henry Fonda; Hips, Hips, Hooray (1934) with Wheeler & Woolsey

DON BRODIE (1899-)

Sons of the Desert (1933)

Other notable films: Little Big Man (1970) with Dustin Hoffman; The Patsy (1964) with Jerry Lewis; On the Town (1948) with Frank Sinatra; Luck of the Irish (1948); Woman in the Window (1945) with Edward G. Robinson, Spanky McFarland; They Got Me Covered (1943) with Bob Hope; Walt Disney's Pinocchio (1940) voice of Barker; Road to Singapore (1940) with Bob Hope, Bing Crosby; Lady in the Morgue (1938); Captains Courageous (1937) with Spencer Tracy; The Toast of New York (1937) with

DON BRODIE *(continued)*

Cary Grant; The Man Who Broke the Bank at Monte Carlo (1935); Little Miss Marker (1934) with Shirley Temple

FRITZI BRUNETTE (1889-1943)

Way Out West (1937)

Other notable films: Meet John Doe (1941) with Gary Cooper, directed by Frank Capra; Stagecoach (1939) with John Wayne, directed by John Ford

BOBBY BURNS

Another Fine Mess (1930): Bicyclist;

Below Zero (1930): "blind" man and the deadbeat at diner

Other notable films: Three Little Pigskins (1934) with The Three Stooges

WILLIAM BURRESS (1866-1948)

Babes in Toyland (1934): Toymaker

Other notable films: The Story of Louis Pasteur (1936) with Paul Muni; Naughty Marietta (1935) with Nelson Eddy, Jeanette MacDonald; Dr. Socrates (1935) with Grady Sutton, Paul Muni; The Little Colonel (1935) with Shirley Temple; Blonde Crazy (1931) with James Cagney

MAE BUSCH (1891-1946)

The Bohemian Girl (1936): Mrs. Hardy; Tit for Tat (1935); The Fixer Uppers (1935); The Live Ghost (1934); Them Thar Hills (1934); Going Bye-Bye! (1934); Oliver the Eighth (1934); Sons of the Desert (1933): Lottie Hardy; Their First Mistake (1932): Mrs. Arabella Hardy; Come Clean (1931): Kate; Chickens Come Home (1931); Unaccustomed As We Are

MAE BUSCH *(continued)*

(1929); Love 'Em and Weep (1927)

Other notable films: Ziegfeld Girl (1941) with James Stewart, Judy Garland; Marie Antoinette (1938) with Norma Shearer, Tyrone Power

JAMES BUSH

The Big Noise (1944): Hartman;
A-Haunting We Will Go (1942): Joe Morgan

Other notable films: Gone With The Wind (1939) with Clark Gable, Vivien Leigh; You Can't Cheat an Honest Man (1939) with W.C. Fields; If I Had a Million (1932) with W.C. Fields

RICHARD CARLE (1871-1941)

Hollywood Party (1934): Knapp; Habeas Corpus (1928): Prof. Padilla

Other notable films: The Devil and Miss Jones (1941) with Bob Cummings, Jean Arthur; The Great McGinty (1940) directed by Preston Sturges; One Night in the Tropics (1940) with Abbott & Costello; It's a Wonderful World (1939) with James Stewart, Claudette Colbert; Ninotchka (1939) with Greta Garbo, nominated best picture; College Holiday (1936) with Jack Benny, Burns & Allen; San Francisco (1936) with Clark Gable; The Trail of the Lonesome Pine (1936) with Henry Fonda, Fred MacMurray, Spanky McFarland; The Old-Fashioned Way (1934) with W.C. Fields; Diplomaniacs (1933) with Wheeler & Woolsey

MARY CARR (1874-1973)

Pack Up Your Troubles (1932): Woman;
One Good Turn (1931): Woman in play

Other notable films: Friendly Persuasion (1956) with Gary Cooper; Gone With the Wind (1939) with Clark Gable, Vivien Leigh; The Wizard of Oz (1925) with Oliver Hardy, Larry Semon

JAMES B. CARSON

Swiss Miss (1938)

Other notable films: Road to Zanzibar (1941) with Bob Hope, Bing Crosby

ALLEN CAVAN

We Faw Down (1928): Pedestrian

Other notable films: Mr. Smith Goes to Washington (1939) with James Stewart, directed by Frank Capra; The Toast of New York (1937) with Cary Grant

NORA CECIL

Hollywood Party (1934): Scientific pedant;
Pack Up Your Troubles (1932): Officers in the Eastside Welfare Association

Other notable films: Sea of Grass (1947) with Spencer Tracy; Miracle of Morgan's Creek, directed by Preston Sturges; I Married a Witch (1942) with Fredric March, Veronica Lake; Stagecoach (1939) with John Wayne, directed by John Ford; Nothing Sacred (1937) with Carole Lombard, Fredric March; College Holiday (1936) with Jack Benny, Burns & Allen; The Fury (1936) with Spencer Tracy; Poppy (1936) with W.C. Fields; Little Miss Marker

NORA CECIL *(continued)*

(1934) with Shirley Temple; The Old-Fashioned Way (1934); You're Telling Me (1934) with W.C. Fields

LANE CHANDLER (1899-1972)

The Devil's Brother (1933): Lieutenant

Other notable films: The Greatest Show on Earth (1952) with Charlton Heston; Samson and Delilah (1950) directed by Cecil B. DeMille; The Paleface (1948) with Bob Hope; Duel in the Sun (1946) with Joseph Cotten, Lillian Gish; It's a Wonderful Life (1946) with James Stewart, directed by Frank Capra; Little Giant (1946) with Abbott & Costello; Laura (1944) with Gene Tierney; They Got Me Covered (1943) with Bob Hope; The Pride of the Yankees (1942) with Gary Cooper; Reap the Wild Wind (1942) with John Wayne; Sergeant York (1941); My Little Chickadee (1940) with W.C. Fields; Angels with Dirty Faces (1938) with James Cagney, Humphrey Bogart

CHARLEY CHASE (1893-1940)

Born Charles Parrott. Started making films in 1912.

Sons of the Desert (1933); On the Wrong Trek (1936); Call of the Cuckoo (1927): Asylum inmate; Now I'll Tell One (1927)

Other notable films: Saved By the Belle (1939), Violent is the Word for Curly (1938), Flat Foot Stooges (1938), Tassels in the Air (1938), and Mutts to You (1938) are Stooges shorts directed by Chase; Kelly the Second (1936); King of the Wild Horses (1924); Tillie's Punctured Romance (1914) with Charlie Chaplin, Milton Berle

JACK CHEFE (1893-1975)

The Flying Deuces (1939): Other Legionnaires

Other notable films: Funny Face (1957) with Fred Astaire; Gentlemen Prefer Blondes (1953) with Marilyn Monroe; My Favorite Spy (1951) with Bob Hope; Abbott & Costello Meet the Killer, Boris Karloff (1949) with Abbott and Costello; My Favorite Brunette (1947) with Bob Hope; Gilda (1946) with Rita Hayworth; The Postman Always Rings Twice (1946); Naughty Nineties (1945) with Abbott and Costello; To Have & Have Not (1944) with Humphrey Bogart, Lauren Bacall; Tales of Manhattan (1942) with Henry Fonda, Edward G. Robinson; My Man Godfrey (1936) with William Powell, Franklin Pangborn, Grady Sutton

DOROTHY CHRISTY (1900-1977)

Sons of the Desert (1933)

Other notable films: Secret Life of Walter Mitty (1947) with Danny Kaye; Little Giant (1946); Laura (1944) with Gene Tierney; East Side of Heaven (1939)

KEN CHRISTY (1894-1962)

The Big Noise (1944): Speaker

Other notable films: Abbott & Costello Go To Mars (1953) with Abbott and Costello; The Greatest Show on Earth (1952) with Charlton Heston; Cheaper by the Dozen (1950) with Clifton Webb; Sunset Boulevard (1950) with William Holden, Buster Keaton; Hit the Ice (1943) with Abbott and Costello; Here Comes Mr. Jordan (1941) with

KEN CHRISTY *(continued)*

Robert Montgomery, Claude Rains; Love Crazy (1941) with William Powell, Myrna Loy; Foreign Correspondent (1940) with Joel McCrea, directed by Alfred Hitchcock

HARVEY CLARK (1885-1938)

Putting Pants on Philip (1927)

Other notable films: The Toast of New York (1937) with Cary Grant; The Fury (1936) with Spencer Tracy; Three Godfathers (1936) with John Wayne; Cracked Nuts (1931) with Wheeler & Woolsey

CHESTER CLUTE (1891-1956)

Nothing But Trouble (1944): Doolittle

Other notable films: Abbott & Costello in Hollywood (1945) with Abbott and Costello; Mildred Pierce (1945) with Joan Crawford; Arsenic and Old Lace (1944) with Cary Grant, directed by Frank Capra; George Washington Slept Here (1942) with Jack Benny, Ann Sheridan; My Favorite Spy (1942) with Bob Hope; Pardon My Sarong (1942) with Abbott and Costello; The Spoilers (1942) with John Wayne; Yankee Doodle Dandy (1942) with James Cagney; Niagara Falls (1941); My Favorite Wife (1940) with Cary Grant, Irene Dunne; You Can't Take It with You (1938) with James Stewart, directed by Frank Capra

CHICK COLLINS (-1981)

The Dancing Masters (1943): Bus Driver

Other notable films: Fuller Brush Man (1948) with Red Skelton, Buster Keaton; Sullivan's Travels (1941) with Joel McCrea, directed by Frank Capra; My Man Godfrey (1936)

CHICK COLLINS *(continued)*
with William Powell; Million Dollar Legs (1932) with W.C. Fields

EDDIE CONRAD (1889-1941)
Saps At Sea (1940): Professor O'Brien
Other notable films: International Squadron (1941), with Ronald Reagan; Road to Zanzibar (1941) with Bob Hope, Bing Crosby; Foreign Correspondent (1940) directed by Alfred Hitchcock

ELISHA COOK JR. (1906-1995)
A-Haunting We Will Go (1942): Frank Lucas
Other notable films: Papa's Delicate Condition (1963) with Jackie Gleason; The Big Sleep (1946) with Humphrey Bogart; Love Crazy (1941) with William Powell, Myrna Loy; The Maltese Falcon (1941) with Humphrey Bogart; Sergeant York (1941) with Gary Cooper; Pigskin Parade (1936) with Jack Haley, Judy Garland

BALDWIN COOKE
Swiss Miss (1938); Our Relations (1936); Thicker Than Water (1936): Hospital visitor; Tit for Tat (1935): Customer; The Live Ghost (1934): Sailor; Hollywood Party (1934): Holding the door for the scientific gentleman; Them Thar Hills (1934): Officer; Going Bye-Bye! (1934); Sons of the Desert (1933); Twice Two (1933): Soda jerk; Scram! (1932): Court Recorder; County Hospital (1932): Orderly; The Chimp (1932); Any Old Port (1932); Pack Up Your Troubles (1932): Doughboys; Beau Hunks (1931); One Good Turn (1931); Chickens Come Home (1931); Be Big! (1931): Cookie;

BALDWIN COOKE *(continued)*

Pardon Us (1931); Below Zero (1930): Man at window; Blotto (1930):Waiter; Night Owls (1930): Policeman; The Hoose-Gow (1929): Prisoner; Perfect Day (1929): Next-door neighbor; Men O'War (1929): Boater; Berth Marks (1929): Train passenger; Two Tars (1928): Motorist

Other notable films: Of Mice and Men (1939) with Burgess Meredith, produced by Hal Roach; The Pip From Pittsburgh (1931) with Charley Chase

NICK COPELAND (1894-1940)

Swiss Miss (1938); Our Relations (1936)

Other notable films: Mr. Smith Goes to Washington (1939) and You Can't Take It With You (1938), both with James Stewart, both directed by Frank Capra; Saratoga (1937) with Clark Gable, Jean Harlow; The Thin Man (1934) with William Powell, Myrna Loy

ELLEN CORBY (1914-)

Worked as script girl for RKO and then at Hal Roach Studios, where she met and married cameraman Francis Corby, but soon divorced. Known for her role as Grandma Walton on the T.V. series 'The Waltons' from 1972 until 1981.

Sons of the Desert (1933): A background extra at convention

Other notable films: Walton's Easter (1997) a T.V. movie; Napoleon and Samantha (1972) with Jodie Foster; Homecoming: A Christmas Story (1971); Support Your Local Gunfighter (1971) with James Garner; Ghost and Mr. Chicken (1966) with Don Knotts; The Family Jewels (1965) with Jerry Lewis; A Pocketful of Miracles (1961)

ELLEN CORBY *(continued)*

with Glenn Ford, Bette Davis, directed by Frank Capra; Vertigo (1958) with James Stewart, directed by Alfred Hitchcock; Sabrina (1954) with Audrey Hepburn; Shane (1953) with Alan Ladd; Caged (1950) with Eleanor Parker; The Gunfighter (1950) with Gregory Peck; Ma & Pa Kettle Go to Town (1950) with Marjorie Main, Percy Kilbride; Mighty Joe Young (1949); I Remember Mama (1948) directed by George Stevens, Oscar-nominated for role; It's A Wonderful Life (1946) with James Stewart, directed by Frank Capra; The Spiral Staircase (1946)

ANNE CORNWALL

Men O'War (1929)

Other notable films: Mr. Smith Goes to Washington (1939); and You Can't Take It With You (1938) both with James Stewart, both directed by Frank Capra

DON COSTELLO (1900-1945)

Air Raid Wardens (1943): Heydrich;
A-Haunting We Will Go (1942): Doc Lake

Other notable films: Here Come the Co-Eds (1945) with Abbott and Costello; Here Comes Mr. Jordan (1941) with Robert Montgomery

DICK CRAMER (1888-1960)

Saps at Sea (1940): Nick Grainger;
The Flying Deuces (1939): Truck driver;
Pack up Your Troubles (1932): Uncle Jack;
Scram! (1932): Judge Beaumont;

Other notable films: Northwest Passage (1940) with

DICK CRAMER *(continued)*

Spencer Tracy; Knights of the Plains (1939), produced by Stan Laurel; The Cat's Paw (1934) with Harold Lloyd; Fatal Glass of Beer (1933) with W.C. Fields; Blonde Crazy (1931) with James Cagney; Platinum Blonde (1931) with Jean Harlow, directed by Frank Capra

JOSEPHINE CROWELL (-1932)

Wrong Again (1929): Henderson's Mother

Other notable films: Birth of a Nation (1915) with D.W. Griffith

BOB CUMMINGS (1910-1990)

Sons of the Desert (1933): Played an extra

Other notable films: Dial M for Murder (1954) with Grace Kelly, Ray Milland, directed by Alfred Hitchcock; Forever and a Day (1943) with Buster Keaton; King's Row (1942) with Ronald Reagan; Saboteur (1942) directed by Alfred Hitchcock; The Devil and Miss Jones (1941); One Night in the Tropics (1940) with Abbott and Costello

PETER CUSHING (1913-1994)

A Chump at Oxford (1940): Student

Other notable films: Star Wars (1977); Horror of Dracula (1958) with Christopher Lee; Moulin Rouge (1952), directed by John Huston; Hamlet (1948) with Laurence Olivier

MICHAEL DALMATOFF

Atoll K (1951): Alecto

Other notable films: For Whom the Bells Tolls (1943) with Gary Cooper

JEAN DARLING (1922-)

Babes in Toyland (1934): Curly Locks

Other notable films: Our Gang Shorts; Jane Eyre (1934)

STEVE DARRELL (1902-1970)

The Bullfighters (1945): Mexican policeman; Nothing But Trouble (1944): Zoo attendant

Other notable films: The Ten Commandments (1956) with Charlton Heston; Angels with Dirty Faces (1938) with James Cagney, Humphrey Bogart

JEAN de BRIAC

Nothing But Trouble (1944): French restaurateur; Swiss Miss (1938): Enrico the waiter

Other notable films: Gentlemen Prefer Blondes (1953) with Marilyn Monroe; Ma and Pa Kettle on Vacation (1953) with Marjorie Main, Percy Kilbride; My Favorite Spy (1951) with Bob Hope; The Razor's Edge (1946) with Tyrone Power; To Have & Have Not (1944) with Humphrey Bogart, Lauren Bacall

EDGAR DEARING (1893-1974)

The Big Noise (1944): Motor policeman; Two Tars (1928)

Other notable films: Pollyanna (1960) with Hayley Mills; The Long, Long Trailer (1954) with Lucille Ball, Desi Arnaz; Ma and Pa Kettle at Home (1954) with Marjorie

EDGAR DEARING *(continued)*

Main, Percy Kilbride; Fancy Pants (1950) with Bob Hope; Samson and Delilah (1950) directed by Cecil B. DeMille; Riding High (1950) with Oliver Hardy, Bing Crosby; Sorrowful Jones (1949) with Bob Hope; The Paleface (1948) with Bob Hope; Road to Utopia (1946) with Bob Hope, Bing Crosby; Abbott & Costello in Hollywood (1945) with Abbott and Costello; The Ghost Catchers (1944) with Olsen and Johnson; In Society (1944) with Abbott and Costello; My Favorite Blonde (1942) with Bob Hope; My Favorite Spy (1942) with Bob Hope; Caught in the Draft (1941) with Bob Hope; Hold That Ghost (1941) with Abbott and Costello; Sullivan's Travels (1941) with Joel McCrea directed by Preston Sturges; One Night in the Tropics (1940) with Abbott and Costello; The Awful Truth (1937) with Cary Grant, Irene Dunne; Million Dollar Legs (1932) with W.C.Fields

JEAN del VAL

The Flying Deuces (1939): Sergeant

Other notable films: Wait Until Dark (1967) with Audrey Hepburn; Funny Face (1957) with Fred Astaire; Sad Sack (1957) with Dean Martin, Jerry Lewis, directed by George Marshall; Gentlemen Prefer Blondes (1953) with Marilyn Monroe; Life with Father (1947) with Elizabeth Taylor, Irene Dunne, Zasu Pitts; Gilda (1946) with Rita Hayworth; Monsieur Beaucaire (1946) with Bob Hope, directed by George Marshall; The Razor's Edge (1946) with Tyrone Power; Passage to Marseilles (1944) with Humphery Bogart; For Whom the Bell Tolls (1943) with Gary Cooper, Ingrid Bergman; Song of Bernadette (1943) with Jennifer

JEAN del VAL *(continued)*

Jones; Gentleman Jim (1942) with Errol Flynn; Sergeant York (1941) with Gary Cooper, Passionate Plumber (1932) with Buster Keaton

SUZY DELAIR (1916-)

Atoll K (1951): Cherie Lamour

Other notable films: Is Paris Burning? (1966),with Glenn Ford, Nominated Best British Film; Rocco and His Brothers (1960); Gervaise (1956) Nominated Best Foreign Film

KAY DESLYS

The Devil's Brother (1933); Below Zero (1930): Woman at window; Perfect Day (1929): Mrs. Hardy; We Faw Down (1928); Should Married Men Go Home (1928); Their Purple Moment (1928): Stan's girlfriend

Other notable films: Pat & Mike (1952) with Spencer Tracy, Katharine Hepburn; Never Give a Sucker an Even Break (1941) with W.C. Fields; You Can't Take it With You (1938) with James Stewart, directed by Frank Capra; The Pip from Pittsburgh (1931) with Charley Chase

DONALD DILLAWAY (1903-1982)

Pack Up Your Troubles (1932): Eddie Smith

Other notable films: Narrow Margin (1952); Cimarron (1930) with Irene Dunne, Best Picture; Min and Bill (1930) with Marie Dressler, Wallace Beery

LESTER DORR (1892-1980)

Swiss Miss (1938): Extra in the Alpenfest; Way Out West (1937): Cowboy

Other notable films: The Greatest Show on Earth (1952) with Charlton Heston; Notorious (1946) with Cary Grant, Ingrid Bergman, directed by Alfred Hitchcock; Gone With the Wind (1939) with Clark Gable, Vivien Leigh; You Can't Take It With You (1938) with James Stewart, directed by Frank Capra; Captains Courageous (1937) with Spencer Tracy; If I Had A Million (1932) with W.C. Fields

GORDON M. DOUGLAS (1909-1993)

Actor and casting director for Hal Roach in the early 1930's. Began directing in 1936, guiding the Little Rascals in 'Bored of Education' and 'Rushin' Ballet', plus their only feature, 'General Spanky.'

Saps at Sea (1940): Director; Beau Hunks (1931): Legionnaire at Fort Arid

Other notable films as Director: Way, Way Out (1966) with Jerry Lewis; Call Me Bwana (1963) with Bob Hope; Zenobia (1939) with Oliver Hardy, Harry Langdon

JOHNNY DOWNS (1913-1994)

Babes in Toyland (1934): Little Boy Blue

Other notable films: Here Come the Girls (1953) with Bob Hope, Jerry Lewis, Dean Martin, Grady Sutton; The Kid from Brooklyn (1946) with Danny Kaye (remake of Harold Lloyd's 'The Milky Way'); Algiers (1938) with Charles Boyer, Alan Hale, Sr.; College Holiday (1936) with Burns & Allen, Jack Benny; Pigskin Parade (1936) with Judy Garland, Jack Haley

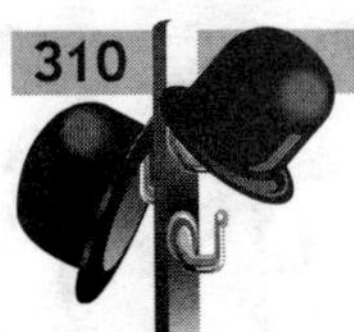

TEX DRISCOLL (1898-1979)

Swiss Miss (1938): Bearded Swiss Peasant; Way Out West (1937), Bearded miner

Other notable films: Giant (1956) with James Dean, Rock Hudson, Elizabeth Taylor; The Ox-Bow Incident (1943) with Henry Fonda; Stagecoach (1939) with John Wayne

ROBERT DUDLEY (1874-1955)

The Big Noise (1944): Grandpa

Other notable films: Mad Wednesday (1950) with Harold Lloyd

MARGARET DUMONT (1889-1965)

The Dancing Masters (1943): Mrs. Harlan

Other notable films: Little Giant (1946) with Abbott & Costello; The Horn Blows at Midnight (1945) with Jack Benny; The Big Store (1941) with the Marx Bros.; Never Give a Sucker an Even Break (1941) with W.C. Fields; At the Circus (1939), A Night at the Opera (1935), Duck Soup (1933), Animal Crackers (1930) and The Coconuts (1929) all with Marx Bros.

BOBBY DUNN (1890-1937)

Way Out West (1937); Our Relations (1936): Messenger boy; Bonnie Scotland (1935); Tit for Tat (1935): Man robbing store; The Bohemian Girl (1936): Bartender; Me and My Pal (1933): Telegraph boy; Pardon Us (1931): Convict; Duck Soup (1927): Removal man; Bacon Grabbers (1929): Construction worker; Why Girls Love Sailors (1927)

Other notable films: Million Dollar Legs (1932) with W.C. Fields

EDDIE DUNN (1896-1951)

Was frequently cast as a police officer in the Hal Roach and Max Sennett comedies.

Nothing But Trouble (1944); Midnight Patrol (1933): Desk sergeant; Me & My Pal (1933): Cabbie; Pardon Us (1931): Convict; Another Fine Mess (1930): Meadows, the butler; The Hoose-Gow (1929): Prisoner

Other notable films: Lost In A Harem (1944) and Hit the Ice (1943) both with Abbott & Costello; Never a Dull Moment (1943) with the Ritz Bros.; Ride 'Em Cowboy (1942) and Abbott & Costello in the Navy (1941) both with Abbott & Costello; The Bank Dick (1940) with W.C. Fields; The Great Dictator (1940) with Charlie Chaplin; One Night in the Tropics (1940) with Abbott & Costello; Of Mice and Men (1939) with Burgess Meredith, produced by Hal Roach; You Can't Cheat an Honest Man (1939) with W.C. Fields; The Milky Way (1936) with Harold Lloyd; Fallen Arches (1933) with Charley Chase; Million Dollar Legs (1932) with W.C. Fields

JAY EATON (1899-1970)

Our Relations (1936)

Other notable films: Love Crazy (1941) with Myrna Loy, William Powell; The Toast of New York (1937); Libeled Lady (1936) with Spencer Tracy, Myrna Loy; A Night at the Opera (1935) with the Marx Bros.

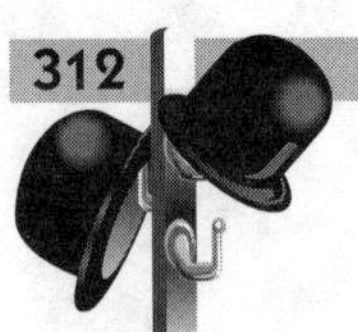

JACK EGAN

Pick A Star (1937): Orchestra conductor; Our Relations (1936)

Other notable films: Nothing But the Truth (1941) with Bob Hope; Mr. Smith Goes to Washington (1939) with James Stewart, directed by Frank Capra; The Toast of New York (1937) with Cary Grant

JOHN ELLIOTT (1875-1956)

Sons of the Desert (1933)

Other notable films: Lady from Shanghai (1948) with Orson Welles, Rita Hayworth; Magnificent Ambersons (1942) with Orson Welles; Jesse James (1939) with Henry Fonda, Tyrone Power; What Happened to Jones (1926) with William Austin, Zasu Pitts

BILLY ENGLE (1888-1966)

The Flying Deuces (1939); Our Relations (1936)

Other notable films: My Favorite Spy (1951) and The Paleface (1948) both with Bob Hope; The Wistful Widow of Wagon Gap (1947) with Abbott and Costello; Mrs. Parkington (1944) and Mrs. Miniver (1942) both with Greer Garson; You Can't Cheat an Honest Man (1939) with W.C. Fields; Test Pilot (1938) with Clark Gable, Spencer Tracy; It Happened One Night (1934) with Clark Gable, Claudette Colbert, Best Picture winner; You're Telling Me (1934), Tillie and Gus (1933), and Million Dollar Legs (1932) all with W.C. Fields

MURIEL EVANS (1912-)

Hollywood Party (1934): Seated at the table during bidding; Pack up Your Troubles (1932): Bride

Other notable films: Mr. Deeds Goes to Town (1936) with Gary Cooper, directed by Frank Capra

CARL FAULKNER

Saps At Sea (1940): Harbor police officer

Other notable films: The Window (1949) with Bobby Driscol

EDITH FELLOWS (1923-)

The Devil's Brother (1933)

Other notable films: Mrs. Wiggs of the Cabbage Patch (1934) with Zasu Pitts, W.C. Fields; Cimarron (1931) with Irene Dunne, Best Picture winner

FRANK FENTON (1905-1957)

The Big Noise (1944): Charlton

Other notable films: Mexican Hayride (1948) with Abbott and Costello

GERALD FIELDING

A Chump at Oxford (1940): Student

Other notable films: New Moon (1940) with Buster Keaton; The Scarlet Empress (1934) with Marlene Dietrich

STANLEY FIELDS (1883-1941)

Way Out West (1937): Sheriff

Other notable films: Pack Up Your Troubles (1939) with the Ritz Bros.; Algiers (1938) with Charles Boyer; The Toast of New York (1937) with Cary Grant; Show Boat (1936) with Irene Dunne; Mutiny on the Bounty (1935) with Clark Gable, Charles Laughton; Girl Crazy (1932) and Cracked Nuts (1931) both with Wheeler & Woolsey; Cimarron (1931) with Irene Dunne, Best Picture winner; Little Caesar (1930) with Edward G. Robinson

FLORA FINCH (1869-1940)

Way Out West (1937): Maw

Other notable films: San Francisco (1936) with Clark Gable

BUDDY FINE

Pack Up Your Troubles (1932); Flying Elephants (1928)

Other notable films: My Favorite Brunette (1947) with Bob Hope; Sea of Grass (1947) with Spencer Tracy; Miracle of Morgan's Creek (1944) directed by Preston Sturges; Only Angels Have Wings (1939) with Cary Grant, directed by Howard Hawks; It's a Gift (1934) with W.C. Fields

ALEX FINLAYSON

Our Relations (1936)

Other notable films: Father Goose (1964) with Cary Grant; Journey to the Center of the Earth (1959) with Pat Boone

FRANCIS FORD (1882-1953)

Older brother of well known director John Ford.

The Big Noise (1944): Station attendant; Jitterbugs (1943): Old-timer

Other notable films: The Quiet Man (1952) with John Wayne; The Wagon Master (1950) with James Arness, Harry Carey Jr.; She Wore a Yellow Ribbon (1949) with John Wayne; Three Godfathers (1948) with John Wayne; My Darling Clementine (1946) with Henry Fonda; Murder, He Says (1945) with Fred MacMurray, Marjorie Main; State Fair (1945) with Vivian Blaine, Dana Andrews; The Princess and the Pirate (1944) with Bob Hope; The Ox-Bow Incident (1943) with Henry Fonda; Tobacco Road (1941) with Charles Grapewin; The Grapes of Wrath (1940) with Henry Fonda; Stagecoach (1939) with John Wayne; A Star is Born (1937) with Janet Gaynor, Fredric March; Frankenstein (1931) with Boris Karloff

PAUL H. FREES (1918-1985)

Provided the voices of many cartoon characters, including Boris Badenov on the television cartoon series Bullwinkle.

Atoll K (1951): English Narrator

Other notable films: Twice Upon a Time (1983), voices; Return of the King (1980), voices; The Time Machine (1960) with Rod Taylor; The Shaggy Dog (1959) with Fred MacMurray, Tommy Kirk; The Harder They Fall (1956) with Humphrey Bogart; War of the Worlds (1953) with Gene Barry; The Big Sky (1952) with Kirk Douglas; The Star (1952) with Bette Davis; A Place in the Sun (1951) with Montgomery Clift, Elizabeth Taylor; The Thing (1951) with James Arness

CHARLES FRENCH (1859-1952)

Chickens Come Home (1931): Judge

Other notable films: Meet John Doe (1941) with Gary Cooper, directed by Frank Capra; The Prisoner of Zenda (1937) with Ronald Coleman; The Milky Way (1936) with Harold Lloyd; The Spoilers (1930) with John Wayne

DICK FRENCH

Our Relations (1936)

Other notable films: You Can't Take It With You (1938) with James Stewart, directed by Frank Capra

OTTO H. FRIES (1887-1938)

Pick A Star (1937); Pardon Us (1931); From Soup To Nuts (1928); Cook; Leave 'Em Laughing (1928): Dentist; Call of the Cuckoos (1927); The Second Hundred Years (1927); French police chief

Other notable films: Alexander's Ragtime Band (1938) with Tyrone Power; The Prisoner of Zenda (1937) with Ronald Coleman; A Night at the Opera (1935) with the Marx Bros.; Monkey Business (1931) with the Marx Bros, directed by Howard Hawks

REGINALD GARDINER (1903-1980)

The Flying Deuces (1939): Francois

Other notable films: Rock-A-Bye Baby (1958) with Jerry Lewis, Snub Pollard; Christmas in Connecticut (1945) with Barbara Stanwyck; The Horn Blows at Midnight (1945) with Jack Benny, Robert Blake; Man Who Came to Dinner (1941) with Bette Davis; The Great Dictator (1940) with Charlie Chaplin

EDWARD GARGAN (1902-1964)

The Bullfighters (1945): Vasso;
A-Haunting We Will Go (1942): Foster

Other notable films: Abbott & Costello Meet the Invisible Man (1951) with Abbott & Costello; Bedtime For Bonzo (1951) with Ronald Reagan; Father of the Bride (1950) with Spencer Tracy, Elizabeth Taylor; Little Giant (1946) with Abbott & Costello; Naughty Nineties (1945) with Abbott & Costello; Hit the Ice (1943) with Abbott & Costello; They Got Me Covered (1943); My Favorite Blonde (1942) with Bob Hope; Northwest Passage (1940) with Spencer Tracy; Bringing up Baby (1938) with Cary Grant, Katharine Hepburn; Mr. Deeds Goes to Town (1936) with Gary Cooper; My Man Godfrey (1936) with William Powell, Carole Lombard; Man on the Flying Trapeze (1935) with W.C. Fields

ANITA GARVIN (1907-1994)

A Chump At Oxford (1940): Mrs. Vandevere; Swiss Miss (1938): Tradesman's bickering wife; Be Big! (1931): Mrs. Laurel; Blotto (1930): Mrs. Laurel; Their Purple Moment (1928): Ollie's girlfriend; From Soup to Nuts (1928); The Battle of the Century (1927); Hats Off (1927); Sailors Beware (1927): Con artist; Why Girls Love Sailors (1927): Captain's wife

Other notable films: Modern Love (1929) with Charley Chase

BUD GEARY (1898-1946)

Saps at Sea (1940)

Other notable films: Talk of the Town (1942) with Cary Grant, directed by George Stevens; Professor Beware (1938) with Harold Lloyd; Dead End (1937) with Humphrey Bogart; High Flyers (1937) with Wheeler & Woolsey; Follow the Fleet (1936) with Fred Astaire, Ginger Rogers; San Francisco (1936) with Clark Gable

CHARLES GEMORA

Swiss Miss (1938): Gorilla; The Chimp (1932): Ethel

Other notable films: War Of The Worlds (1953) with Gene Barry; Road To Utopia (1946) and Road To Zanzibar (1941) both with Bob Hope, Bing Crosby

JOHN GEORGE (1897-1968)

Babes in Toyland (1934): Barnaby's minion

Other notable films: Son of Paleface (1952) with Bob Hope, Roy Rogers; If I Were King (1938) with Ronald Colman; Island of Lost Souls (1932) with Bela Lugosi; Condemned (1929) Ronald Colman; Unknown (1927); Don Juan (1926) with Mary Astor

CHARLES GERRARD

Another Fine Mess (1930): Lord Leopold Ambrose Plumtree

Other notable films: Dracula (1931) with Bela Lugosi

SUMNER GETCHELL

Babes in Toyland (1934): Tom Thumb

Other notable films: Island in the Sky (1953) with John Wayne, Carl 'Alfalfa' Switzer

BILLY GILBERT (1894-1971)

Block-Heads (1938): Mr. Gilbert; Them Thar Hills (1934): Doctor; Sons of the Desert (1933): Voice of steamship official; Towed in a Hole (1932): Joe; Their First Mistake (1932): Process server; Pack Up Your Troubles (1932): Doctor; The Chimp (1932): Landlord; The Music Box (1932): Prof. von Schwarzenhoffen; On the Loose (1932); One Good Turn (1931): Drunk

Other notable films: Made appearances on the TV series Make Room for Daddy (1955) with Danny Thomas; Walt Disney's Fun and Fancy Free (1947): Cartoon voice of the Giant; The Villain Still

Pursued Her (1941) with Buster Keaton; The Great Dictator (1940) with Charlie Chaplin; His Girl Friday (1940) with Cary Grant; Destry Rides Again (1939) with James Stewart; Million Dollar Legs (1939) with Betty Grable; Peck's Bad Boy with the Circus (1938) with Spanky McFarland; Walt Disney's Snow White and the Seven Dwarfs (1937), Cartoon voice of Sneezy; Broadway Melody of 1938 (1937) with Judy Garland; The Toast of New York (1937) with Cary Grant; Captains Courageous (1937) with Spencer Tracy; A Night at the Opera (1935) with the Marx Bros.; Pardon My Scotch (1935) with the Three Stooges; Curly Top (1935) with Shirley Temple; Men in Black (1934) with the Three Stooges; Cockeyed Cavaliers (1934) with Wheeler & Woolsey; The Count of Monte Cristo (1934); Million Dollar Legs (1932) with W.C. Fields; Free Eats (1932) with Our Gang

CONNIE GILCHRIST (1901-1985)

Nothing But Trouble (1944): Mrs. Flannagan

Other notable films: The Monkey's Uncle (1965) with Tommy Kirk, Annette Funicello; Auntie Mame (1958) with Rosalind Russell; Woman of the Year (1942) with Spencer Tracy, Katharine Hepburn

WILLIAM GILLESPIE

Sons of the Desert (1933)

Other notable films: Why Worry? (1923) with Harold Lloyd, Sam Lufkin; Doctor Jack (1922) with Harold Lloyd; Grandma's Boy (1922) with Harold Lloyd

MINNA GOMBELL (1892-1973)

Block-Heads (1938): Mrs. Hardy

Other notable films: The Best Years of Our Lives (1946) with Dana Andrews; High Sierra (1941) with Humphrey Bogart; The Hunchback of Notre Dame (1939) with Charles Laughton, Maureen O'Hara; The Count of Monte Cristo (1934); The Lemon Drop Kid (1934); The Thin Man (1934) with William Powell, Myrna Loy

MARY GORDON (1882-1963)

Played Mrs. Hudson, Sherlock Holmes' housekeeper at 221B Baker Street, opposite Basil Rathbone in the films of the 1930's and '40's.

Saps at Sea (1940): Mrs. O'Riley; Pick A Star (1937): Undertaker's wife; Way Out West (1937); Bonnie Scotland (1935): Mrs. Bickerdike; Pack up Your Troubles (1932): Mrs. MacTavish

Other notable films: Fort Apache (1948) with John

MARY GORDON *(continued)*

Wayne, Henry Fonda, Shirley Temple; Little Giant (1946) with Abbott and Costello; Kitty (1945) with Paulette Goddard; The Spider Woman (1944) with Basil Rathbone; Forever and a Day (1943); Gentleman Jim (1942); The Pride of the Yankees (1942) with Gary Cooper; How Green was My Valley (1941), directed by John Ford; The Invisible Man Returns (1940); When the Daltons Rode (1940); Adventures of Sherlock Holmes (1939) and The Hound of the Baskervilles (1939) both with Basil Rathbone; Mr. Smith Goes to Washington (1939) with James Stewart, directed by Frank Capra; Angels with Dirty Faces (1938) with James Cagney, Humphrey Bogart; The Toast of New York (1937) with Cary Grant; The Bride of Frankenstein (1935); Mutiny on the Bounty (1935) with Clark Gable, Charles Laughton; The Whole Town's Talking (1935) with Edward G. Robinson; She Done Him Wrong (1933) with Mae West, Cary Grant

DOROTHY GRANGER (1911-1995)

One Good Turn (1931): A Community Player; The Laurel-Hardy Murder Case (1930): Young woman; Hog Wild (1930): Tillie

** Note: Her photograph is used as the Landlord's wife in 'The Chimp'*

Other notable films: The Paleface (1948) with Bob Hope; The Secret Life of Walter Mitty (1947) with Danny Kaye; The Southerner (1945); In Society (1944) with Abbott and Costello; Romeo and Juliet (1936) directed by George Cukor; Show Boat (1936) with Irene Dunne; The Count of Monte Cristo (1934); Punch Drunks (1934) with the

DOROTHY GRANGER *(continued)*

Three Stooges; The Dentist (1932) with W.C. Fields; The Pip from Pittsburgh (1931) with Charley Chase

ETHEL GRIFFIES (1877-1975)

Great Guns (1941): Aunt Agatha

Other notable films: The Birds (1963) with Tippi Hedren, directed by Alfred Hitchcock; Jane Eyre (1944) with Orson Wells, Joan Fontaine; Mrs. Wiggs of the Cabbage Patch (1942) with W.C. Fields

KIT GUARD (1893-1961)

The Flying Deuces (1939)

Other notable films: It Ain't Hay (1943) with Abbott and Costello; Sergeant York (1941) with Gary Cooper; Professor Beware (1938) with Harold Lloyd; You Can't Take It With You (1938) with James Stewart, directed by Frank Capra

WILLIAM HAADE (1903-1966)

The Dancing Masters (1943): Truck driver

Other notable films: Abbott & Costello Meet the Keystone Cops (1955) with Abbott and Costello; Father of the Bride (1950) with Spencer Tracy, Elizabeth Taylor; Key Largo (1948) with Humphrey Bogart; Buck Privates Come Home (1947) with Abbott & Costello; The Secret Life of Walter Mitty (1947) with Danny Kaye; I Married a Witch (1942) with Fredric March, Veronica Lake; The Spoilers (1942) with John Wayne; You're Tellin' Me (1942) with W.C. Fields; Sergeant York (1941) with Gary Cooper; The Grapes of Wrath (1940) with Henry Fonda

FRANK S. HAGNEY (1884-1973)

Pack Up Your Troubles (1932)

Other notable films: Gunfight at the O.K. Corral (1957) with Burt Lancaster, Kirk Douglas; Kettles on Old MacDonald's Farm (1957) with Marjorie Main; Friendly Persuasion (1956) with Gary Cooper; My Favorite Spy (1951) with Bob Hope; The Paleface (1948) with Bob Hope; Road to Rio (1947) with Bob Hope, Bing Crosby; Sea of Grass (1947) with Spencer Tracy; The Wistful Widow of Wagon Gap (1947) with Abbott and Costello; It's a Wonderful Life (1946) with James Stewart, directed by Frank Capra; Northwest Passage (1940) with Spencer Tracy; Angels with Dirty Faces (1938) with James Cagney, Humphrey Bogart; Professor Beware (1938) with Harold Lloyd; Treasure Island (1934) with Wallace Beery, Jackie Cooper; If I Had A Million (1932) with W.C. Fields

ALAN HALE, SR. (1892-1950)

Our Relations (1936): Joe Groagan, the waiter

Other notable films: The Adventures of Robin Hood (1938) with Errol Flynn; The Prince and the Pauper (1937); A Message to Garcia (1936) with Wallace Beery; Broadway Bill (1934) directed by Frank Capra; It Happened One Night (1934) with Clark Gable, Claudette Colbert

CHARLIE HALL (1890-1959)

Appeared 47 times with the Boys. Was a contestant twice on Groucho Marx's 'You Bet Your Life' T.V. game show in the 1950's.

Saps at Sea (1940): Desk clerk; A Chump at Oxford (1940): Hector; Pick a Star (1937); Our Relations(1936) Bonnie Scotland (1935); Thicker Than Water (1935): Bank teller; Tit for Tat (1935): Grocer; The Live Ghost (1934): Sailor; Them Thar Hills (1934): Mr. Hall; Busy Bodies (1933): Shop workman; Midnight Patrol (1933): Tire thief's partner; Me and My Pal (1933): Delivery boy; Twice Two (1933): Delivery boy; Pack Up Your Troubles (1932): Janitor; The Music Box (1932): Postman; Any Old Port (1932): Stan's second; On the Loose (1932); Beau Hunks (1931): New recruit number 13; Come Clean (1931): Soda jerk; Pardon Us (1931): Dental assistant; Laughing Gravy (1931):Landlord; Be Big (1931): Bellboy; Below Zero (1930): Street cleaner; Blotto (1930): Cabdriver; Angora Love (1929): Neighbor; The Hoose-Gow (1929): Look-out; Bacon Grabbers (1929); They Go Boom (1929): Landlord; Men O'War (1929): Boater; Berth Marks (1929): Train passenger; Double Whoopee (1929): Cabdriver; Big Business (1929): Neighbor; That's My Wife (1929): Waiter; Wrong Again (1929): Neighbor; Two Tars (1928): Shopkeeper; Should Married Men Go Home (1928); You're Darn Tootin' (1928): Musician; Leave 'Em Laughing (1928); The Battle of the Century (1927): Pie delivery man; Call of the Cuckoos (1927); The Second Hundred Years (1927); Sugar Daddies (1927); Love 'Em and Weep (1927)

Other notable films: Cockeyed Cavaliers (1934) with Wheeler & Woolsey; Diplomaniacs (1933) with Wheeler & Woolsey; Fallen Arches (1933), and Hold Your Temper

CHARLIE HALL *(continued)*
(1933) both with Charley Chase; Bear Shooters (1930) and Pups is Pups (1930) both with Our Gang; Skirt Shy (1930) with Harry Langdon; Boxing Gloves (1929) with Our Gang

SHERRY HALL
The Dancing Masters (1943)
Other notable films: Father of the Bride (1950) with Spencer Tracy, Elizabeth Taylor; They Were Expendable (1945) with John Wayne; Captains Courageous (1937) with Spencer Tracy; Libeled Lady (1936) with Myrna Loy, Spencer Tracy; San Francisco (1936) with Clark Gable; It Happened One Night (1934) with Clark Gable, Claudette Colbert, directed by Frank Capra, Best Picture winner; The Thin Man (1934) with William Powell, Myrna Loy

CHARLES HALTON (1876-1959)
Jitterbugs (1943): Cass; Pick a Star (1937): Malheimer
Other notable films: Friendly Persuasion (1956) with Gary Cooper; A Star is Born (1954) with Judy Garland; Three Godfathers (1948) with John Wayne; The Best Years of Our Lives (1946) with Fredric March; It's a Wonderful Life (1946) with James Stewart; Heaven Can Wait (1943) with Don Ameche; Saboteur (1942) with Bob Cummings, directed by Alfred Hitchcock; To Be or Not to Be (1942) with Jack Benny; Mr. & Mrs. Smith (1941), directed by Alfred Hitchcock; Tobacco Road (1941) with Charley Grapewin; Foreign Correspondent (1940) with Joel McCrea, directed by Alfred Hitchcock; Room Service (1938) with the Marx Bros.

CARL HARBAUGH (1885-1960)

The Devil's Brother (1933): Second woodchopper

Other notable films: High Sierra (1941) with Humphrey Bogart; Steamboat Bill, Jr. (1928) with Buster Keaton

JEAN HARLOW (1911-1937)

Bacon Grabbers (1929): Target's wife; Double Whoopee (1929): Swanky blonde; Liberty (1929): Woman in cab

** Note: Her photograph is used as 'Jeanie Weanie' in Beau Hunks and is seen on the mantelpiece in Brats*

Other notable films: Saratoga (1937) with Clark Gable; Libeled Lady (1936) with Myrna Loy, Spencer Tracy; Dinner at Eight (1933) with Lionel Barrymore; City Lights (1931) with Charlie Chaplin

PAT HARMON (1887-1958)

Berth marks (1929): Stationmaster; Pack Up Your Troubles (1932): Doughboy; Sons of the Desert (1933): Doorman

Other notable films: Mad Wednesday (1950) with Harold Lloyd, Franklin Pangborn; The Freshman (1925) with Harold Lloyd, Grady Sutton; Hot Water (1924) with Harold Lloyd

JACK HERRICK (1890-1952)

Pardon Us (1931)

Other notable films: The Gold Rush (1925) with Charlie Chaplin

FORRESTER HARVEY (1889-1945)

A Chump at Oxford (1940): Meredith

Other notable films: Mrs. Miniver (1942) with Greer Garson, Best Picture winner; This Above All (1942) with Tyrone Power; Meet John Doe (1941) with Gary Cooper, directed by Frank Capra; The Invisible Man Returns (1940) with Vincent Price; Rebecca(1940) with Joan Fontaine, directed by Alfred Hitchcock; The Private Lives of Elizabeth and Essex (1939) with Bette Davis, Errol Flynn; A Tale of Two Cities (1935) with Ronald Coleman; The Invisible Man (1933) with Claude Rains; Shanghai Express (1932) with Marlene Dietrich; Smilin' Through (1932) with Norma Shearer; Guilty Hands (1931) with Spencer Wilson , Lionel Barrymore; The Ring (1927), written and directed by Alfred Hitchcock

PAUL HARVEY (1884-1955)

Great Guns (1941): Gen. Essick

Other notable films: Sabrina (1954) with Audrey Hepburn; Father's Little Dividend (1951); and Father of the Bride (1950) both with Spencer Tracy, Elizabeth Taylor; Riding High (1950) with Oliver Hardy, Bing Crosby; Stella (1950) with Joan Fontaine; The Horn Blows at Midnight (1945) with Jack Benny, Robert Blake; The Southerner (1945); Spellbound (1945) with Gregory Peck, directed by Alfred Hitchcock; State Fair (1945) with Vivian Blaine; High Sierra (1941) with Humphrey Bogart; Algiers (1938) with Charles Boyer; The Petrified Forest (1936) with Humphrey Bogart, Bette Davis; Broadway Bill (1934) directed by Frank Capra; The Awful Truth (1932) with Cary Grant, Irene Dunne

HARRY HAYDEN (1882-1955)

The Big Noise (1944): Butler; Saps at Sea (1940): Mr. Sharp

Other notable films: Abbott & Costello Meet the Killer, Boris Karloff (1949) with Abbott and Costello; Out of the Past (1947) with Robert Mitchum; Notorious (1946) with Cary Grant, Ingrid Bergman, directed by Alfred Hitchcock; The Ziegfeld Follies (1946) with William Powell; Hail the Conquering Hero (1944) directed by Preston Sturges; Since You Went Away (1944) with Claudette Colbert; Thirty Seconds over Tokyo (1944) with Spencer Tracy; True to Life (1943) directed by George Marshall; The Palm Beach Story (1942) with Claudette Colbert; Tales of Manhattan (1942) with Henry Fonda, Charles Boyer; This Gun for Hire (1942); Yankee Doodle Dandy (1942) with James Cagney; High Sierra (1941) with Humphrey Bogart; Hold That Ghost (1941) with Abbott & Costello; Christmas in July (1940) with Dick Powell, directed by Preston Sturges; The Great McGinty (1940) directed by Preston Sturges; I Love You Again (1940) with William Powell, Myrna Loy; Angels with Dirty Faces (1938) with Humphrey Bogart, James Cagney; In Old Chicago (1938) with Tyrone Power; College Holiday (1936) with Burns & Allen, Jack Benny; The Fury (1936) with Spencer Tracy

DELL HENDERSON (1883-1956)

Our Relations (1936): Judge Polk; The Laurel-Hardy Murder Case (1930): Transvestite; Wrong Again (1929): Millionaire owner of 'Blue Boy'

Other notable films: State of the Union (1948) with Spencer Tracy, Katharine Hepburn; A Message to Garcia (1936) with Wallace Beery; Poppy (1936) with W.C. Fields; Ruggles of Red Gap (1935) with Charlie Ruggles; Mrs. Wiggs of the Cabbage Patch (1934), and You're Telling Me (1934) both with W.C. Fields

BEN HENDRICKS, JR. (1893-1938)

Pack Up Your Troubles (1932)

Other notable films: Angels With Dirty Faces (1938) with James Cagney, Humphrey Bogart; Stage Door (1937) with Katharine Hepburn, Ginger Rogers; Dr. Socrates (1935) with Paul Mini; Little Caesar (1930) with Edward G. Robinson

CHARLOTTE HENRY (1913-1980)

Babes in Toyland (1934): Bo-Peep

Other notable films: Alice in Wonderland (1933) with Cary Grant, W.C. Fields

JACK HERRICK (1890-1952)

Pardon Us (1931)

Other notable films: The Cat's Paw (1934) with Harold Lloyd; The Gold Rush (1925) with Charlie Chaplin

RUSSELL HICKS (1895-1957)

Air Raid Wardens (1943): Major Scanion; Great Guns (1941): Gen. Burns; Pick a Star (1937): J. Aubrey Stone

Other notable films: As You Were (1951) produced by Hal Roach, Jr.; Samson and Delilah (1950)directed by Cecille B. DeMille; The Noose Hangs High (1948); Scarlet Street (1945) with Edward G. Robinson; Valley of Decision (1945) with Greer Garson; Ride 'em Cowboy (1942) with Abbott and Costello; Hold That Ghost (1941) with Abbott and Costello; The Big Store (1941) with the Marx Bros.; Little Foxes (1941) with Bette Davis; Man Betrayed (1941) with John Wayne; Sergeant York (1941) with Gary Cooper; The Bank Dick (1940) with W.C. Fields; Hollywood Cavalcade (1939) with Buster Keaton; Stanley and Livingstone (1939) with Spencer Tracy; The Three Musketeers (1939) with Don Ameche; In Old Chicago (1938) with Tyrone Power; You Can't Take It With You (1938) with James Stewart, directed by Frank Capra; The Big Broadcast of 1938 (1937) with W.C. Fields, Bob Hope; The Toast of New York (1937) with Cary Grant; Mr. Deeds Goes to Town (1936) with Gary Cooper, directed by Frank Capra

FRANK HOLLIDAY

County Hospital (1932): Hospital visitor; Pardon Us (1931): Officer in classroom; Chickens Come Home (1931): Dinner guest; Blotto (1930): Singer; Below Zero (1930): Cop

Other notable films: It Happened One Night (1934) with Clark Gable, Claudette Colbert; The Pip from Pittsburgh (1930) with Charley Chase

FRED HOLMES

Our Relations (1936): Bailiff; Going Bye-Bye! (1934); Wrong Again(1929): Stableboy; Two Tars (1928): Motorist

Other notable films: If I Had a Million (1932) with W.C. Fields

ROBERT E. HOMANS (1875-1947)

Nothing But Trouble (1944): Jailer;
Pack Up Your Troubles (1932): Detective

Other notable films: They Were Expendable (1945) with John Wayne; It Ain't Hay (1943) with Abbott and Costello; Holiday Inn (1942); The Spoilers (1942) and Reap the Wild Wind (1942) both with John Wayne; The Maltese Falcon (1941) with Humphrey Bogart; The Grapes of Wrath (1940) with Henry Fonda; Stagecoach (1939) with John Wayne, directed by John Ford; Angels with Dirty Faces (1938) with James Cagney, Humphrey Bogart; A Star Is Born (1937) with Janet Gaynor; The Fury (1936) with Spencer Tracy; The Whole Town's Talking (1935) with Edward G. Robinson; The Thin Man (1934) with William Powell, Myrna Loy; She Done Him Wrong (1933) with Mae West, Cary Grant; If I Had a Million (1932) with W.C. Fields

DARLA HOOD (1931-1979)

The Bohemian Girl (1936): Arline as child

Other notable films: Little Rascals' Christmas Special (1979): Cartoon voice of Miss Crabtree; Our Gang comedies (1935-1941)

ARTHUR HOUSMAN (1890-1942)

Our Relations (1936): Inebriated stroller; The Fixer Uppers (1935): The drunk; The Live Ghost (1934): Drunk sailor; Scram (1932)

Other notable films: Go West (1940) with the Marx Bros.; Step Lively, Jeeves (1937) with Arthur Treacher, David Niven; Show Boat (1936) with Irene Dunne; The Count of Monte Cristo (1934); Mrs. Wiggs of the Cabbage Patch (1934) with W.C. Fields; She Done Him Wrong (1933) with Mae West, Cary Grant; Punch Drunks (1934) with Three Stooges; Movie Crazy (1932) with Harold Lloyd

ESTHER HOWARD (1892-1965)

The Big Noise (1944): Aunt Sophie

Other notable films: Hail the Conquering Hero (1944) directed by Preston Sturges; The Miracle of Morgan's Creek (1944) directed by Preston Sturges; My Favorite Blonde (1942) with Bob Hope; The Palm Beach Story (1942) with Claudette Colbert; Sullivan's Travels (1941) with Joel McCrea, directed by Preston Sturges

JOHN E. INCE (1879-1947)

Way Out West (1937)

Other notable films: Here Comes Mr. Jordan (1941) with Robert Montgomery; Meet John Doe (1941) with Gary Cooper, directed by Frank Capra; Hollywood Cavalcade (1939) with Don Ameche, Buster Keaton; Mr. Smith Goes to Washington (1939) with James Stewart, directed by Frank Capra; You Can't Take It With You (1938) with James Stewart, directed by Frank Capra; Grand Slam Opera

JOHN E. INCE *(continued)*

(1936) with Buster Keaton; Three on a Limb (1936) with Buster Keaton; The Cat's Paw (1934) with Harold Lloyd

WILLIAM IRVING (1893-1943)

You're Darn Tootin' (1928): Band Stand musician

Other notable films: My Favorite Blonde (1942) with Bob Hope; Ninotchka (1939) with Greta Garbo; Idiot's Delight (1939) with Norma Shearer, Clark Gable; Calling All Doctors (1937) with Charley Chase; Whoops, I'm an Indian (1936), Hoi Polloi (1935), Pop Goes the Easel (1935), Restless Knights (1935) and the Three Little Pigskins (1934) all with the Three Stooges; The Cat's Paw (1934) with Harold Lloyd; Diplomaniacs (1933) with Wheeler & Woolsey; Tillie and Gus (1933) with W.C. Fields

SELMAR JACKSON (1888-1971)

The Big Noise (1944): Manning

Other notable films: Mighty Joe Young (1949); Sorrowful Jones (1949) with Bob Hope; The Fuller Brush Man (1948) with Red Skelton, Buster Keaton; The Time of Their Lives (1946) with Abbott and Costello; It Ain't Hay (1943) with Abbott and Costello; My Favorite Spy (1942) with Bob Hope; Saboteur (1942) with Bob Cummings, directed by Alfred Hitchcock; Buck Privates (1941) with Abbott and Costello; Here Comes Mr. Jordan (1941) with Robert Montgomery; Love Crazy (1941) with William Powell, Myrna Loy; Meet John Doe (1941) with Gary Cooper, directed by Frank Capra; Sergeant York (1941) with Gary Cooper; The Grapes of Wrath (1940) with

SELMAR JACKSON *(continued)*

Henry Fonda; Libeled Lady (1936) with Spencer Tracy, Myrna Loy; My Man Godfrey (1936) with Carole Lombard; A Night at the Opera (1935) with the Marx Brothers

ED JOHNSON

Swiss Miss (1938): Bellboy at the Alpen hotel

Other notable films: My Favorite Brunette (1947) with Bob Hope

CHARLES JUDELS (1882-1969)

Swiss Miss (1938): Emile

Other notable films: Samson and Delilah (1950), directed by Cecil B. DeMille; Walt Disney's Pinocchio (1940): Cartoon voice of Stromboli; Idiot's Delight (1939) with Norma Shearer, Clark Gable; San Francisco (1936) with Clark Gable

EDDIE KANE (1887-1969)

Swiss Miss (1938): Village tradesman; Pick A Star (1937): Albert, Headwaiter

Other notable films: Meet John Doe (1941) with Gary Cooper, directed by Frank Capra; Mr. Smith Goes to Washington (1939) and You Can't Take It With You (1938) both with James Stewart and both directed by Frank Capra; A Star Is Born (1937) with Janet Gaynor, Fredric March; It Happened One Night (1934) with Clark Gable, Claudette Colbert, directed by Frank Capra; The Mummy (1932) with Boris Karloff

BORIS KARLOFF (1887-1969)

Pardon Us (1931) In French version of film

Other notable films: How The Grinch Stole Christmas (1965) Narrator and voice of the Grinch in the Chuck Jones' classic cartoon; Abbott & Costello Meet Dr. Jekyll & Mr. Hyde (1952) and Abbott & Costello Meet the Killer, Boris Karloff (1949) both with Abbott & Costello; The Secret Life of Walter Mitty (1947) with Danny Kaye; House of Rothschild (1934) with George Arliss; The Mummy (1932); Cracked Nuts (1931) with Wheeler & Woolsey; Frankenstein (1931); Scarface (1931) with Paul Muni

ROBERT EMMETT KEANE (1883-1981)

The Dancing Masters (1943): Auctioneer; Jitterbugs (1943): Henry Corcoran; A-Haunting We Will Go (1942): Phillips

Other notable films: My Favorite Blonde (1942) with Bob Hope; Abbott & Costello in the Navy (1941) with Abbott & Costello; The Devil and Daniel Webster (1941) with Walter Huston; The Devil and Miss Jones (1941) with Bob Cummings; High Sierra (1941) with Humphrey Bogart; Mr. & Mrs. Smith (1941) directed by Alfred Hitchcock; Mr. Smith Goes to Washington (1939) with James Stewart, directed by Frank Capra; Pack up Your Troubles (1939) with the Ritz Bros.; Boys Town (1938) with Spencer Tracy; Saratoga (1937) with Clark Gable, Jean Harlow

CORNELIUS KEEFE (1900-1972)

Saps at Sea (1940); Swiss Miss (1938); Pick a Star (1937): Dress extra; Way Out West (1937): Worker at Mickey Finn's; Our Relations (1936); The Devil's Brother (1933); Pack Up Your Troubles (1932): New recruit;

CORNELIUS KEEFE *(continued)*

Pack Up Your Troubles (1932): Pedestrian; Pardon Us (1931)

Other notable films: Stagecoach (1939) with John Wayne; The Whole Town's Talking (1935) with Edward G. Robinson; Treasure Island (1934) with Wallace Beery, Jackie Cooper; Three's a Crowd (1927) with Harry Langdon

JOHN KELLY (1900-1947)

Our Relations (1936): First Mate

Other notable films: My Little Chickadee (1940) with W.C. Fields; Bringing Up Baby (1938) with Cary Grant, Katharine Hepburn; San Francisco (1936) with Clark Gable

FRED KELSEY (1884-1961)

Was type-cast as a comedy cop so firmly throughout his career, that in the 1944 MGM cartoon classic 'Who Killed Who?' animator Tex Avery deliberately designed his detective to look like Kelsey.

The Laurel-Hardy Murder Case (1930)

Other notable films: The Noose Hangs High (1948) with Abbott & Costello; Christmas in Connecticut (1945) with Barbara Stanwyck; If A Body Meets A Body (1945) with The Three Stooges; King's Row (1942) with Ronald Reagan; My Favorite Blonde (1942) with Bob Hope; Yankee Doodle Dandy (1942) with James Cagney; If I Had a Million (1932) with W.C. Fields

EDGAR KENNEDY (1890-1948)

Comedian acknowledged as master of the "slow burn" when antagonized; brother is actor Tom Kennedy.

Air Raid Wardens (1943): Joe Bledsoe; Night Owls (1930): Officer Kennedy; Angora Love (1929): Landlord; Bacon Grabbers (1929): Uncle Edgar; Unaccustomed As We Are (1929): Officer Kennedy; Should Married Men Go Home (1928): Golfer; The Finishing Touch (1928): Cop; Leave 'Em Laughing (1928): Cop

Other notable films: Unfaithfully Yours (1948) with Rex Harrison; The Sin of Harold Diddlebock (1947) with Harold Lloyd; It's a Wonderful World (1939) with Claudette Colbert, James Stewart; Peck's Bad Boy with the Circus (1938) with Spanky McFarland; A Star is Born (1937) with Janet Gaynor, Fredric March; San Francisco (1936) with Clark Gable; Twentieth Century (1934) with Carol Lombard; Diplomaniacs (1933) with Wheeler & Woolsey; Duck Soup (1933) with the Marx Bros.; Tillie and Gus (1933) with W.C. Fields; Hold 'em Jail (1932) with Wheeler & Woolsey; Better 'ole (1926) with Sydney Chaplin (Charlie's half-brother); Oh, What a Nurse (1926) with Sydney Chaplin; Tillie's Punctured Romance (1914) with Charlie Chaplin, Milton Berle

TOM KENNEDY (1884-1965)

The older brother of comedian Edgar Kennedy

Hollywood Party (1934): Beavers, the doorman; Pack Up Your Troubles (1932): Recruiting sergeant; Liberty (1929): Prison warden

Other notable films: It's A Mad, Mad, Mad, Mad World (1963) with Spencer Tracy; Some Like It Hot (1959) with Tony Curtis, Jack Lemmon, Marilyn Monroe, directed by Billy Wilder; The Paleface (1948) with Bob Hope, Jane Russell; The Princess and the Pirate (1944) with Bob Hope, Virginia Mayo; Poppy (1936) with W.C. Fields; If I Had a Million (1932) with W.C. Fields; Monkey Business (1931) with the Marx Bros.; Tillie's Punctured Romance (1928) with W. C. Fields

WALTER WOOLF KING (1899-1984)

Swiss Miss (1938): Victor Albert

Other notable films: The Ten Commandments (1956) with Charlton Heston; Go West (1940) and A Night At The Opera (1935) both with the Marx Bros.

BOB KORTMAN (1887-1967)

On The Wrong Trek (1936): Hold-up man; Beau Hunks (1931): New recruit; The Midnight Patrol (1933): Tries to steal police car spare tire; Pardon Us (1931); Duck Soup (1927)

Other notable films: Fancy Pants (1950) with Bob Hope, Lucille Ball; Samson and Delilah (1950) directed by Cecil B. DeMille; Sorrowful Jones (1949); and The Paleface (1948) both with Bob Hope; You Can't Take It With You (1938) with James Stewart, directed by Frank Capra; The

BOB KORTMAN *(continued)*

Trail of the Lonesome Pine (1936) with Henry Fonda, Fred MacMurray, Spanky McFarland

ADIA KUZNETZOFF (1889-1954)

Swiss Miss (1938): Franzelhuber

Other notable films: Lost In A Harem (1944) with Abbott and Costello; The Princess and the Pirate (1944) with Bob Hope, Virginia Mayo; For Whom The Bell Tolls (1943) with Gary Cooper

ALAN LADD (1913-1964)

Great Guns (1941): Soldier

Other notable films: Saskatchewan (1954); Shane (1953), Oscar winner for best cinematography; Lucky Jordan (1942); Star Spangled Rhythm (1942); This Gun For Hire (1942); Citizen Kane (1941) with Orson Wells; Helltown (1938) with John Wayne; Pigskin Parade (1936) with Jack Haley, Judy Garland; Island of Lost Souls (1932) with Charles Laughton; Once in a Lifetime (1932) with Zazu Pitts

FLORENCE LAKE (1904-1980)

The Rogue Song (1930): Nadja

Other notable films: The Day of the Locust (1975) with Donald Sutherland; Little Giant (1946) with Abbott and Costello; Stagecoach (1939) with John Wayne, directed by John Ford

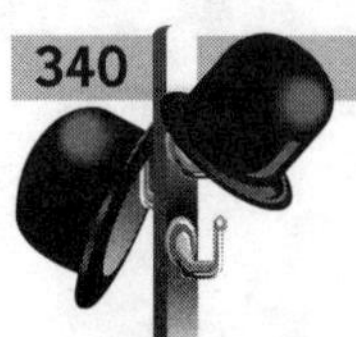

RICHARD LANE (1899-1940)

The Bullfighters (1945): Hot Shot Coleman; A-Haunting We Will Go (1942): Parker

Other notable films: Here Come the Co-Eds (1945) with Abbott and Costello; It Ain't Hay (1943) with Abbott and Costello; Bringing up Baby (1938) with Cary Grant, Katharine Hepburn

JUNE LANG (1915-)

Bonnie Scotland (1935): Lorna McLaurel

Other notable films: Zenobia (1939) with Oliver Hardy, Harry Langdon; Wee Willie Winkle (1937) with Shirley Temple

ROSE LANGDON (1881-1962)

Our Relations (1936)

Other notable films: National Velvet (1944) with Mickey Rooney, Elizabeth Taylor

ROSINA LAWRENCE (1912-1997)

Appeared as the teacher in 'Our Gang' comedies (1936-1937). Married to Laurel & Hardy biographer, John McCabe

Pick A Star (1937): Cecila Moore; Way Out West (1937): Mary Roberts; On the Wrong Trek (1936)

Other notable films: General Spanky (1936) with Spanky McFarland, Carl 'Alfafa' Switzer, produced by Hal Roach; On the Wrong Trek (1936); Kelly the Second (1936) with Charley Chase; The Great Ziegfeld (1936) with Myrna Loy, William Powell

REX LEASE (1901-1966)

A Chump at Oxford (1940): Bank robber

Other notable films: Abbott & Costello Go to Mars (1953), Abbott & Costello Meet Captain Kidd (1952), Lost in Alaska (1952) all with Abbott and Costello; Ma and Pa Kettle at the Fair (1952), Ma and Pa Kettle Go to Town (1950), Ma and Pa Kettle (1949) all with Marjorie Main, Percy Kilbride; The Wistful Widow of Wagon Gap (1947); The Time of Their Lives (1946) and Naughty Nineties (1945) both with Abbott and Costello; In Old California (1942) with John Wayne; Saboteur (1942) with Bob Cummings, directed by Alfred Hitchcock; The Grapes of Wrath (1940) with Henry Fonda; Professor Beware (1938) with Harold Lloyd

OTTO LEDERER (1885-1965)

You're Darn Tootin' (1928): Orchestra leader

Other notable films: The Jazz Singer (1927) with Al Jolsen (first talking picture); The Wizard of Oz (1925) with Oliver Hardy, Larry Semon

GUS LEONARD (1855-1939)

Babes in Toyland (1934): Candle snuffer

Other notable films: Maytime (1937) with Nelson Eddy, Jeanette MacDonald; The Milky Way (1936) with Harold Lloyd; The Petrified Forest (1936) with Humphrey Bogart, Bette Davis; Movie Crazy (1932), Speedy (1928), Kid Brother (1927), The Freshman (1925), Safety Last (1923), Grandma's Boy (1922), and Sailor-Made Man (1921) all with Harold Lloyd

MITCHELL LEWIS (1879-1956)

The Bohemian Girl (1936): Salinas

Other notable films: Meet John Doe (1941) with Gary Cooper, directed by Frank Capra; Go West (1940) with the Marx Bros.; Idiot's Delight (1939) with Clark Gable, Norma Shearer; The Wizard of Oz (1939) with Judy Garland, Jack Haley

LUCIEN LITTLEFIELD (1895-1960)

Sons of the Desert (1933): Dr. Horace Meddick;
Dirty Work (1933): Professor Noodle

Other notable films: In Old Sacramento (1946) with Robert Blake, Ellen Corby; Little Foxes (1941); Early to Bed (1936) with Charlie Ruggles, written by Littlefield; The Man on the Flying Trapeze (1935) with W.C. Fields, Grady Sutton; Ruggles of Red Gap (1935) with Charlie Ruggles, directed by Leo McCarey ; Alice in Wonderland (1933) with W.C. Fields; If I Had a Million (1932) with W.C. Fields; Tom Sawyer (1930) with Jackie Coogan; My Best Girl (1927) with Mary Pickford; Charley's Aunt (1925) with Sydney Chaplin (Charlie's half-brother); Round Up (1920) with Fatty Arbuckle; Joan the Woman (1916) directed by Cecil B. DeMille

GEORGE LLOYD

The Dancing Masters (1943): Jasper

Other notable films: The Fuller Brush Girl (1950) with Lucille Ball; The Egg & I (1947) with Fred MacMurray, Claudette Colbert; My Favorite Brunette (1947) with Bob Hope; The Secret Life of Walter Mitty (1947) with Danny Kaye; Destination Tokyo (1943); The Ox-Bow Incident

GEORGE LLOYD *(continued)*

(1943) with Henry Fonda; Road to Morocco (1942) with Bob Hope, Bing Crosby; Slight Case of Murder (1938) with Edward G. Robinson

JEAN 'BABE' LONDON (1900-1980)

Our Wife (1931): Dulcy

Other notable films: The Paleface (1948) with Bob Hope; Road to Rio (1947) with Bob Hope, Bing Crosby; Tillie's Punctured Romance (1928) with W.C. Fields

WALTER LONG (1879-1952)

Pick a Star (1937); The Live Ghost (1934): Captain; Going Bye-Bye! (1934): Butch; Any Old Port (1932): Mugsy Long; Pardon Us (1931): the Tiger

Other notable films: Three Little Pigskins (1934) with the Three Stooges; Six of a Kind (1934) with W.C. Fields; The Thin Man (1934) with William Powell, Myrna Loy; I Am a Fugitive from a Chain Gang (1932) with Paul Mini; The Maltese Falcon (1931) with Humphrey Bogart; The Birth of a Nation (1916) directed by D. W. Griffith

LOU LUBIN

A-Haunting We Will Go (1942): Dixie Beeler

Other notable films: Pat & Mike (1952) with Spencer Tracy, Katharine Hepburn; They Got Me Covered (1943) with Bob Hope; Saboteur (1942) with Bob Cummings, directed by Alfred Hitchcock

WILFRED LUCAS (1871-1940)

A Chump At Oxford (1940): Dean Williams; The Devil's Brother (1933): Allessandro; Pardon Us (1931): The Warden

Other notable films: Sea Wolf (1941) with Edward G. Robinson; They Drive By Night (1940) with Humphrey Bogart; Waterloo Bridge (1940) with Vivien Leigh; Accidents Will Happen (1939) with Ronald Reagan; The Adventures of Robin Hood (1938) with Errol Flynn; Angels with Dirty Faces (1938) with James Cagney, Humphrey Bogart; Charge of the Light Brigade (1936) with Errol Flynn; Modern Times (1936) with Charlie Chaplin; The Story of Louis Pasteur (1936) with Paul Muni; Cracked Nuts (1931) with Wheeler & Woolsey

SAM LUFKIN (1892-1952)

Saps at Sea (1940); A Chump at Oxford (1940): Water wagon driver; The Flying Deuces (1939): Legionnaire knocked out by corks; Block-Heads (1938): Veteran; Swiss Miss (1938); Pick a Star (1938): Mexican hit with a chair; Way Out West (1937): Stagecoach baggage man; Our Relations (1936); The Bohemian Girl (1936): Shopkeeper, guard, Pickpocket victim; The Live Ghost (1934): Sailor; Them Thar Hills (1934): Man with warning; Sons of the Desert (1933); Scram (1932): Policeman; County Hospital (1932): Policeman; Any Old Port (1932): Referee; The Music Box (1932): Policeman; Pardon Us (1931); The Hoose-Gow (1929): Prison camp officer; Bacon Grabbers (1929); They Go Boom (1929): Policeman; Double Whoopee (1929): Man poked in eye; That's My Wife (1929): Waiter; Wrong Again (1929): Sullivan; Liberty (1929); Two Tars (1928): Pedestrian, motorist

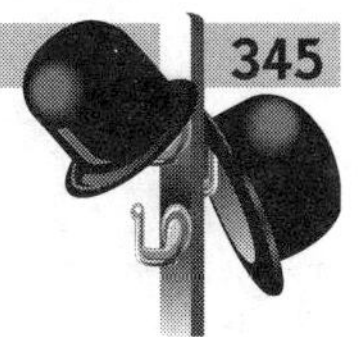

SAM LUFKIN *(continued)*

Should Married Men Go Home (1928); Their Purple Moment (1928): Waiter; You're Darn Tootin (1928): Man in restaurant; From Soup to Nuts (1928); The Finishing Touch (1928); The Battle of the Century (1927); Putting Pants on Philip (1927); Hats Off (1927); Sugar Daddies (1927)

Other notable films: Tycoon (1947) with John Wayne; Goofs and Saddles (1937) and Grips, Grunts and Groans (1937) both with Three Stooges; Life Hesitates at 40 (1936) with Charley Chase; Man on the Flying Trapeze (1935) with W.C. Fields; Six of a Kind (1934) with W.C. Fields; Part Time Wife (1930) directed by Leo McCarey; Speedy (1928) with Harold Lloyd, Babe Ruth; Why Worry? (1923) with Harold Lloyd; A Pleasant Journey (1923) with Our Gang

GEORGE LYNN

A-Haunting We Will Go (1942): Darby Mason

Other notable films: The Day the Earth Stood Still (1951); My Favorite Spy (1951) with Bob Hope; Notorious (1946) with Cary Grant, Ingrid Bergman, directed by Alfred Hitchcock; To Be or Not to Be (1942) with Jack Benny

EDMUND MacDONALD (1810-1951)

Great Guns (1941): Hippo

Other notable films: The Flying Tigers (1942) with John Wayne; Who Done It? (1942) with Abbott & Costello

WALLACE MacDONALD (1891-1978)

The Rogue Song (1930): Hassan

Other notable films: Tillie's Punctured Romance (1914) with Charlie Chaplin, Milton Berle

JAMES T. MACK (1870-1948)

Bonnie Scotland (1935): Butler

Other notable films: Libeled Lady (1936) with Myrna Loy, Spencer Tracy

NOEL MADISON (1898-1975)

Jitterbugs (1943): Tony Queen; Our Relations (1936): Gangsters

Other notable films: Little Caesar (1930) with Edward G. Robinson

JERRY MANDY (1892-1945)

Pardon Us (1931): Convict who can't add; With Love and Kisses (1927): Soldier with appetite; Forty-five Minutes From Hollywood (1926): Trashman

Other notable films: One Night in the Tropics (1940) with Abbott and Costello; It's a Gift (1934) with W.C. Fields

HANK MANN (1888-1971)

The Dancing Masters (1943): Vegetable Man

Other notable films: Man of a Thousand Faces; Abbott & Costello Meet the Keystone Cops (1955) and Abbott & Costello Meet the Mummy (1955) both with Abbott & Costello; Son of Paleface (1952) and My Favorite Spy (1951) both Bob Hope; Arsenic and Old Lace (1944) with Cary Grant, directed by Frank Capra; George Washington Slept Here (1942) with Jack Benny; King's Row (1942) with Ronald Reagan; The Maltese Falcon (1941) with Humphrey Bogart; The Man Who Came to Dinner (1941) with Gary Cooper; Meet John Doe (1941) with Gary Cooper, directed by Frank Capra; Saratoga (1937) with Clark Gable, Jean Harlow; Modern Times (1936) with Charlie Chaplin; Million Dollar Legs (1932) with W.C. Fields; City Lights (1931) with Charlie Chaplin; Tillie's Punctured Romance (1914) with Charlie Chaplin, Milton Berle

MICHAEL MARK (1886-1975)

Swiss Miss (1938): Astonished Swiss villager

Other notable films: She Done Him Wrong (1933) with Mae West, Cary Grant; Frankenstein (1931) with Boris Karloff

MAE MARSH (1895-1968)

Great Guns (1941): Aunt Martha

Other notable films: Donovan's Reef (1963) with John Wayne, Lee Marvin, directed by John Ford; The Searchers (1956) with John Wayne, Natalie Wood; A Star Is Born (1954) with Judy Garland, directed by George Cukor; The

MAE MARSH *(continued)*

Robe (1953) with Richard Burton; The Titanic (1953) with Clifton Webb, Barbara Stanwyck; The Quiet Man (1952) with John Wayne; The Model and the Marriage Broker (1951) directed by George Cukor; The Gunfighter (1950) with Gregory Peck; The Fighting Kentuckian (1949) with John Wayne, Oliver Hardy; It Happens Every Spring (1949) with Ray Milland; Fort Apache (1948) with John Wayne, Henry Fonda; Three Godfathers (1948) with John Wayne; Leave Her To Heaven (1946) with Gene Tierney; My Darling Clementine (1946) with Henry Fonda; A Tree Grows in Brooklyn (1945); Jane Eyre (1944) with Joan Fontaine, Orson Welles; Song of Bernadette (1943) with Jennifer Jones; Tales of Manhattan (1942) with Charles Boyer; How Green Was My Valley (1942) directed by John Ford; The Grapes of Wrath (1940) with Henry Fonda; Drums Along the Mohawk (1939) with Henry Fonda, directed by John Ford; Alice in Wonderland (1933) with W.C. Fields; White Rose (1923); Intolerance(1916), Birth of a Nation (1915), Mother and the Law (1914) and Judith of Bethulia (1914) with Lillian Gish, all directed by D.W. Griffith

GEORGE MARSHALL (1891-1975)

Pack Up Your Troubles (1932): Cook, also directed by Marshall; Their First Mistake (1932): Neighbor, also directed by Marshall; Towed in a Hole (1932) directed by Marshall

Other notable films he directed: Hook, Line and Sinker (1969) with Jerry Lewis; Boy, Did I Get A Wrong Number (1966) with Bob Hope; How the West Was Won (1963) with Henry Fonda, Gregory Peck; Papa's Delicate

GEORGE MARSHALL *(continued)*

Condition (1963); The Sad Sack (1957) with Jerry Lewis; Money from Home (1953), Scared Stiff (1953), and My Friend Irma (1949), all with Dean Martin, Jerry Lewis; Murder, He Says (1945) with Fred MacMurray, Marjorie Main; The Ghost Breakers (1940) with Bob Hope, You Can't Cheat An Honest Man (1939) with W.C. Fields; A Message to Garcia (1936) with Wallace Beery

TRUDY MARSHALL (1922-)

The Dancing Masters (1943): Mary Harlan

Other notable films: The Fuller Brush Man (1948) with Red Skelton, Buster Keaton; Heaven Can Wait (1943) with Don Ameche

CHARLES McAVOY (1884-1953)

Sons of the Desert (1933)

Other notable films: My Favorite Blonde (1942) with Bob Hope; The Mad Doctor (1941) with Basil Rathbone; Meet John Doe (1941) with Gary Cooper, directed by Frank Capra

PHILO McCULLOUGH (1893-1981)

Sons of the Desert (1933): Assistant Exhausted Ruler

Other notable films: They Shoot Horses, Don't They? (1969) with Jane Fonda; Lady Godiva (1955) with Henry Brandon, Clint Eastwood, Maureen O'Hara; Father of the Bride (1950) with Spencer Tracy, Elizabeth Taylor; Samson and Delilah (1950) directed by Cecil B. De Mille; Bedtime for Bonzo (1951) with Ronald Reagan; Life with Father (1947) with William Powell, Elizabeth Taylor; Possessed

PHILO McCULLOUGH *(continued)*

(1947) with Joan Crawford; Hail the Conquering Hero (1944) directed by Preston Sturges; Love Crazy (1941) with William Powell, Myrna Loy; Destry Rides Again (1939) with James Stewart; Mr. Smith Goes to Washington (1939) with James Stewart, directed by Frank Capra; Captains Courageous (1937) with Spencer Tracy; Dick Turpin (1925) with Tom Mix

MATT McHUGH (1894-1971)

The Devil's Brother (1933)

Other notable films: My Favorite Brunette (1947) with Bob Hope; The Bell's of St. Mary's (1945) with Bing Crosby, directed by Leo McCarey; The Pride of the Yankees (1942) with Gary Cooper; The Devil and Miss Jones (1941); Mr. Smith Goes to Washington (1939) with James Stewart, directed by Frank Capra; Professor Beware (1938) with Harold Lloyd

BOB McKENZIE

Saps at Sea (1940): Captain McKenzie

Other notable films: Duel in the Sun (1946) with Gregory Peck, Joseph Cotten; The More The Merrier (1943) directed by George Stevens; The Spoilers (1942) with John Wayne; My Little Chickadee (1940) with W.C. Fields, Mae West; Destry Rides Again (1939) with James Stewart; San Francisco (1936) with Clark Gable; Mississippi (1935) with W.C. Fields, Bing Crosby; Six of a Kind (1934) with W.C. Fields, Burns & Allen, Charlie Ruggles; You're Telling

BOB McKENZIE *(continued)*

Me (1934) with W.C. Fields; Old-Fashioned Way (1934) with W.C. Fields; Viva Villa (1934) with Wallace Beery; Tillie and Gus (1933) with W.C. Fields

CHARLES McMURPHY (1891-1969)

Pick A Star (1937); Below Zero (1930): Grubby extra in restaurant; Hog Wild (1930): Streetcar conductor; Night Owls (1930): Officer; Two Tars (1928): Countryside motorist

Other notable films: The Spoilers (1942) with John Wayne; You're Telling Me (1942) with W.C. Fields; Love Crazy (1941) with William Powell, Myrna Loy; Never Give a Sucker an Even Break (1941) and My Little Chickadee (1940) both with W.C. Fields, Mae West; You Can't Take It With You (1938) with James Stewart, directed by Frank Capra; The Milky Way (1936) with Harold Lloyd; Poppy (1936) with W.C. Fields; If I Had a Million (1932) with W.C. Fields

PHILIP MERIVALE (1886-1946)

Nothing But Trouble (1944): Prince Saul

Other notable films: The Stranger (1946) with Orson Welles; Mr. & Mrs. Smith (1941) directed by Alfred Hitchcock

JOHN MERTON (1901-1959)

Sons of the Desert (1933)

Other notable films: The Ten Commandments (1956) with Charlton Heston; The Greatest Show on Earth (1952) with Charlton Heston; Gold Raiders (1951) with The Three Stooges; Samson and Delilah (1950) directed by

JOHN MERTON *(continued)*
Cecil B. DeMille; Gilda (1946) with Rita Hayworth; Northwest Passage (1940) with Spencer Tracy; Knights of the Plains (1939) produced by Stan Laurel; Running Wild (1927) with W.C. Fields; It's the Old Army Game (1926) with W.C. Fields

BUDDY MESSINGER (1906-1965)
Our Relations (1936)
Other notable films: Idiot's Delight (1939) with Norma Shearer, Clark Gable; College Holiday (1936) with Jack Benny, Burns & Allen

GERTRUDE MESSINGER (1893-1940)
Our Relations (1936)
Other notable films: The Greatest Show on Earth (1952) with Charlton Heston; Samson and Delilah (1950) directed by Cecil B. DeMille; Sunset Boulevard (1950) with Gloria Swanson, William Holden, directed by Billy Wilder

CHARLES MIDDLETON (1879-1949)
Flying Deuces ((1939): Commandant;
Pack Up Your Troubles (1932)
Other notable films: Road to Rio (1947) with Bob Hope, Bing Crosby; Sea of Grass (1947) with Spencer Tracy; Sergeant York (1941) with Gary Cooper; Purple Death from Outer Space (1940), a Flash Gordon Serial with Buster Crabbe; Good Earth (1937) with Paul Mini; Spaceship to the Unknown (1936), a Flash Gordon Serial with Buster Crabbe; The Trail of the Lonesome Pine (1936) with Henry Fonda, Fred MacMurray, Spanky

CHARLES MIDDLETON *(continued)*

MacFarland; Mrs. Wiggs of the Cabbage Patch (1934) with W.C. Fields; Duck Soup (1933) with the Marx Bros., directed by Leo McCarey; I Am a Fugitive From a Chain Gang (1932) with Paul Muni

ART MILES

Our Relations (1936)

Other notable films: My Favorite Blonde (1942) with Bob Hope

FRANK MILLS (1869-)

Way Out West (1937)

Other notable films: Sorrowful Jones (1949) with Bob Hope; I Married a Witch (1942) with Fredric March, Veronica Lake; My Favorite Blonde (1942) with Bob Hope; Mr. & Mrs. Smith (1941), directed by Alfred Hitchcock; Sullivan's Travels (1941) with Joel McCrea, directed by Preston Sturges; You Can't Take It with You (1938) with James Stewart, directed by Frank Capra; The Toast of New York (1937) with Cary Grant; The Milky Way (1936) with Harold Lloyd

HOWARD M. MITCHELL

Nothing But Trouble (1944); Air Raid Wardens (1943): Huxton Officer

Other notable films: Narrow Margin (1952); The Egg and I (1947) with Claudette Colbert, Fred MacMurray; The Cockeyed Miracle (1946) with Frank Morgan; Notorious (1946) with Ingrid Bergman, Cary Grant, directed by Alfred Hitchcock; The Palm Beach Story (1942) Claudette

HOWARD M. MITCHELL *(continued)*

Colbert; The Mad Doctor (1941) with Basil Rathbone; Of Mice and Men (1939) with Burgess Meredith, Nominated for Best Picture and Score, produced by Hal Roach

ROBERT MITCHUM (1917-1997)

The Dancing Masters (1943)

Other notable films: Cape Fear (1991) with Robert DeNiro, Nick Nolte; Longest Day (1962) with Henry Fonda; Cape Fear (1961) with Gregory Peck; Heaven Knows Mr. Allison (1957) with Deborah Kerr, directed by John Huston; Story of G. I. Joe (1945) with Burgess Meredith, Bill Benedict (Nominated for Best Supporting Actor); Thirty Seconds over Tokyo (1944) with Spencer Tracy

ANTONIO MORENO (1887-1967)

The Bohemian Girl (1936): Devilshoof

Other notable films: The Searchers (1956) with John Wayne; The Creature from the Black Lagoon (1954); Saskatchewan (1954) with Alan Ladd

GENE MORGAN (1892-1940)

Saps at Sea (1940); Pack Up Your Troubles (1932); Pardon Us (1931); From Soup to Nuts (1928): Party guest; The Battle of the Century (1928): Ring announcer

Other notable films: Meet John Doe (1941) with Gary Cooper, directed by Frank Capra; Mr. Smith Goes to Washington (1939) with James Stewart, directed by Frank Capra; You Can't Take It With You (1938) with James Stewart, directed by Frank Capra; Mr. Deeds Goes to Town

GENE MORGAN *(continued)*

(1936) with Gary Cooper, directed by Frank Capra; Alibi Ike (1935) with Joe E. Brown; G-Men (1935) with James Cagney; Dr. Socrates (1935) with Paul Muni; Elmer the Great (1933) with Joe E. Brown

KEWPIE MORGAN

Babes in Toyland (1934): Old King Cole;
The Rogue Song (1930): Frolov
Other notable films: Other Men's Women (1931) with Mary Astor, James Cagney, directed by Lionel Barrymore

JAMES C. MORTON

Block-Heads (1938): James; Pick a Star (1937); Our Relations (1936); The Bohemian Girl (1936): Constable; The Fixer Uppers (1935): Policeman; Tit for Tat (1935): Policeman; The Midnight Patrol (1933): Policeman; The Devil's Brother (1933): Cunning woodchopper; Me and My Pal (1933): Traffic cop
Other notable films: My Little Chickadee (1940) with W.C. Fields, Mae West; You Can't Cheat an Honest Man (1939) with W.C. Fields; Three Little Sew and Sews (1938), The Sitter-Downers (1937), Dizzy Doctors (1937), Pain in the Pullman (1936), Disorder in the Court (1936), Ants in the Pantry (1936) all with The Three Stooges; Modern Times (1936) with Charlie Chaplin; Pardon My Scotch (1935) with The Three Stooges; Circus Hoodoo (1934) with Harry Langdon ; You're Telling Me (1934) with W.C. Fields; Fallen Arches (1933) with Charley Chase

FERDINAND MUNIER (1889-1945)

Babes in Toyland (1934): Santa Claus

Other notable films: Road to Utopia (1946) with Bing Crosby, Bob Hope; Northwest Passage (1940) with Spencer Tracy; Three Comrades (1938) with Robert Young; Confession (1937); Every Day's a Holiday (1937) with Mae West; Swing Time (1936) with Fred Astaire, Ginger Rogers; China Seas (1935) with Clark Gable, Jean Harlow; The Whole Town's Talking (1935) with Edward G. Robinson, Lucille Ball; The Barretts of Wimpole Street (1934) with Charles Laughton, Norma Shearer; The Count of Monte Cristo (1934); Queen Christina (1933) with Greta Garbo

FORBES MURRAY

Nothing But Trouble (1944); A Chump at Oxford (1940): Banker

Other notable films: Monkey Business (1952) with Cary Grant, Katharine Hepburn; The Wistful Widow of Wagon Gap (1947) with Abbott and Costello; The Big Sleep (1946) with Humphrey Bogart; Gilda (1946) with Rita Hayworth; The Razor's Edge (1946) with Tyrone Power; They Were Expendable (1945) with John Wayne; Laura (1944) with Gene Tierney; Tales of Manhattan (1942) with Henry Fonda; Meet John Doe (1941) with Gary Cooper, directed by Frank Capra; New Moon (1940); Only Angels Have Wings (1939) with Cary Grant, directed by Howard Hawks; Test Pilot (1938) with Clark Gable, Spencer Tracy; Saratoga (1937) with Jean Harlow, Clark Gable; They Won't Forget (1937) with Claude Rains

MAYO NEWHALL (1889-1958)

Nothing But Trouble (1944)

Other notable films: The Razor's Edge (1946) with Tyrone Power; Meet Me in St. Louis (1944) with Judy Garland; For Whom the Bell Tolls (1943) with Gary Cooper

JACK NORTON (1889-1958)

The Big Noise (1944): Drunk;
Pick a Star (1937): Oscar the souse

Other notable films: Mad Wednesday (1950) with Harold Lloyd; Naughty Nineties (1945) with Abbott and Costello; Ghost Catchers (1944) with Olsen and Johnson; Hail the Conquering Hero (1944) directed by Preston Sturges; The Miracle of Morgan's Creek (1944) directed by Preston Sturges; It Ain't Hay (1943) with Abbott and Costello; My Favorite Spy (1942) with Bob Hope; The Palm Beach Story (1942) with Claudette Colbert; The Spoilers (1942) with John Wayne; The Bank Dick (1940) with W.C. Fields; The Ghost Breakers (1940) with Bob Hope; A Day at the Races (1937) with the Marx Brothers; Ruggles of Red Gap (1935) with Charlie Ruggles; Cockeyed Cavaliers (1934) with Wheeler and Woolsey

JAY NOVELLO (1905-1982)

The Bullfighters (1945): Lusi

Other notable films: A Pocketful of Miracles (1961) with Glenn Ford, Bette Davis directed by Frank Capra; Ma and Pa Kettle on Vacation (1953) with Marjorie Main, Percy Kilbride

W.J. O'BRIEN (1893-1940)

Pack Up Your Troubles (1932): Butler

Other notable films: San Francisco (1936) with Clark Gable; Movie Crazy (1932) with Harold Lloyd

PATSY O'BYRNE (1885-1968)

Saps at Sea (1940): Mother; Chickens Come Home (1931): Old gossip; Their Purple Moment (1928): Old gossip

Other notable films: Sorrowful Jones (1949) with Bob Hope; Road to Rio (1947) with Bob Hope; The Pride of the Yankees (1942) with Gary Cooper; Abbott and Costello in the Navy (1941) with Abbott and Costello; It's a Gift (1934) with W.C. Fields; Dr. Bull (1933)

ROBERT E. O'CONNOR (1884-1962)

Nothing But Trouble (1944): Mulligan; Air Raid Wardens (1943): Charlie Beaugart

Other notable films: Sunset Boulevard (1950) with Gloria Swanson, William Holden directed by Billy Wilder; Abbott & Costello in Hollywood (1945) with Abbott and Costello; They Were Expendable (1945) with John Wayne; Meet Me in St. Louis (1944) with Judy Garland; The Human Comedy (1943) with Mickey Rooney; Professor Beware (1938) with Harold Lloyd; A Star is Born (1937) with Janet Gaynor, Fredric March; A Night at the Opera (1935) with the Marx Brothers;

SPEC O' DONNELL

Call of the Cuckoos (1927): Love's greatest mistake

Other notable films: College Holliday (1936) with Jack Benny, Burns & Allen; San Francisco (1936) with Clark Gable

BRODERICK O'FARRELL

Beau Hunks (1931): Commander at Fort Arid

Other notable films: The Secret Life of Walter Mitty (1947) with Danny Kaye; Love Crazy (1941) with William Powell, Myrna Loy; The Milky Way (1936) with Harold Lloyd

HENRY O'NEILL (1891-1961)

Nothing But Trouble (1944): Basil Hawkley;
Air Raid Wardens (1936): Rittenhaus

Other notable films: A Guy Named Joe (1944) with Spencer Tracy; Girl Crazy (1943) with Mickey Rooney; Jezebel (1938) with Bette Davis, Henry Fonda, Matthew 'Stymie' Beard

VIVIAN OAKLAND (1894-1958)

Way Out West (1937): Stagecoach passenger, Molly; Scram! (1932): Mrs. Beaumont; That's My Wife (1929): Mrs. Hardy; We Faw Down (1928); Love 'Em and Weep (1927)

Other notable films:
The Tenderfoot (1932) with Joe E. Brown

GARRY OWEN (1897-1951)

Nothing But Trouble (1944): Periwinkle

Other notable films: State of the Union (1948) with Spencer Tracy, Katharine Hepburn; My Favorite Brunette (1947) with Bob Hope; It's a Wonderful Life (1946) with James Stewart, directed by Frank Capra; Notorious (1946) with Cary Grant, Ingrid Bergman; The Postman Always Rings Twice (1946) with John Garland, Lana Turner; Mildred Pierce (1945) with Joan Crawford; Arsenic and Old Lace (1944) with Cary Grant, directed by Frank Capra,; Yankee Doodle Dandy (1942) with James Cagney; High Sierra (1941) with Humphrey Bogart; Meet John Doe (1941) with Gary Cooper, directed by Frank Capra,; Idiot's Delight (1939) with Clark Gable, Norma Shearer; The Thin Man (1934) with William Powell, Myrna Loy

NESTOR PAIVA (1905-1966)

The Dancing Masters (1943): Silvio

Other notable films: Girls! Girls! Girls! (1962) with Elvis Presley; Three Stooges in Orbit (1962) with Three Stooges; Casanova's Big Night (1954) with Bob Hope; Creature from the Black Lagoon (1954); My Favorite Spy (1951) with Bob Hope; Mighty Joe Young (1949); The Paleface (1948) with Bob Hope; Road to Rio (1947) with Bob Hope, Bing Crosby; Road to Utopia (1946) with Bob Hope, Bing Crosby; The Southerner (1945); Reap the Wild Wind (1942) with John Wayne; Road to Morocco (1942) with Bob Hope, Bing Crosby; Hold That Ghost (1941) with Abbott and Costello

EUGENE PALLETTE (1889-1954)

Sugar Daddies (1927); The Battle of the Century (1927): Insurance man; The Second Hundred Years (1927): Dinner guest

Other notable films: Heaven Can Wait (1943) with Don Ameche; It Ain't Hay (1943) with Abbott & Costello; Lady Eve (1941) with Barbara Stanwyck, Henry Fonda, directed by Preston Sturges; The Adventures of Robin Hood (1938) with Errol Flynn; Topper (1937) with Cary Grant, produced by Hal Roach, Nominated for Best Picture; My Man Godfrey (1936) with William Powell; Intolerance (1916) directed by D. W. Griffith

EDDIE PARKER

Our Relations (1936)

Other notable films: Abbott and Costello Meet the Mummy (1955); Abbott and Costello Meet Dr. Jekyll & Mr. Hyde (1952); Hit the Ice (1943) with Abbott and Costello; Northwest Passage (1940) with Spencer Tracy

JEAN PARKER (1915-)

The Flying Deuces (1939): Georgette

Other notable films: Black Tuesday (1955) with Edward G. Robinson; The Gunfighter (1950) with Gregory Peck

EMORY PARNELL (1894-1979)

The Dancing Masters (1943): Featherstone

Other notable films: The Delicate Delinquent (1956) with Jerry Lewis; Pardners (1956) with Dean Martin, Jerry Lewis; The Long, Long Trailer (1954) with Lucille Ball, Desi Arnaz; Ma and Pa Kettle at Home (1954) with Marjorie Main, Percy Kilbride; Lost in Alaska (1952) with Abbott and Costello; Ma and Pa Kettle at the Fair (1952), Ma and Pa Kettle Back on the Farm (1951), Ma and Pa Kettle Go to Town (1950) and Ma and Pa Kettle (1949) all with Marjorie Main, Percy Kilbride; State Fair (1945) with Janet Gaynor; King's Row (1942) with Ronald Reagan; Saboteur (1942) with Bob Cummings, directed by Alfred Hitchcock; The Maltese Falcon (1941) with Humphrey Bogart; Mr. & Mrs. Smith (1941) directed by Alfred Hitchcock; Sullivan's Travels (1941)with Joel McCrea, directed by Preston Sturges; Foreign Correspondent (1940) with Joel McCrea, directed by Alfred Hitchcock; Idiot's Delight (1939) with Clark Gable, Norma Shearer; Angels with Dirty Faces (1938) with Humphrey Bogart, James Cagney

LEE PATRICK (1906-1982)

Jitterbugs (1943): Dorcas

Other notable films: Pillow Talk (1959) with Rock Hudson, Doris Day; Auntie Mame (1958) with Rosalind Russell; Vertigo (1958) with James Stewart, directed by Alfred Hitchcock; The Fuller Brush Girl (1950) with Lucille Ball; Mildred Pierce (1945) with Joan Crawford; George Washington Slept Here (1942) with Jack Benny; The Maltese Falcon (1941) with Humphrey Bogart

BLANCHE PAYSON

Helpmates (1932): Mrs. Hardy; Our Wife (1931): Mrs. Gladding; Below Zero (1930): Formidable woman who destroys instruments

Other notable films: You Can't Take It With You (1938) with James Stewart, directed by Frank Capra

LEE PHELPS (1894-1953)

Air Raid Wardens (1943): Moving Man; Our Relations (1936): Bartender; Putting Pants on Philip (1927): Extra in crowd

Other notable films: Father of the Bride (1950) with Spencer Tracy, Elizabeth Taylor; Duel in the Sun (1946) with Jennifer Jones, Gregory Peck; Arsenic and Old Lace (1944) with Cary Grant, directed by Frank Capra; Saboteur (1942) with Bob Cummings , directed by Alfred Hitchcock; High Sierra (1941) with Humphrey Bogart; Love Crazy (1941) with William Powell, Myrna Loy; The Philadelphia Story (1940) with Cary Grant, Katharine Hepburn, James Stewart, directed by George Cukor; Gone With the Wind (1939) with Clark Gable, Vivien Leigh; Idiot's Delight (1939) with Clark Gable, Norma Shearer; You Can't Cheat an Honest Man (1939) with W.C. Fields; Angels with Dirty Faces (1938) with James Cagney, Humphrey Bogart; You Can't Take It With You (1938) with James Stewart, directed by Frank Capra; Nothing Sacred (1937) with Carole Lombard, Fredric March; A Star Is Born (1937) with Janet Gaynor; The Trail of the Lonesome Pine (1936) with Henry Fonda, Fred MacMurray, Spanky McFarland; Six of a Kind (1934) with W.C. Fields, Burns & Allen, Charlie Ruggles; You're Telling Me (1934) with

LEE PHELPS *(continued)*

W. C. Fields; Grand Hotel (1932) with Greta Garbo; Why Worry? (1923) with Harold Lloyd

ZASU PITTS (1900-1963)

Way Out West (1937)

Other notable films: It's a Mad, Mad, Mad, Mad World (1963) with Spencer Tracy; Life with Father (1947) with William Powell, Irene Dunne, Elizabeth Taylor; Ruggles of Red Gap (1935) with Charlie Ruggles; Mrs Wiggs of the Cabbage Patch (1934) with W.C. Fields; Greed (1925), an eight hour long film

LON POFF (1869-1952)

The Laurel-Hardy Murder Case (1930): Elderly man;
Habeas Corpus (1928): Graveyard keeper;
Two Tars (1928): Countryside motorist

Other notable films: Father's Little Dividend (1951) with Spencer Tracy, Elizabeth Taylor; Madame Bovary (1949) with Jennifer Jones; The More the Merrier (1943) with Jean Arthur, directed by George Stevens; The Toast of New York (1937) with Cary Grant; Tillie and Gus (1933) with W.C. Fields; Greed (1925) with Zasu Pitts; Dante's Inferno (1924)

SNUB POLLARD (1886-1962)

Played comic support to Harold Lloyd in dozens of one-reel comedies. In 1919 made his own one-reel comedy series, directed by Charles Parrott. Was brother of Daphne Pollard.

The Midnight Patrol (1932); One Good Turn (1931): A community player

Other notable films: The Errand Boy (1961) with Jerry Lewis; A Pocketful of Miracles (1961) with Glenn Ford, Bette Davis, directed by Frank Capra; Man of a Thousand Faces (1957) with James Cagney; Limelight (1952) with Charlie Chaplin; Miracle on 34th Street (1947) with Edmond Gywnn; Monkey Businessmen (1946), Three Pests in a Mess (1945), both with The Three Stooges; Cockeyed Cavaliers (1934) with Wheeler & Woolsey

PAUL PORCASI (1878-1946)

Nothing But Trouble (1944): Italian Restaurateur

Other notable films: Casablanca (1942) with Humphrey Bogart, Ingrid Bergman; Road To Zanzibar (1941) with Bob Hope, Bing Crosby; Mr. Deeds Goes to Town (1936) with Gary Copper, directed by Frank Capra

JOHN QUALEN (1899-1987)

The Devil's Brother (1933): Man who owned the bull

Other notable films: The Sons of Katie Elder (1965) with John Wayne; The Man Who Shot Liberty Valance (1962) with John Wayne; Elmer Gantry (1960) with Burt Lancaster; North to Alaska (1960) with John Wayne; Anatomy of a Murder (1959) with James Stewart; The Searchers (1956) with John Wayne, Natalie Wood; Sea

JOHN QUALEN *(continued)*

Chase (1955) with John Wayne; High and the Mighty (1954) with John Wayne; Casablanca (1942) with Humphrey Bogart, Ingrid Bergman; The Devil and Daniel Webster (1941) with Walter Huston, Edward Arnold; The Grapes of Wrath (1940) with Henry Fonda; His Girl Friday (1940) with Cary Grant, directed by Howard Hawks; Nothing Sacred (1937) with Carole Lombard, Fredric March

ANDERS RANDOLF (1870-1930)

Night Owls (1930)

Other notable films: The Jazz Singer (1927) with Al Jolsen

HERBERT RAWLINSON (1885-1953)

He came out of retirement in 1953 to do one more film for the inept director Ed Wood Jr., who is known for making the worst film of all time, *Plan 9 From Outer Space*

Slipping Wives (1927): Leon, Taz

Other notable films: Jail Bait (1954); Joan of Arc (1948); Swiss Family Robinson(1940) with Freddie Bartholomew

JACK RAYMOND (1902-1951)

Liberty (1929): Getaway driver

Other notable films: Abbott & Costello in the Foreign Legion (1950)

FRANK RICE (1891-1936)

Pack Up Your Troubles (1932): Parkins, the butler

Other notable films: The Trail of the Lonesome Pine (1936) with Henry Fonda, Fred MacMurray, Spanky McFarland; Ruggles of Red Gap (1935) with Charlie Ruggles; The Gold Rush (1925) with Charlie Chaplin

DICK RICH (1908-1967)

Great Guns (1941): Post cook

Other notable films: Jailhouse Rock (1957) with Elvis Presley; Black Tuesday (1955) with Edward G. Robinson; Seven Brides for Seven Brothers (1954), Nominated for Best Picture; The Story of G. I. Joe (1945) with Robert Mitchum; The Princess and the Pirate (1944) with Bob Hope; In Old Oklahoma (1943) with John Wayne; The Ox-Bow Incident (1943)and The Grapes of Wrath (1940) both with Henry Fonda; Rio Rita (1942) with Abbott and Costello; Angels with Dirty Faces (1938) with Humphrey Bogart, James Cagney

ADDISON RICHARDS (1887-1964)

A-Haunting We Will Go (1942): Malcolm Kilgore

Other notable films: The Ten Commandments (1956) with Charlton Heston; Mighty Joe Young (1949); Anna and the King of Siam (1946) with Irene Dunne, Rex Harrison; Spellbound (1945) with Gregory Peck, directed by Alfred Hitchcock; A Guy Named Joe (1944) with Spencer Tracy; The Flying Tigers (1942) with John Wayne; My Favorite Blonde (1942) with Bob Hope; The Pride of the Yankees (1942) with Gary Cooper; Northwest Passage (1940) with Spencer Tracy; My Little Chickadee (1940) with W.C.

ADDISON RICHARDS *(continued)*

Fields, Mae West; Boys Town (1938) with Spencer Tracy; The Petrified Forest (1936) with Humphrey Bogart, Bette Davis

BERT ROACH (1891-1971)

The Battle of the Century (1927): Ring of spectators

Other notable films: Duel in the Sun (1946) with Jennifer Jones, Gregory Peck; Little Giant (1946) with Abbott & Costello; The Princess and the Pirate (1944) with Bob Hope; My Favorite Spy (1942) with Bob Hope; Hellzapoppin' (1941) with Olsen & Johnson; Algiers (1938) with Charles Boyer; Saratoga (1937) with Clark Gable, Jean Harlow; The Fury (1936) with Spencer Tracy; San Francisco (1936) with Clark Gable; The Thin Man (1934) with William Powell, Myrna Loy

FLORENCE ROBERTS (1861-1940)

Babes in Toyland (1934): Widow Peep

Other notable films: Abe Lincoln in Illinois (1940); The Life of Emile Zola (1937) with Paul Muni; Nobody's Baby (1937) with Patsy Kelly, Rosina Lawrence, produced by Hal Roach; The Prisoner of Zenda (1937) with Mary Astor, Ronald Coleman, Douglas Fairbanks, Jr., directed by George Cukor, produced by David Selznick; Accent on Youth (1935) with Patsy Kelly; Les Miserables (1935) with Fredric March; Cleopatra (1934) with Claudette Colbert

CONSTANTINE ROMANOFF

Saps at Sea (1940); Our Relations (1936): Tuffy

Other notable films: The Princess and the Pirate (1944) with Bob Hope; Reap the Wild Wind (1942) with John Wayne; The Long Voyage Home (1940); Professor Beware (1938) with Harold Lloyd; Judge Priest (1934); Island of Lost Souls (1932); Movie Crazy (1932) with Harold Lloyd; Kid Brother (1927) with Harold Lloyd

SHEILA RYAN (1921-1975)

Was married to character actor Pat Buttram

A-Haunting We Will Go (1942): Margo; Great Guns (1941): Ginger Hammonds

Other notable films: Caged Fury (1948) with Buster Crabbe

TINY SANDFORD (1894-1961)

Our Relations(1936); Going Bye-Bye! (1934); Busy Bodies (1933): Shop foreman; The Midnight Patrol (1933): Policeman; The Devil's Brother (1933): Woodchopper; The Chimp (1932): Destructo; Beau Hunks (1931): Legion officer; Come Clean (1931): Doorman; Pardon Us (1931): Prison guard; The Laurel-Hardy Murder Case (1930): Policeman; Below Zero (1930): Pete; Blotto (1930): Head waiter; The Hoose-Gow (1929); Double Whoopee (1929): Policeman; Big Business (1929); Their Purple Moment (1928): Waiter; From Soup to Nuts (1928); The Second Hundred Years (1927); Sailors, Beware! (1927) Flying Elephants(1927); Forty-five Minutes from Hollywood (1926)

Other notable films: Modern Times (1936) with Charlie Chaplin

RALPH SANFORD (1898-1963)

The Bullfighters (1945): Muldoon

Other notable films: The Seven Year Itch (1955) with Marilyn Monroe; River of No Return (1954) with Robert Mitchum, Marilyn Monroe; My Favorite Spy (1951) with Bob Hope; State Fair (1945) with Vivian Blaine, Dana Andrews; Lost in a Harem (1944) with Abbott & Costello; High Sierra (1941) with Humphrey Bogart; Mr. & Mrs. Smith (1941) directed by Alfred Hitchcock; You Can't Cheat an Honest Man (1939) with W.C. Fields; Angels with Dirty Faces (1938) with James Cagney, Humphrey Bogart

HARRY SCHULTZ (1882-1935)

Beau Hunks (1931): Capt. Schultz

Other notable films: Dante's Inferno (1935) with Spencer Tracy; Tillie and Gus (1933) with W.C. Fields

ROLFE SEDAN (1896-1982)

The Devil's Brother (1933): Customer at La Taverne del Cucu; Double Whoopee (1929): Hotel desk clerk; You're Darn Tootin' (1928): Drunk

Other notable films: Gentlemen Prefer Blondes (1953) with Marilyn Monroe, Jane Russell; My Favorite Spy (1951) with Bob Hope; Ninotchka (1939) with Greta Garbo; A Night at the Opera (1935) with the Marx Bros.; Ruggles of Red Gap (1935) with Charlie Ruggles; The Thin Man (1934) with William Powell, Myrna Loy; Grand Hotel (1932) with Greta Garbo, John Barrymore; If I Had a Million (1932) with W.C. Fields; Trouble in Paradise (1932)

HARRY SEMELS (1887-1946)

Swiss Miss (1938): Organ grinder

Other notable films: Ninotchka (1939) with Greta Garbo; You Can't Take It With You (1938) with James Stewart, directed by Frank Capra; Viva Villa (1934) with Wallace Beery

DAVID SHARPE (1909-1980)

Our Relations (1936)

Other notable films: War of the Worlds (1953) with Gene Barry; The Fuller Brush Man (1948) with Red Skelton, Buster Keaton; The Wistful Widow of Wagon Gap (1947) with Abbott and Costello; Never Give a Sucker an Even Break (1941) with W.C. Fields; Pigskin Parade (1936) with Jack Haley, Judy Garland

MONTAGUE SHAW (1882-1968)

Pack Up Your Troubles (1932): Groom's father

Other notable films: The Pride of the Yankees (1942) with Gary Cooper; Charley's Aunt (1941) with Jack Benny; Stanley and Livingstone (1939) with Spencer Tracy; The Three Musketeers (1939) with Don Ameche; Little Miss Broadway (1938) with Shirley Temple; The Story of Louis Pasteur (1936) with Paul Muni; Sylvia Scarlett (1935) with Cary Grant, Katharine Hepburn, directed by George Cukor

KATHRUN SHELDON (1878-1975)

Bonnie Scotland (1935): School teacher

Other notable films: The Kettles in the Ozarks (1956) with Marjorie Main; I Married a Witch (1942) with Fredric

KATHRUN SHELDON *(continued)*

March, Veronica Lake; Never Give a Sucker an Even Break (1941) with W.C. Fields; Nothing Sacred (1937) with Carole Lombard, Fredric March

JOHN SHELTON (1814-1972)

A-Haunting We Will Go (1942): Tommy White

Other notable films: The Time of Their Lives (1946) with Abbott & Costello

FLORENCE SHIRLEY (1892-1967)

The Dancing Masters (1943): Dowager

Other notable films: Ninotchka (1939) with Greta Garbo

GEORGE SOREL (1899-1948)

Swiss Miss (1938): Joseph The Chauffeur

Other notable films: The Razor's Edge (1946) with Tyrone Power; To Have & Have Not (1944) with Humphrey Bogart, Lauren Bacall; For Whom the Bell Tolls (1943) with Gary Cooper; Angels with Dirty Faces (1938) with James Cagney, Humphrey Bogart

ARTHUR SPACE (1909-1983)

The Big Noise (1944): Hartley; The Dancing Masters (1943): Director

Other notable films: The Shakiest Gun in the West (1968) with Don Knotts; The Spoilers (1955) with John Wayne; The Fuller Brush Girl (1950) with Lucille Ball; Sorrowful Jones (1949) with Bob Hope, Lucille Ball; The Fuller Brush Man (1948) with Red Skelton, Buster Keaton; The Pale Face (1948) with Bob Hope; The Cockeyed Miracle (1946)

ARTHUR SPACE *(continued)*
with Frank Morgan; Abbott & Costello in Hollywood (1945) with Abbott and Costello; A Guy Named Joe (1944) with Spencer Tracy

WILL STANTON (1884-1969)
Any Old Port (1932): Drunken wagerer; Pardon Us (1931); Do Detectives Think? (1927): Slasher's pal; Sailors, Beware! (1927): Baron Behr; With Love & Kisses (1927): Soldier sleeping next to Stan
Other notable films: Mr. Skeffington (1944) with Bette Davis; Charley's Aunt (1941) with Jack Benny; Little Princess (1939) with Shirley Temple; The Last of the Mohicans (1936) with Randolph Scott; The Fury (1936) with Spencer Tracy; Mutiny on the Bounty (1935) with Clark Gable, Charles Laughton

VERNON STEELE (1882-1955)
Bonnie Scotland (1935)
Other notable films: They Were Expendable (1945) with John Wayne; Mrs. Miniver (1942) with Greer Garson; Captain Blood (1935) with Errol Flynn

RAFAEL STORM
The Bullfighters (1945): Hotel Clerk
Other notable films: Ruggles of Red Gap (1935) with Charlie Ruggles, Mary Boland, directed by Leo McCarey

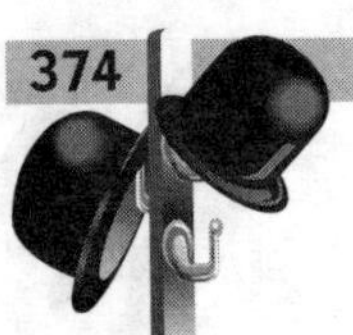

LUDWIG STOSSEL (1883-1973)

Great Guns (1941): Dr. Hugo Schickel

Other notable films: G.I. Blues (1960) with Elvis Presley; Casablanca (1942) with Humphrey Bogart, Ingrid Bergman; King's Row (1942) with Ronald Reagan; The Pride of the Yankees (1942); Who Done It? (1942) with Abbott and Costello; Woman of the Year (1942) with Spencer Tracy, Katharine Hepburn, directed by George Stevens; Testament of Dr. Mabuse (1933) directed by Fritz Long

GERTRUDE SUTTON

Another Fine Mess (1930): Real maid

Other notable films: Captains Courageous (1937) with Spencer Tracy; The Fury (1936) with Spencer Tracy; Poppy (1936) with W.C. Fields

GRADY SUTTON (1908-1995)

Pack Up Your Troubles (1932): Eddie, the groom

Other notable films: Rock 'n' Roll High School (1979); Support Your Local Gunfighter (1971) with James Garner; My Fair Lady (1964) with Rex Harrison, Audrey Hepburn, directed by George Cukor, Nominated for Best Picture; A Star Is Born (1954) with Judy Garland, directed by George Cukor; White Christmas (1954) with Bing Crosby, Danny Kaye; The More the Merrier (1943) with Jean Arthur, directed by George Stevens; The Bank Dick (1940) with W.C. Fields; It's a Wonderful World (1939) with Claudette Colbert, James Stewart; You Can't Cheat an Honest Man (1939) with W.C. Fields; Alexander's Ragtime Band (1938) with Tyrone Power; Vivacious Lady (1938) with James

GRADY SUTTON *(continued)*

Stewart, directed by George Stevens; Stage Door (1937) with Katharine Hepburn, Ginger Rogers; My Man Godfrey (1936) with William Powell; Pigskin Parade (1936) with Judy Garland, Jack Haley; Dr.Socrates (1935) with Paul Muni; The Man on the Flying Trapeze (1935) with W.C. Fields; Movie Crazy (1932) with Harold Lloyd; The Pharmacist (1932) with W.C. Fields

RAY TEAL (1902-1976)

Nothing But Trouble (1944): Officer

Other notable films: Chisum (1970) with John Wayne; Judgment at Nuremberg (1961) with Spencer Tracy; Inherit the Wind (1960) with Spencer Tracy; Winchester '73 (1950) with James Stewart; My Favorite Brunette (1947) with Bob Hope; Road to Rio (1947) with Bob Hope, Bing Crosby; The Best Years of Our Life (1946) with Fredric March; The Princess and the Pirate (1944) with Bob Hope; Woman of the Year (1942) with Spencer Tracy, Katharine Hepburn; Northwest Passage (1940) with Spencer Tracy

ROSEMARY THEBY

Our Relations (1936): Nightclub extra;
The Second Hundred Years (1927): Dinner guest

Other notable films: One Million B.C. (1940) directed by Hal Roach; You Can't Take It with You (1938) with James Stewart, directed by Frank Capra; San Francisco (1936) with Clark Gable; The Man on the Flying Trapeze (1935), Fatal Glass of Beer (1933) both with W.C. Fields

AL THOMPSON

Sons of the Desert (1933)

Other notable films: In Society (1944) with Abbott and Costello

ZEFFIE TILBURY (1862-1950)

The Bohemian Girl (1936): Gypsy queen

Other notable films: Tobacco Road (1941) with Charles Grapewin; The Grapes of Wrath (1940) with Henry Fonda

THELMA TODD (1905-1935)

The Bohemian Girl (1936): Gypsy Queen's Daughter; The Devil's Brother (1933): Lady Pamela Rocburg; On the Loose (1932); Chickens Come Home (1931): Mrs. Hardy; Another Fine Mess (1930): Lady Plumtree; Unaccustomed As We Are (1929): Mrs. Kennedy

Other notable films: Three Chumps Ahead (1934); Cockeyed Cavaliers (1934) with Wheeler & Woolsey; Hip, Hips, Hooray (1934) with Wheeler & Woolsey; Horse Feathers (1932) with the Marx Bros.; On the Loose (1932) with Marx Bros.; Speak Easily (1932) with Buster Keaton; The Maltese Falcon (1931) with Humphrey Bogart; Monkey Business (1931) with the Marx Bros.; The Pip From Pittsburgh (1931) with Charley Chase; High C's (1930), Looser than Loose (1930), All Teed Up (1930), Whispering Whoopee (1930), The Real McCoy (1930) and Dollar Dizzy (1930), all with Charley Chase

SIDNEY TOLER (1874-1947)

Starred as Charlie Chan from 1938-1944.

Our Relations (1936): Captain of the S.S. Periwinkle

Other notable films: Three Godfathers (1936) with John Wayne

FRED 'SNOWFLAKE' TOONES

Way Out West (1937): Janitor

Other notable films: The Lost Weekend (1945) with Ray Milland; The Palm Beach Story (1942) with Claudette Colbert; Mr. Smith Goes to Washington (1939) with James Stewart, directed by Frank Capra; Saratoga (1937) with Clark Gable, Jean Harlow

DAVID TORRENCE (1880-1942)

Bonnie Scotland (1935): Mr. Miggs

Other notable films: Stanley and Livingstone (1939) with Spencer Tracy; Captain Blood (1935) with Errol Flynn; Mutiny on the Bounty (1935) with Charles Laughton, Clark Gable; Smilin' Through (1932) with Norma Shearer;

LUIGI TOSI

Atoll K (1951): Lt. Jack Frazer

Other notable films: Earth Cries Out (1949)

CHARLES TROWBRIDGE (1882-1967)

Great Guns (1941): Col. Ridley

Other notable films: Last Hurrah (1958) with Spencer Tracy; The Paleface (1949) with Bob Hope; Private Affairs of Bel Ami (1947); The Secret Life of Walter Mitty (1947) with Danny Kaye; They Were Expendable (1945) with

CHARLES TROWBRIDGE *(continued)*

John Wayne, directed by John Ford; Mildred Pierce (1945) with Joan Crawford; Madame Curie (1943) with Greer Garson, Walter Pidgeon; The Great Lie (1941) with Bette Davis; Sergeant York (1941) with Gary Cooper ; Meet John Doe (1941) with Gary Cooper, directed by Frank Capra; The Fighting 69th (1940) with James Cagney; Our Town (1940) with William Holden; Angels with Dirty Faces (1938) with James Cagney, Humphrey Bogart; Holiday (1938) with Katharine Hepburn, Cary Grant, directed by George Cukor; Captains Courageous (1937) with Spencer Tracy; A Day at the Races (1937) with the Marx Bros.; Libeled Lady (1936) with Jean Harlow, William Powell

GLENN TRYON (1894-1970)

Became a producer at Universal Studios in the 1940's.

Forty-Five Minutes From Hollywood (1926): Orville

Other notable films: Hold That Ghost (1941) and Keep 'em Flying (1941) Abbott & Costello films he produced

RICHARD TUCKER (1884-1942)

Pack Up Your Troubles (1932): Bank president

Other notable films: Libeled Lady (1936) with Spencer Tracy, Myrna Loy; Shadow of a Doubt (1935) with Joseph Cotten, directed by Alfred Hitchcock; The Jazz Singer (1927) with Al Jolson, first talking picture

BEN TURPIN (1869-1940)

Had his eyes insured by "Lloyd's of London" in case they might come uncrossed.

Saps at Sea (1940): Mixed-up plumber; Our Wife (1931): Henry

Other notable films: Chasing Those Depression Blues (1935) with Danny Kaye; Million Dollar Legs (1932) with W.C. Fields; Cracked Nuts (1931) with Wheeler & Woolsey; Love Parade (1929) with Maurice Chevalier; Burlesque of Carmen (1916),The Champion (1915), A Night Out (1915), His New Job (1915), all with Charlie Chaplin

HARRY TYLER (1888-1961)

The Dancing Masters (1943): Man on crutches

Other notable films: Pillow Talk (1959) with Rock Hudson, Doris Day; Abbott & Costello Meet the Keystone Cops (1955) with Abbott & Costello; Guys and Dolls (1955) with Frank Sinatra, Marlon Brando; The Quiet Man (1952) with John Wayne; Bedtime for Bonzo (1951) with Ronald Reagan; The Lemon Drop Kid (1949) with Bob Hope; Ma and Pa Kettle (1949) with Marjorie Main, Percy Kilbride; Sorrowful Jones (1949) with Bob Hope; Abbott & Costello in Hollywood (1945) with Abbott & Costello; I Married a Witch (1942) with Fredric March, Veronica Lake; The Palm Beach Story (1942) with Claudette Colbert; Sullivan's Travels (1942) with Joel McCrea, directed by Preston Sturges; Tobacco Road (1941) with Charles Grapewin; The Grapes of Wrath (1940) with Henry Fonda; A Night at the Opera (1935) with the Marx Bros.

GEORGE TYNE (1917-)

The Dancing Masters (1943): Gangster

Other notable films: Skin Game (1971) with James Garner, Louis Gossett, Jr.; Marlowe (1969)with James Garner, Bruce Lee (his character's name was Oliver Hardy); The Boston Strangler (1968) with Henry Fonda; The Sands of Iwo Jima (1949) with John Wayne; Objective, Burma (1945) with Errol Flynn

MINERVA URECAL (1894-1966)

Bonnie Scotland (1935): Storekeeper

Other notable films: Mr. Hobbs Takes a Vacation (1962) with James Stewart; Lost in Alaska (1952) with Abbott & Costello; Niagara (1952) with Marilyn Monroe, Joseph Cotten; The Secret Life of Walter Mitty (1947) with Danny Kaye; State Fair (1945) with Vivian Blaine, Dana Andrews; Mr. Skeffington (1944) with Bette Davis; Hit the Ice (1943) with Abbott & Costello; Shadow of a Doubt (1943) with Joseph Cotten, directed by Alfred Hitchcock; My Favorite Blonde (1942) with Bob Hope; Never Give a Sucker an Even Break (1941), You Can't Cheat an Honest Man (1939) and The Man on the Flying Trapeze (1935) all with W.C. Fields

ELLINOR VAN DER VEER

Going Bye-Bye! (1934); Pack Up Your Troubles (1932): Wedding Guest; The Hoose-Gow (1929): Party guest; From Soup to Nuts (1928); The Battle of the Century (1927); The Second Hundred Years (1927)

Other notable films: Movie Crazy (1932) with Harold Lloyd

PHILIP VAN ZANDT (1904-1958)

The Big Noise (1944): Dutchy; Air Raid Wardens (1943): Herman

Other notable films: Man of a Thousand Faces (1957) with James Cagney; To Catch a Thief (1955) with Cary Grant, Grace Kelly, directed by Alfred Hitchcock,; The High and the Mighty (1954) with John Wayne; Life with Father (1947) with William Powell, Irene Dunne, Elizabeth Taylor; A Guy Named Joe (1944) with Spencer Tracy; Citizen Kane (1941) with Orson Welles

ROBERT VATTIER (1905-1982)

Atoll K (1951)

Other notable films: Letters from My Windmill (1954); LaRonde (1950); Caesar (1935); The Baker's Wife (1933); Fanny (1932); Marius (1931)

MICHAEL VISAROFF (1892-1951)

The Flying Deuces (1939): Innkeeper

Other notable films: For Whom the Bell Tolls (1943) with Gary Cooper; Madame Curie (1943) with Greer Garson; Woman of the Year (1942) with Spencer Tracy, Katharine Hepburn, directed by George Stevens; Never Give a Sucker an Even Break (1941) and The Man on the Flying Trapeze (1935) both with W.C. Fields; Sylvia Scarlett (1935) with Cary Grant, Katharine Hepburn; The Cat's Paw (1934) with Harold Lloyd; Viva Villa!(1934) with Wallace Beery; The Man Who Played God (1932) with Bette Davis; Dracula (1931); The Last Command (1928) with William Powell

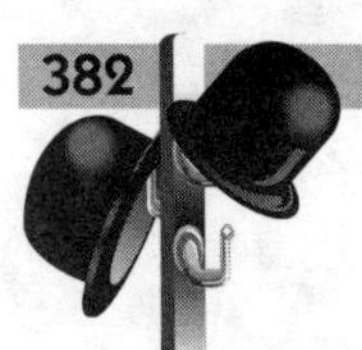

EMMETT VOGAN (1893-1964)

The Bullfighters (1945): Prosecutor

Other notable films: The Long, Long Trailer (1954) with Lucille Ball, Desi Arnaz; Sabrina (1954) with Audrey Hepburn; Sorrowful Jones (1949) with Lucille Ball, Bob Hope; The Big Sleep (1946) with Humphrey Bogart, Lauren Bacall; Notorious (1946) with Cary Grant, Ingrid Bergman; directed by Alfred Hitchcock; The Lost Weekend (1945) with Ray Milland; They Were Expendable (1945) with John Wayne; Never Give a Sucker an Even Break (1941) with W.C. Fields; The Bank Dick (1940) with W.C. Fields; Ghost Breakers (1940) with Bob Hope

GUSTAV von SEYFFERTITZ (1863-1943)

Swiss Miss (1938)

Other notable films: Mr. Deeds Goes to Town (1936) with Gary Cooper, directed by Frank Capra

JUDITH VOSSELLI

The Rogue Song (1930): Countess Tatiana

Other notable films: Roberta (1935) with Lucille Ball, Fred Astaire; Madame Butterfly (1932) with Cary Grant

MAX WAGNER

The Bullfighters (1945): Attendant

Sons of the Desert (1933)

Other notable films: Country Girl (1954) with Bing Crosby; Mad Wednesday (1950) with Harold Lloyd; Possessed (1947) with Joan Crawford; Tycoon (1947) with John Wayne; My Favorite Blonde (1942) with Bob Hope; The Palm Beach Story (1942) with Claudette Colbert; The

MAX WAGNER *(continued)*

Talk of the Town (1942) with Cary Grant; Ghost Breakers (1940) with Bob Hope; They Drive by Night (1940) with Humphrey Bogart; Professor Beware (1938) with Harold Lloyd; Step Lively, Jeeves (1937) with Arthur Treacher; The Toast of New York (1937) with Cary Grant

RUTH WARREN

Our Relations (1936): Mrs. Addlequist

Other notable films: The Last Hurrah (1958) with Spencer Tracy; The Long, Long Trailer (1954) with Lucille Ball, Desi Arnaz; Monkey Business (1952) with Ginger Rogers, Cary Grant, directed by Howard Hawk; Song of Bernadette (1943); State Fair (1933) with Janet Gaynor, Will Rogers

PIERRE WATKIN (1889-1960)

Great Guns (1941): Col. Wayburn

Other notable films: Pal Joey (1957) with Frank Sinatra, Rita Hayworth; Samson and Delilah (1950) directed by Cecil B. DeMille; Incident (1948) with Anthony Caruso; State of the Union (1948) with Spencer Tracy, Katharine Hepburn; Monsieur Verdoux (1947) with Charlie Chaplin; The Secret Life of Walter Mitty (1947) with Danny Kaye; The Kid From Brooklyn (1946) with Danny Kaye; Little Giant (1946), and It Ain't Hay (1943) both with Abbott and Costello; The Pride of the Yankees (1942) with Gary Cooper; Meet John Doe (1941) with Gary Cooper, directed by Frank Capra; The Bank Dick (1940) with W.C. Fields; I Love You Again (1940) with William Powell, Myrna Loy; Road to Singapore (1940) with Bob Hope, Bing Crosby;

PIERRE WATKIN *(continued)*

Mr. Smith Goes to Washington (1939), and You Can't Take It With You (1938), both with James Stewart and both directed by Frank Capra; Confession (1937) with Basil Rathbone; Life of Emile Zola (1937) with Paul Muni; Stage Door (1937) with Katharine Hepburn; Mr. Deeds Goes to Town (1936) with Gary Cooper, directed by Frank Capra; Swing Time (1936) with Fred Astaire, Ginger Rogers, directed by George Stevens

DOODLES WEAVER (1912-1983)

Uncle of Sigourney Weaver

Swiss Miss (1938): Driver of the ancient taxi

Other notable films: Cancel My Reservation (1972) with Bob Hope; It's a Mad, Mad, Mad, Mad World (1963) with Spencer Tracy; A Pocketful Of Miracles (1961) with Bette Davis, Glenn Ford, directed by Frank Capra; Topper (1937) with Cary Grant, Roland Young

LEO WHITE (1882-1948)

The Devil's Brother (1933)

Other notable films: Arsenic and Old Lace (1944) with Cary Grant, directed by Frank Capra; Meet John Doe (1941) with Gary Cooper, directed by Frank Capra; A Night at the Opera (1935) with the Marx Bros.; Viva Villa (1934) with Wallace Beery; Why Worry? (1923) with Harold Lloyd; Burlesque of Carmen (1916) with Charlie Chaplin

BLACKIE WHITEFORD

Pardon Us (1931)

Other notable films: The Man Who Shot Liberty Valance (1962) with John Wayne, James Stewart, directed by John Ford; King Kong (1933); Tillie and Gus (1933) with W.C. Fields; Movie Crazy (1932) with Harold Lloyd

CRANE WHITLEY (1899-1957)

The Flying Deuces (1939): Corporal

Other notable films: My Favorite Spy (1951) with Bob Hope; Samson and Delilah (1950) directed by Cecil B. DeMille; Mr. Skeffington (1944) with Bette Davis; The Princess and the Pirate (1944) with Bob Hope; Till We Meet Again (1944) with Ray Milland; To Have and Have Not (1944) with Humphrey Bogart, Lauren Bacall; My Favorite Blonde (1942) with Bob Hope; Who Done It? (1942) with Abbott and Costello, Shemp Howard

LEO WILLIS (1889-1952)

Beau Hunks (1931): New recruit; Pardon Us (1931): Pal of 'The Tiger'; Below Zero (1930): Crook; The Hoose-Gow (1929): Man with apples; Their Purple Moment (1928): Cab driver; Flying Elephants (1928): Fisherman; Call of the Cuckoos (1927): Couple at housewarming

Other notable films: Six of a Kind (1934) with W.C. Fields

DAVE WILLOCK (1909-1990)

Great Guns (1941): Recruit at target practice

Other notable films: Frankie and Johnny (1965) with Elvis Presley; The Patsy (1964) with Jerry Lewis; Send Me

DAVE WILLOCK *(continued)*

No Flowers (1964) with Doris Day, Rock Hudson; The Nutty Professor (1963) with Jerry Lewis; What Ever Happened to Baby Jane? (1962) with Bette Davis, Joan Crawford; The Buster Keaton Story (1957) with Donald O'Conner; The Delicate Delinquent (1956) with Jerry Lewis; Ma and Pa Kettle on Vacation (1953) with Marjorie Main, Percy Kilbride; State of the Union (1948) with Spencer Tracy, Katherine Hepburn; Pride of the Marines (1945) with John Garfield; Spellbound (1945) with Gregory Peck, Ingrid Bergman, directed by Alfred Hitchcock; Let's Face It (1943); and Caught in the Draft (1941), both with Bob Hope; Never Give a Sucker an Even Break (1941) with W.C. Fields

CHILL WILLS (1903-1978)

Way Out West (1937)

Other notable films: McClintock (1963) with John Wayne; The Alamo (1960) with John Wayne; Where the Boys Are (1960) with Connie Francis; Giant (1956) with James Dean, Rock Hudson, Elizabeth Taylor; Meet Me in St. Louis (1944) with Judy Garland; It's a Gift (1934) with W.C. Fields

CHARLES WILSON (1894-1948)

The Big Noise (1944):Conductor

Other notable films: Crime on Their Hands (1948) with The Three Stooges; Road to Utopia (1946) with Bob Hope, Bing Crosby; Meet John Doe (1941) with Gary Cooper; Angels with Dirty Faces (1938) with James Cagney, Humphrey Bogart; Pigskin Parade (1936) with Jack Haley,

CHARLES WILSON *(continued)*

Judy Garland; The Nitwits (1935) with Wheeler & Woolsey; It Happened One Night (1934) with Clark Gable, Claudette Colbert, winner of Best Picture

HARRY WILSON (1897-1978)

Our Relations (1936): Seaman

Other notable films: Some Like It Hot (1959) with Tony Curtis, Jack Lemmon, Marilyn Monroe, directed by Billy Wilder; Guys and Dolls (1955) with Frank Sinatra, Marlon Brando; Hold That Ghost (1942) with Abbott and Costello; One Million B.C. (1940) directed by Hal Roach

MARIE WILSON (1916-1972)

Babes in Toyland (1934): Mary Quite Contrary

Other notable films: Klute (1971) with Jane Fonda, Donald Sutherland; Mr. Hobbs Takes a Vacation (1962) with James Stewart, Maureen O'Hara; Marry Me Again (1953) with Bob Cummings; Girl in Every Port (1952) with Groucho Marx; Never Wave at a WAC (1952) with Rosalind Russell; My Friend Irma Goes West (1950);and My Friend Irma (1949) both with Dean Martin, Jerry Lewis; Private Affairs of Bel Ami (1947)

HANK WORDEN (1901-1992)

The Bullfighters (1945): Texan

Other notable films: Bronco Billy (1980)and Every Which Way But Loose (1978) both with Clint Eastwood; Smokey and the Bandit (1977) with Burt Reynolds; Cahill, United States Marshal (1973), Big Jake (1971), Chisum (1970), Rio Lobo (1970), True Grit (1969), McClintock! (1963),

HANK WORDEN *(continued)*

The Alamo (1960), The Horse Soldiers (1959), and The Searchers (1956), all with John Wayne; Ma and Pa Kettle at Home (1954) with Marjorie Main, Percy Kilbride; Big Sky (1952) with Kirk Douglas; The Quiet Man (1952) with John Wayne; The Wagon Master (1950) with James Arness, Harry Carey Jr.; The Fighting Kentuckian (1949) with John Wayne, Oliver Hardy; Three Godfathers (1948) with John Wayne; Angel and the Badman (1947) with John Wayne; The Secret Life of Walter Mitty (1947) with Danny Kaye; Duel in the Sun (1946) with Joseph Cotten, Jennifer Jones; Northwest Passage (1940) with Spencer Tracy

NOAH YOUNG (1887-1958)

Bonnie Scotland (1935); The Fixer Uppers (1935): Bartender; The Battle of the Century (1927): Stan's opponent; Do Detectives Think? (1927): Escaped convict; Sugar Daddies (1927)

Other notable films: The Cat's Paw (1934), Movie Crazy (1932), Feet First (1930), Welcome Danger (1929), Safety Last (1923), Grandma's Boy (1922), Sailor-Made Man (1921), Don't Shove (1919) all with Harold Lloyd

JOE YULE (1888-1950)

Nothing But Trouble (1944)

Other notable films: A Picture of Dorian Gray (1945); Woman of the Year (1942) with Spencer Tracy, Katharine Hepburn; Go West (1940), with the Marx Brothers, directed by Buster Keaton; Idiot's Delight (1939) with Clark Gable, Norma Shearer

GENERAL TRIVIA
The Films

1. Not counting any of the cameo roles in films, can you name three of the seven films where Stan does not cry?

2. Which film contains the most head scratches by Stan?

3. How many head clunks did the Boys have for their entire career?

4. What film contains the most head clunks?

5. What three films contain auctions?

6. In which film does Ollie fall into the bottomless pit the most times?

7. Name the three films in which the 'Pink Pup Cafe' appears.

8. What is the name of the club in 'Blotto'?

9. What phrase does Ollie say the most times in their films?

10. In which Hal Roach films does Ollie appear without his moustache?

11. Name the three films in which Ollie is a father.

12. The Boys play sailors in eight films. How many can you name?

13. In how many films does Dinah the mule make an appearance?

14. Name the two films in which Stan has dental problems.

15. Ollie drives a car into a bottomless mudhole twice. Can you name the films?

16. Ollie pretends to be talking to his boss on the telephone to dupe his wife. Can you name the two films this happens?

17. The Boys have trouble getting into bed in what two films?

18. Stan and Ollie hide a girl in the trunk in two films. Name them.

19. How many film titles contain exclamation points?

20. How many film titles contain question marks?

21. Name the two films in which Stan wears a kilt.

22. The Boys lie to their wives about where they are going in what two films?

23. Stan has problems getting ice cream in which two films?

24. Name the two films in which an attempt is made on Ollie's life.

25. What does Ollie always say he's going to break?

26. In what film does Fin wear a toupee?

27. In 'Block-Heads,' there is a mountain of bean cans. What is there a mountain of in 'The Flying Deuces'?

28. Whom was never married to Mae Busch in any of the films?

a. Oliver Hardy
b. Arthur Housman
c. Charles Middleton
d. Walter Long

29. Which one of the following cab companies did not appear in the Boys films:

a. Black and White Cab Co.
b. ABC Cab Co.
c. Yellow Cab Co.

30. Name the two films in which a bat flies in Stan's face.

31. Billy Gilbert is Ollie's doctor in which two films?

32. Which of the following does not have a dream sequence in the film?

a. The Laurel~Hardy Murder Case
b. Lucky Dog
c. Early To Bed
d. Oliver The Eighth

33. Name the three films in which the Boys play dual roles.

34. Which film is the Boys' first opera?

35. It rains in six films. How many can you name?

36. What's your favorite film of the Boys and who's your favorite; Stan or Ollie?

GENERAL TRIVIA
Answers

1. Lucky Dog
   Busy Bodies
   Swiss Miss
   Midnight Patrol
   Me and My Pal
   The Music Box
   The Bullfighters

2. Bonnie Scotland (15)

3. 16

4. Our Relations (5)

5. One Good Turn, Thicker Than Water, The Dancing Masters

6. Way Out West (3)

7. Putting Pants On Philip, Their Purple Moment and That's My Wife

8. Rainbow Club

9. "Do something to help me!" (26 times)
   "Here's another nice mess" (18 times)

10. Brats, Twice Two, Wild Poses, Thicker Than Water

11. Brats, The Bohemian Girl and Their First Mistake

12. Why Girls Love Sailors
    Sailors Beware!
    Two Tars
    Men O' War
    Any Old Port
    The Live Ghost
    Our Relations
    Saps At Sea

13. Two; Way Out West and Swiss Miss

14. Leave 'Em Laughing and Pardon Us

15. Leave 'Em Laughing and Perfect Day

16. We Faw Down and Their First Mistake

17. Berth Marks and The Big Noise

18. Unaccustomed As We Are and Block-Heads

19. Three; Sailors Beware!, Going Bye-Bye! and Scram!

20. Two; Do Detectives Think? and Should Married Men Go Home?

21. Putting Pants On Philip and Bonnie Scotland

22. We Faw Down and Sons Of The Desert

23. Come Clean and Twice Two

24. Oliver The Eighth and The Big Noise

25. Stanley's neck

26. Our Relations

27. Dirty laundry

28. **D.** Walter Long

29. **B.** ABC Cab Co.

30. The Laurel~Hardy Murder Case and Habeas Corpus

31. Them Thar Hills and County Hospital

32. **C.** Early To Bed

33. Brats, Twice Two and Our Relations

34. The Devil's Brother

35. Scram!, Sons Of The Desert, Helpmates, (The Rogue Song), The Laurel~Hardy Murder Case, and Atoll K

36. You can't get this one wrong!!! (But picking only one film as your favorite might be tough.)